DEMON

DEM⬤N

VOLUME 1

JASON SHIGA

:01

First Second

New York

First Second

Copyright © 2016 by Jason Shiga

Penciled with a Bic ballpoint on letter-size copy paper. Inked with a size 2 Windsor & Newton brush and black India ink on more copy paper. Colored digitally with Photoshop. Production help from Jackie Lo.

Published by First Second
First Second is an imprint of Roaring Brook Press,
a division of Holtzbrinck Publishing Holdings Limited Partnership
175 Fifth Avenue, New York, New York 10010
All rights reserved

Library of Congress Control Number: 2015958711

ISBN 978-1-62672-452-5

Our books may be purchased in bulk for promotional, educational, or business use. Please contact your local bookseller or the Macmillan Corporate and Premium Sales Department at (800) 221-7945 ext. 5442 or by e-mail at MacmillanSpecialMarkets@macmillan.com.

FIRST
EDITION

First edition 2016
Book design by John Green

Printed in China
10 9 8 7 6 5 4 3 2 1

FOREWORD

As cartoonists and readers, we live in an extremely exciting time for comics. In just the past ten years, we've seen the medium grow from a niche form of pop culture to a respectable and full-fledged art form. Since 2000, comics have found their way into libraries, bookstores, and the *New York Times* bestsellers list. They've been nominated for the National Book Award, the Printz Award, and even a Tony.

The book you now hold in your hands represents roughly none of that change. From the suicide depicted on the first page of the story to the climactic bloodbath three volumes later, *Demon* is my gleeful homage to the lurid and pulpy entertainment rags that make up the detritus of our childhoods. It's been a dream come true working on this project, pushing past the limits of common decency—of good taste—with every new page.

Readers of my previous work may recognize the main character, Jimmy Yee, who has been the star of my last few books, including the Choose Your Own Adventure-style children's book, *Meanwhile*. If you are a child, please put this book down slowly and walk away. The characters use a lot of profanity and deal with some very adult themes such as murder, camel sex, and drug use. Also, stay in school.

But if you're an adult, oooh, let me tell ya, this story is going to blow your mind! You are in for such a treat! You will not believe all the completely depraved mischief Jimmy gets into...and out of. Ooooh. I really want to tell you everything but I hate spoilers myself so for now the less said, the better.

In case you couldn't tell, *Demon* is a different kind of comic, both in form and content. It's been my goal to construct the story like a jet engine, pulling you across 750 pages, 4 volumes, and 21 chapters, each one more intense, twisted, and needlessly gratuitous than the previous. But at the end of the day, it's personal. Ultimately, Jimmy is me. When he leaps in front of a semi-trailer, it's really me who secretly wants to do that. When he acts in a deliberately amoral and antisocial manner, that's me, too. And when he expresses his feelings about the universe being a meaningless and chaotic miasma and consciousness as the ultimate cruel joke on humanity, he's really speaking for me.

Anyway, I hope you enjoy the book and will laugh, love, and cry along with Jimmy as he embarks upon his journey. Thank you so much.

—Jason

To my wife, Alina,
who begged me not to dedicate this book to her

CHAPTER 1

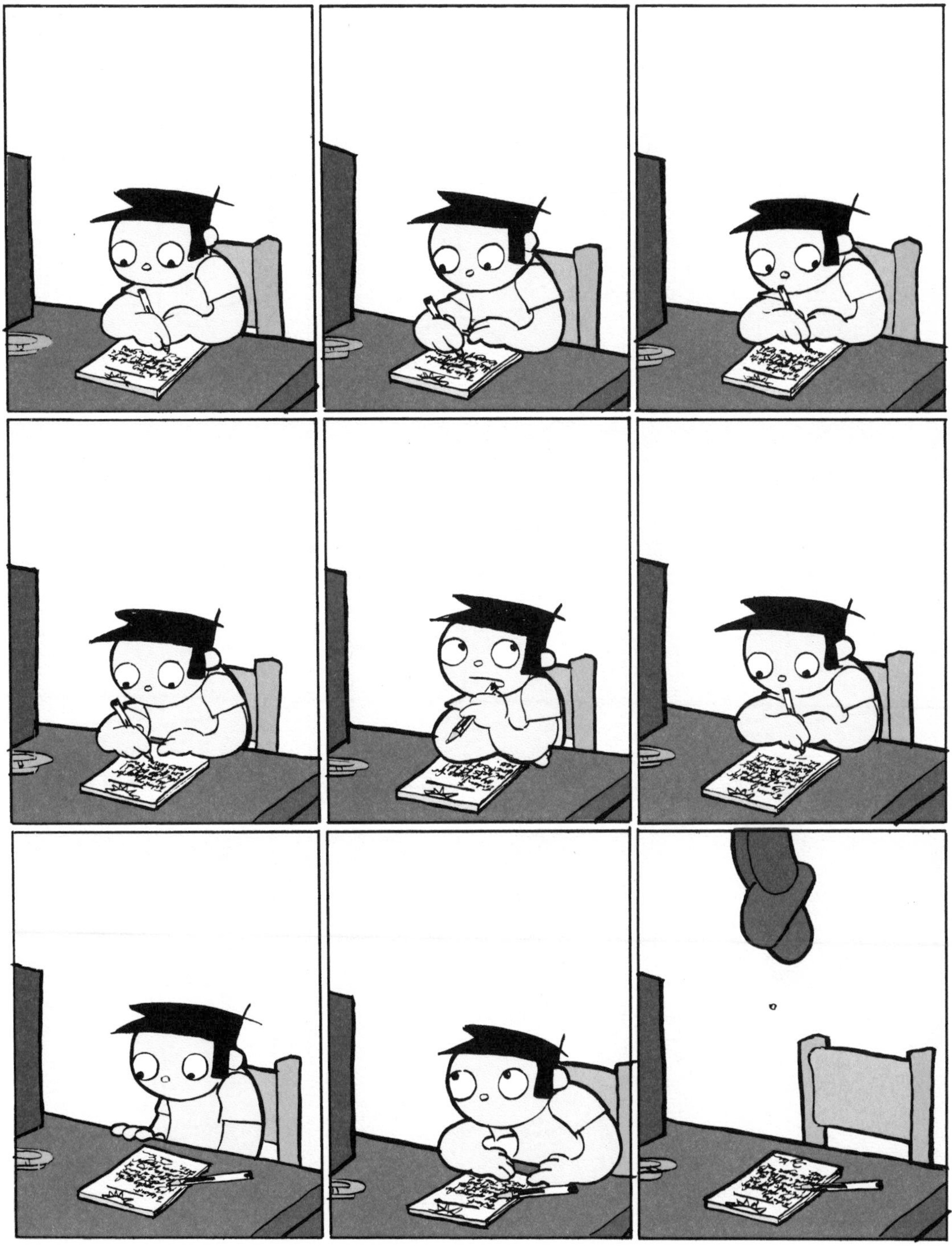

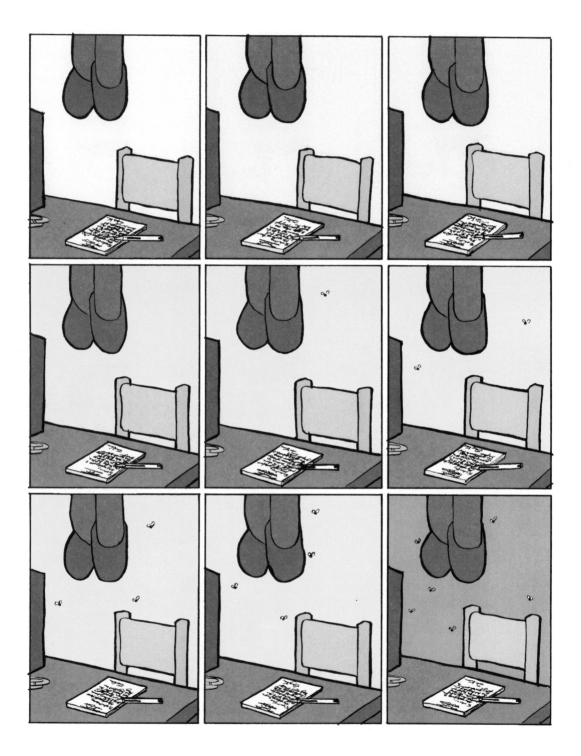

DEMON

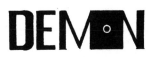

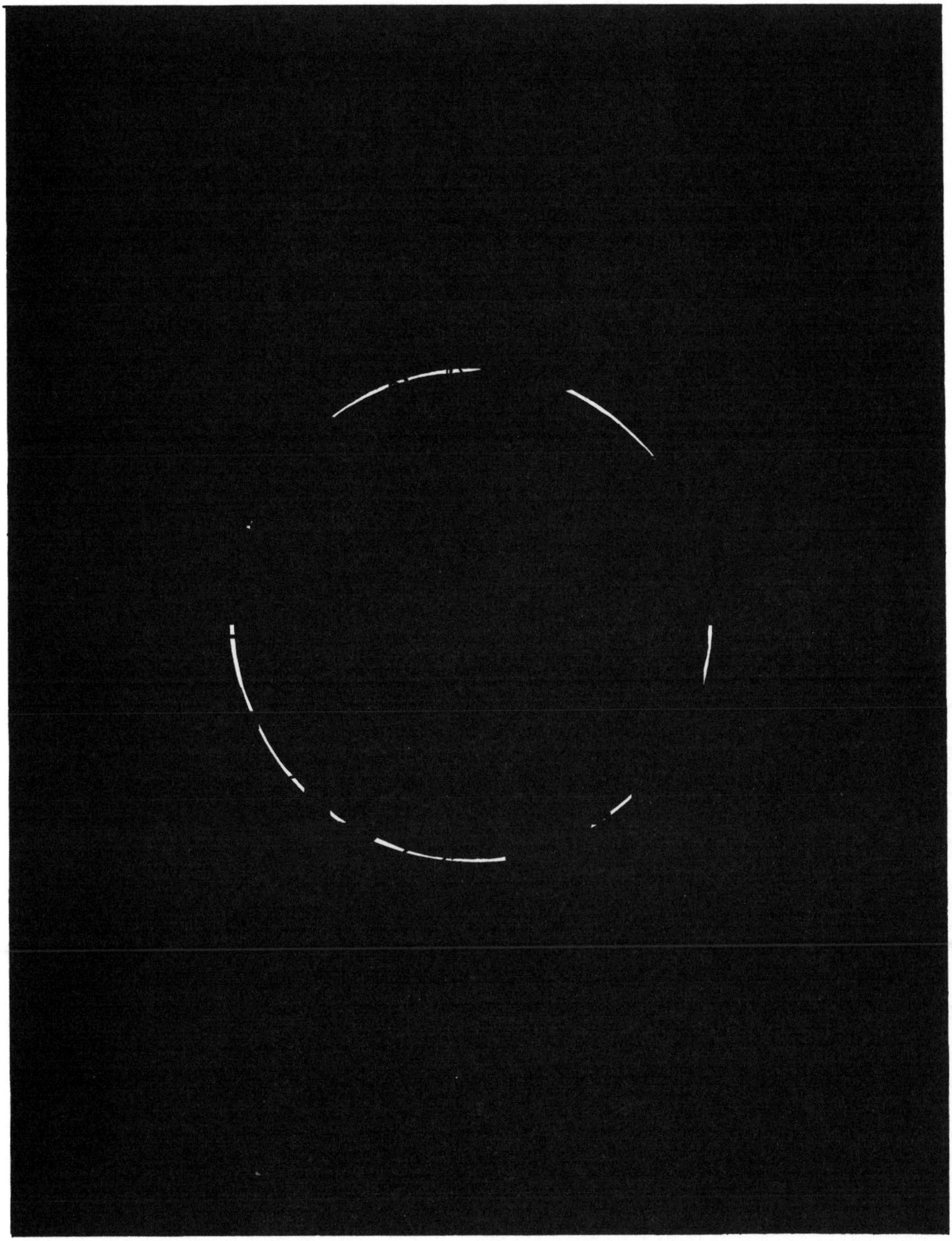

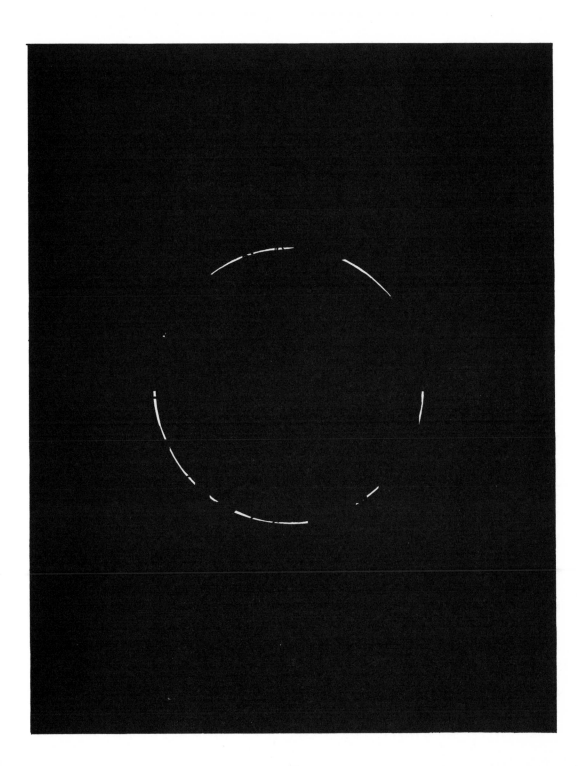

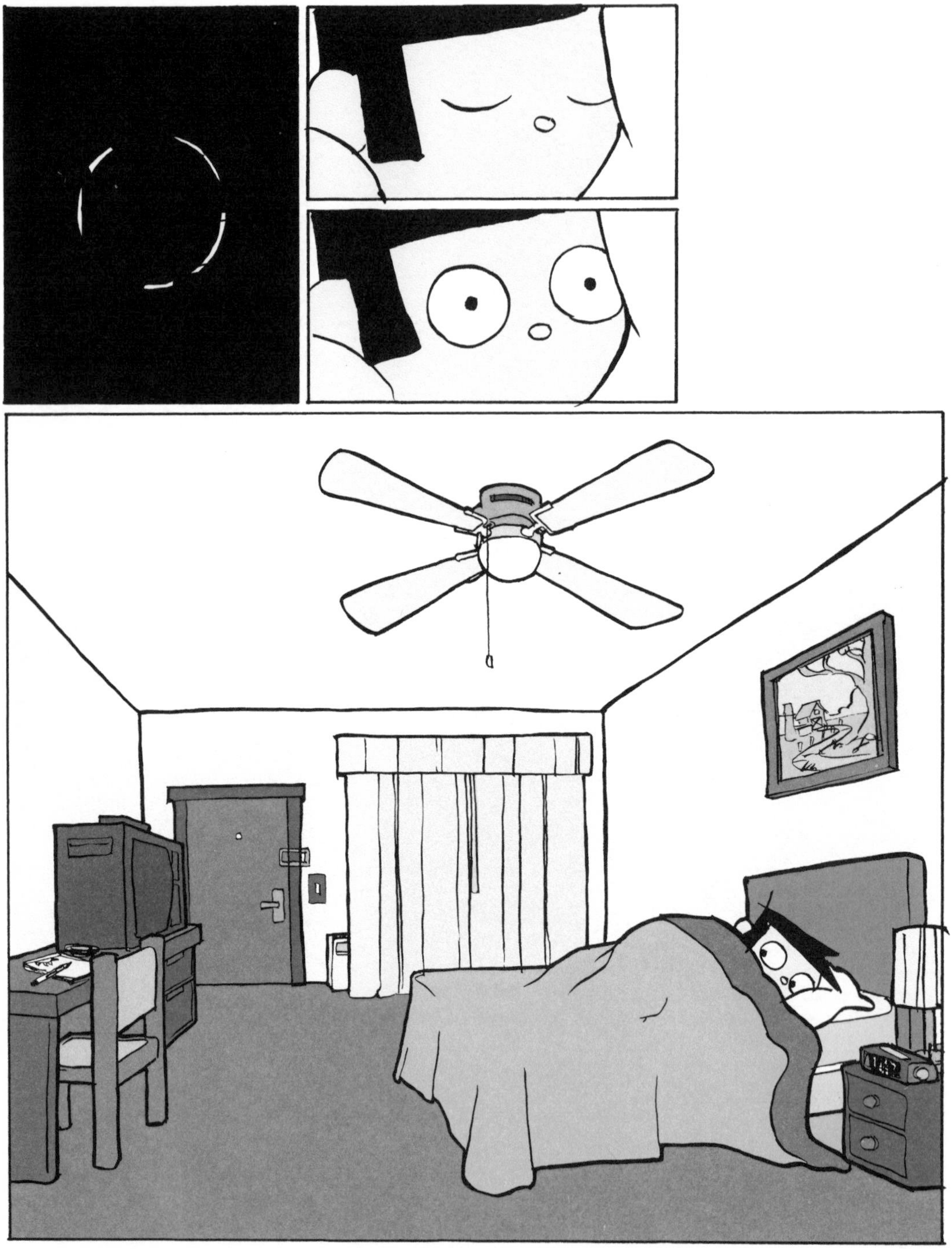

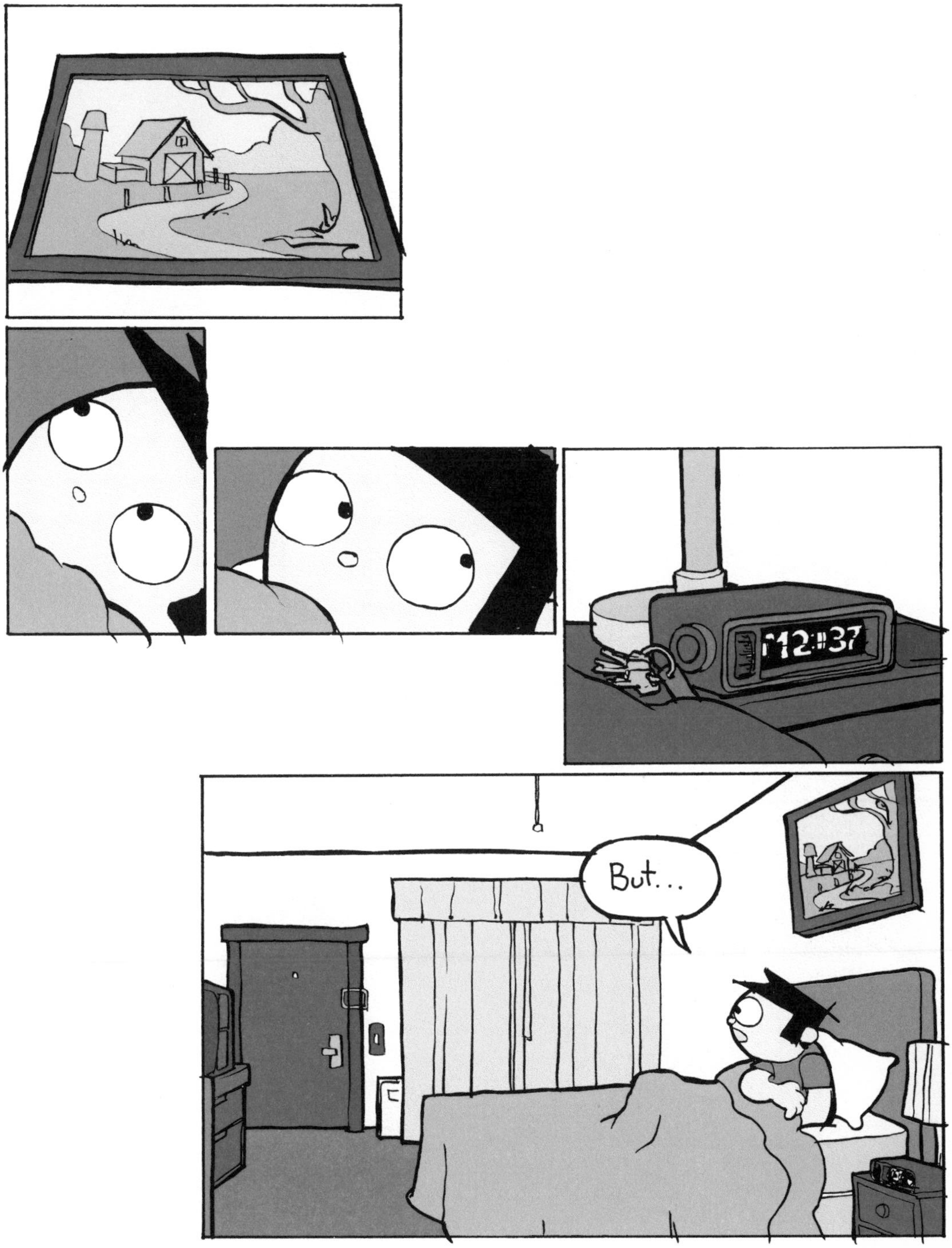
But...

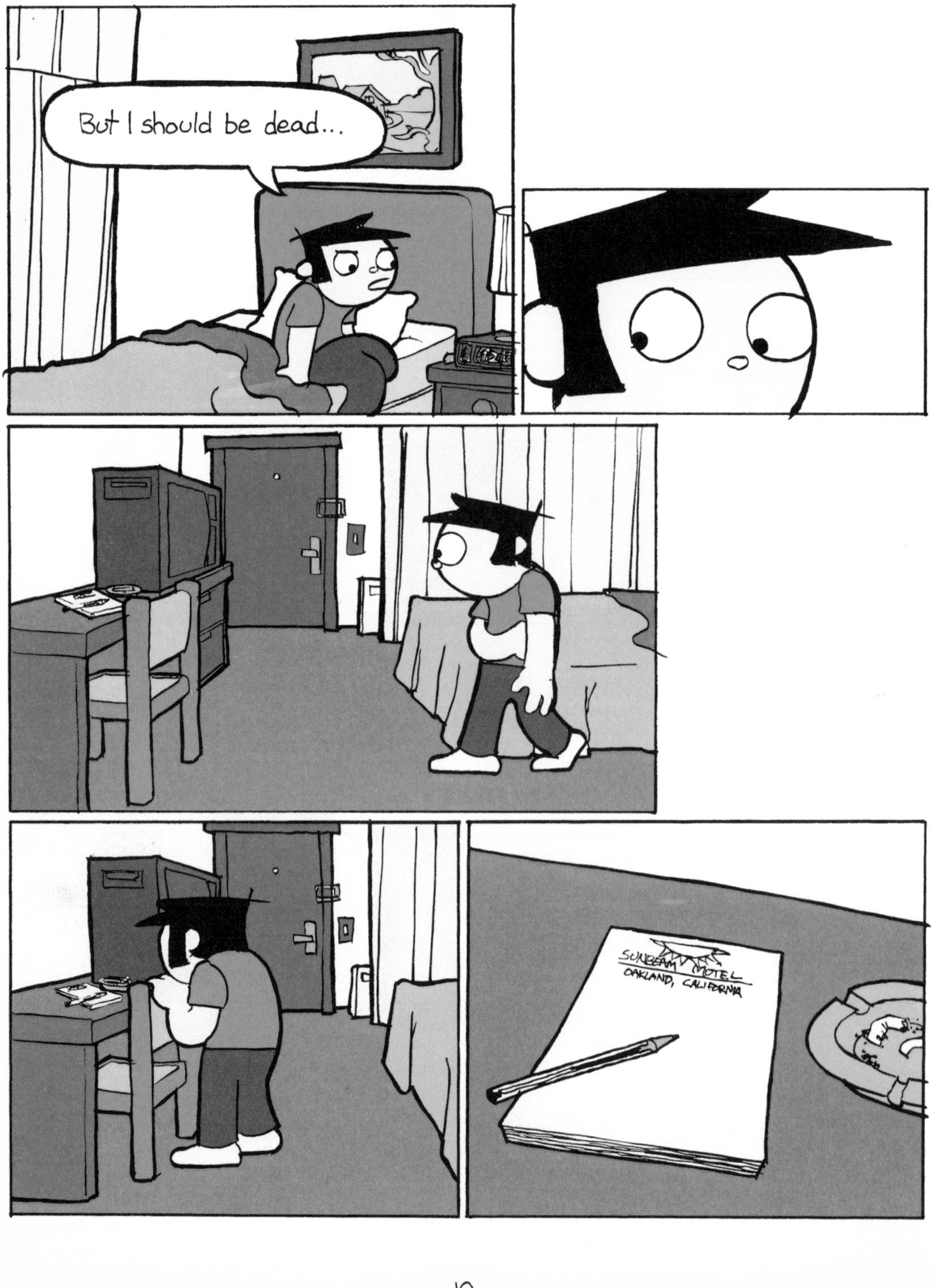
But I should be dead...
SUNBEAM MOTEL
OAKLAND, CALIFORNIA

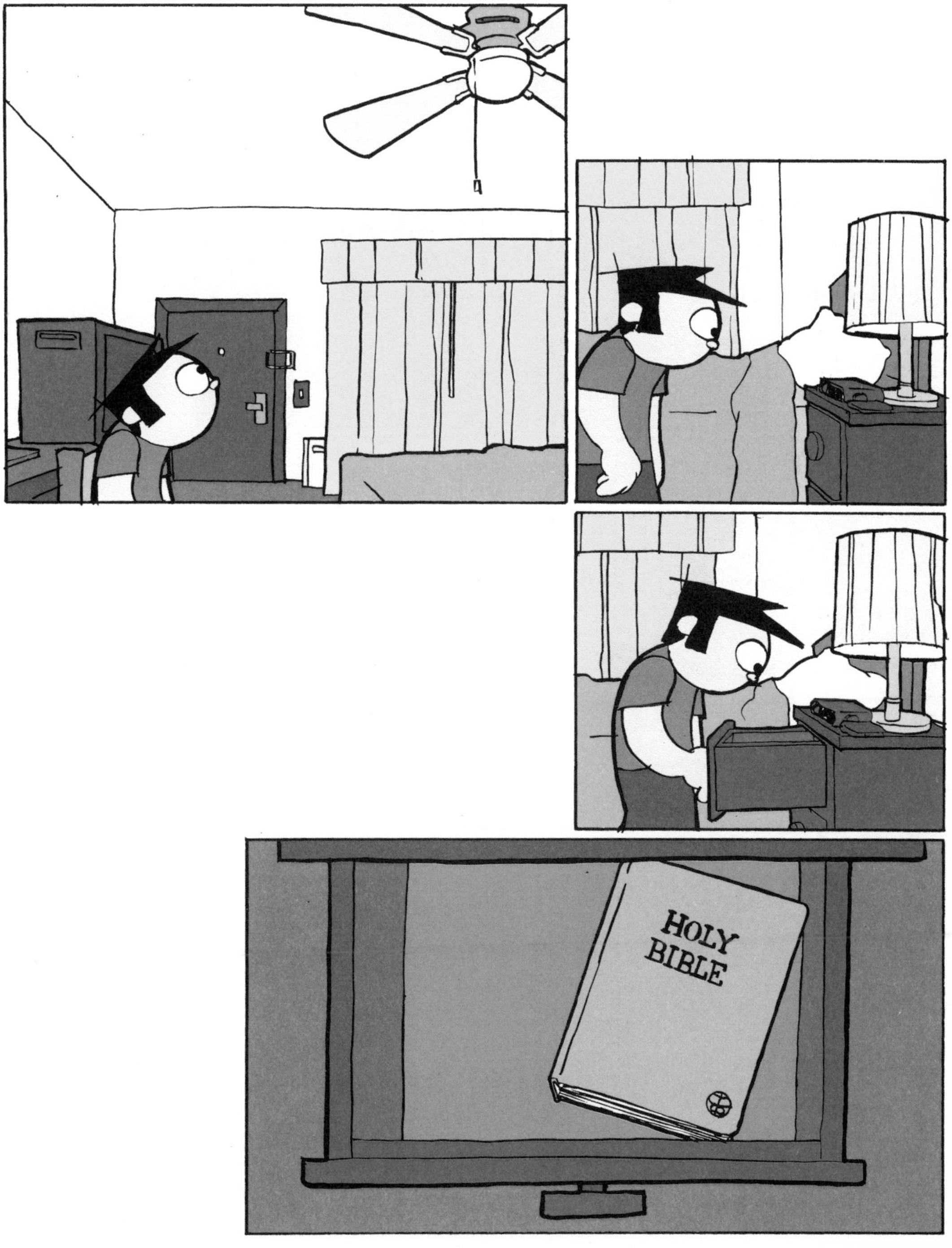
HOLY
BIBLE

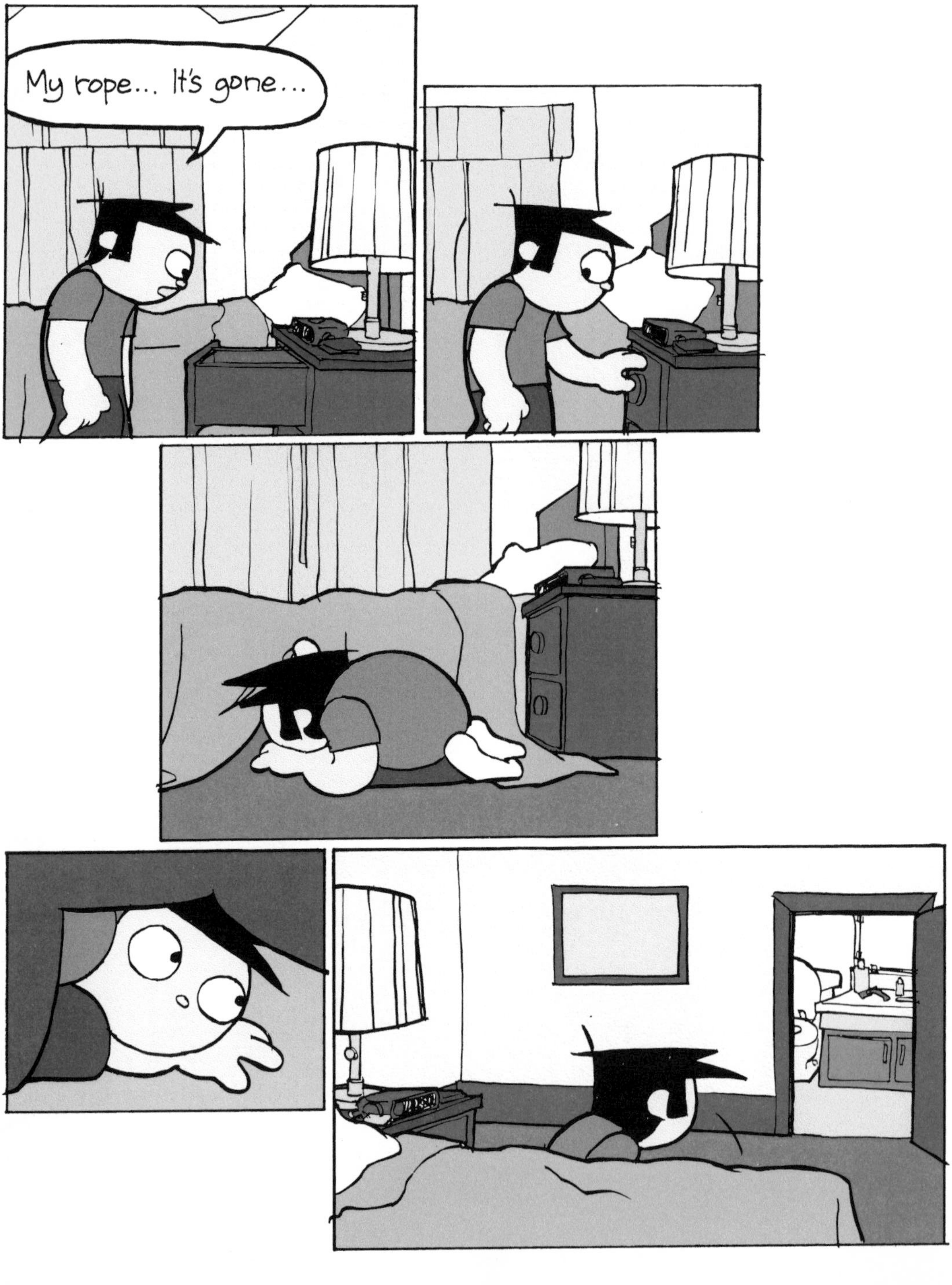
My rope... It's gone...

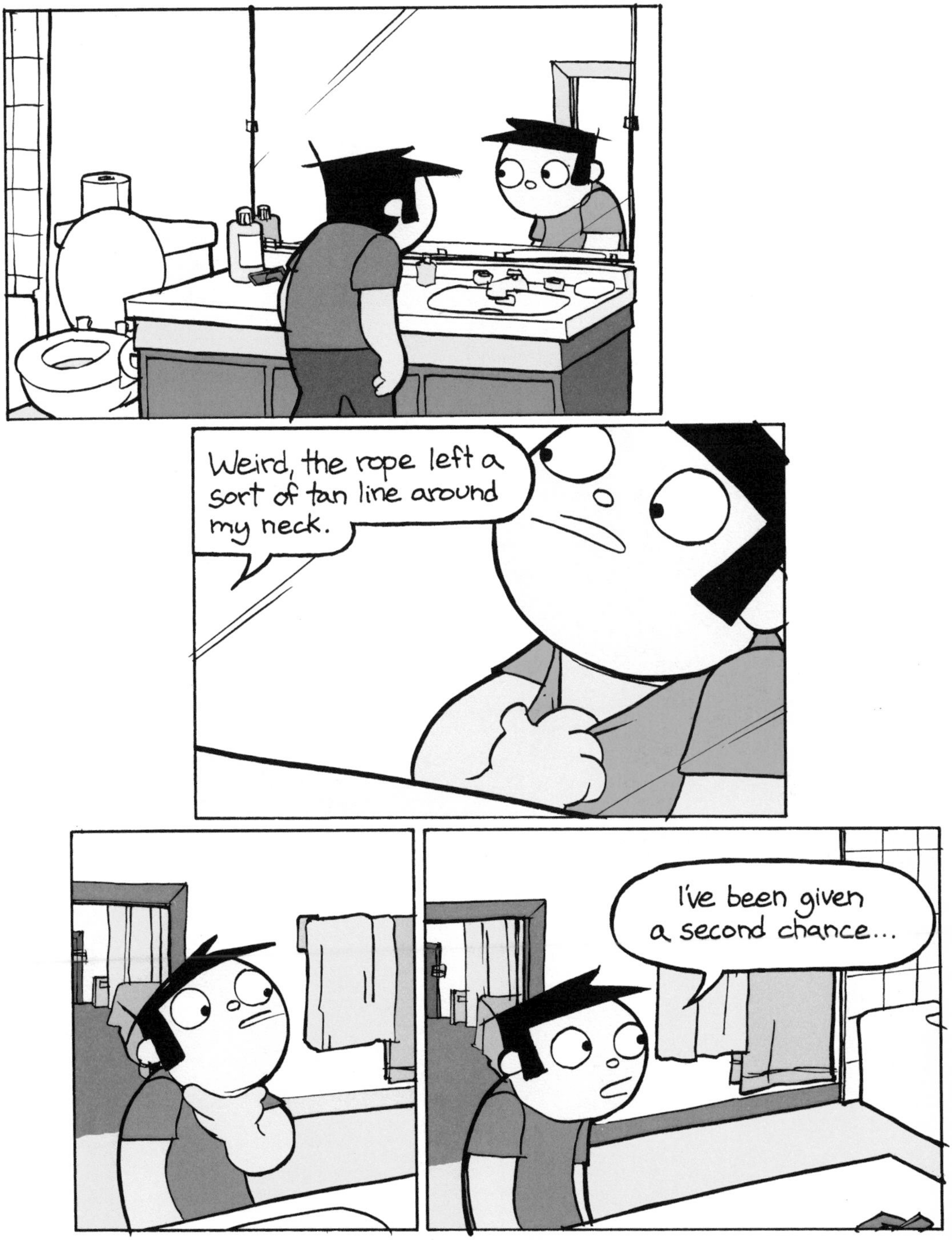
Weird, the rope left a sort of tan line around my neck.
I've been given a second chance...

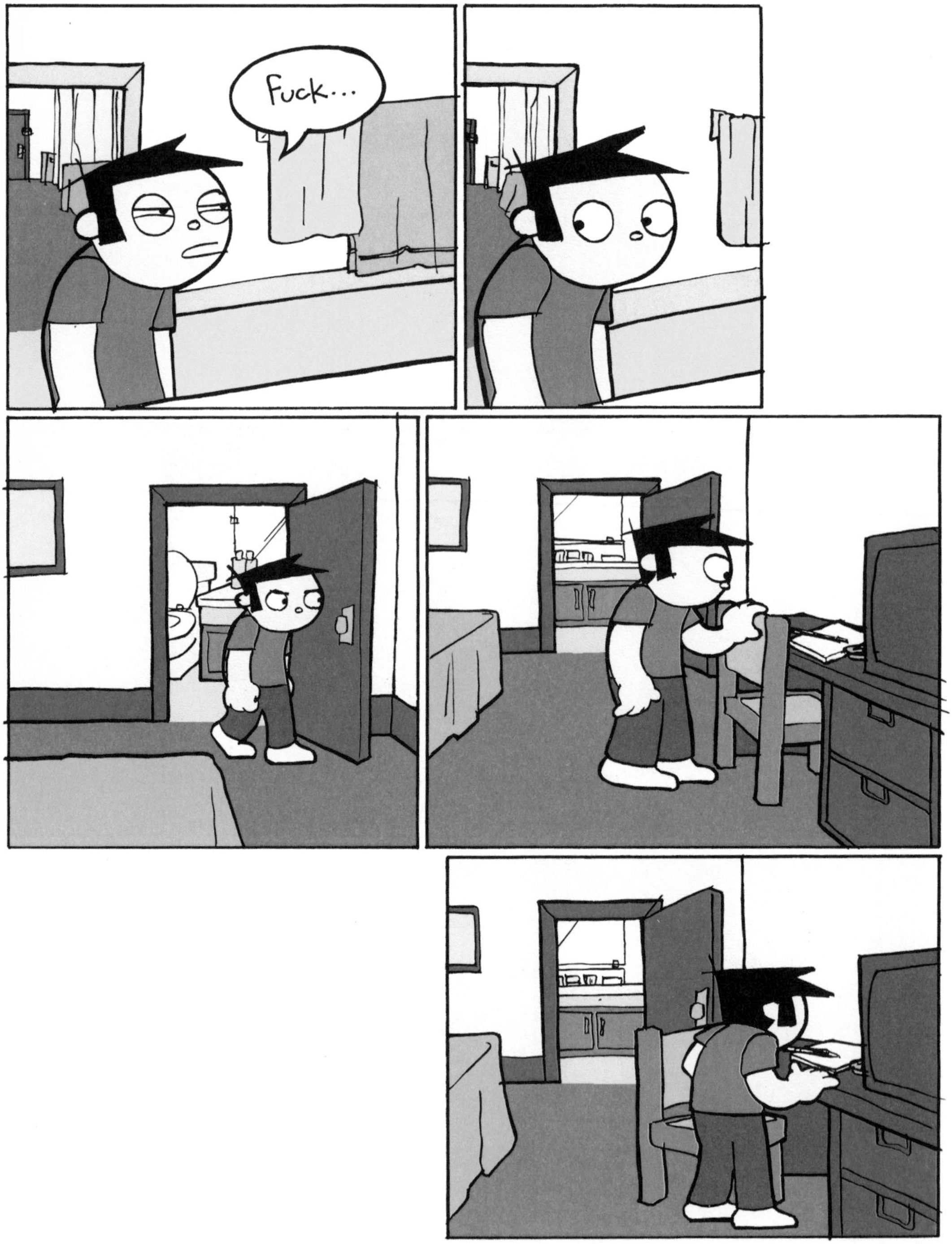
Fuck...

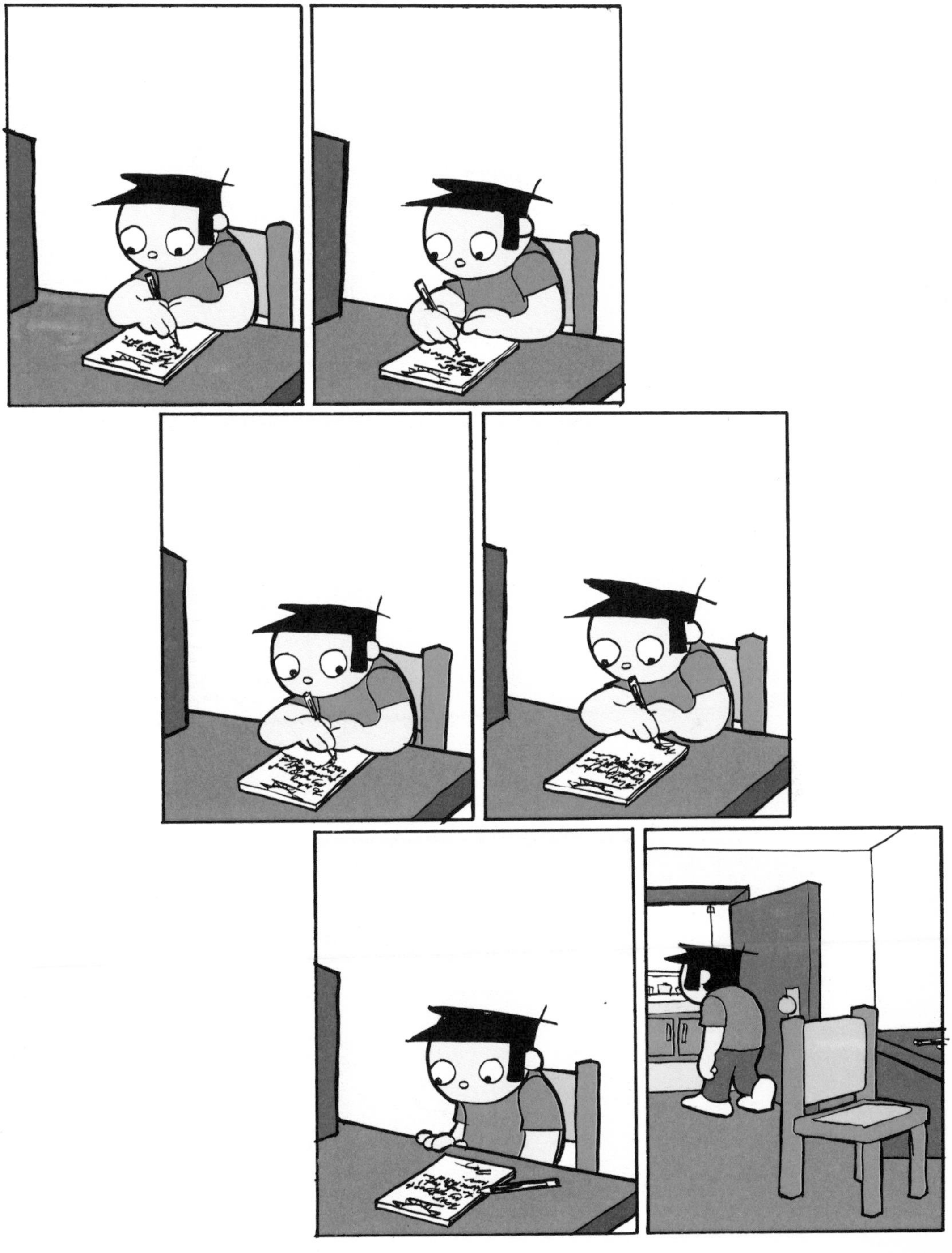

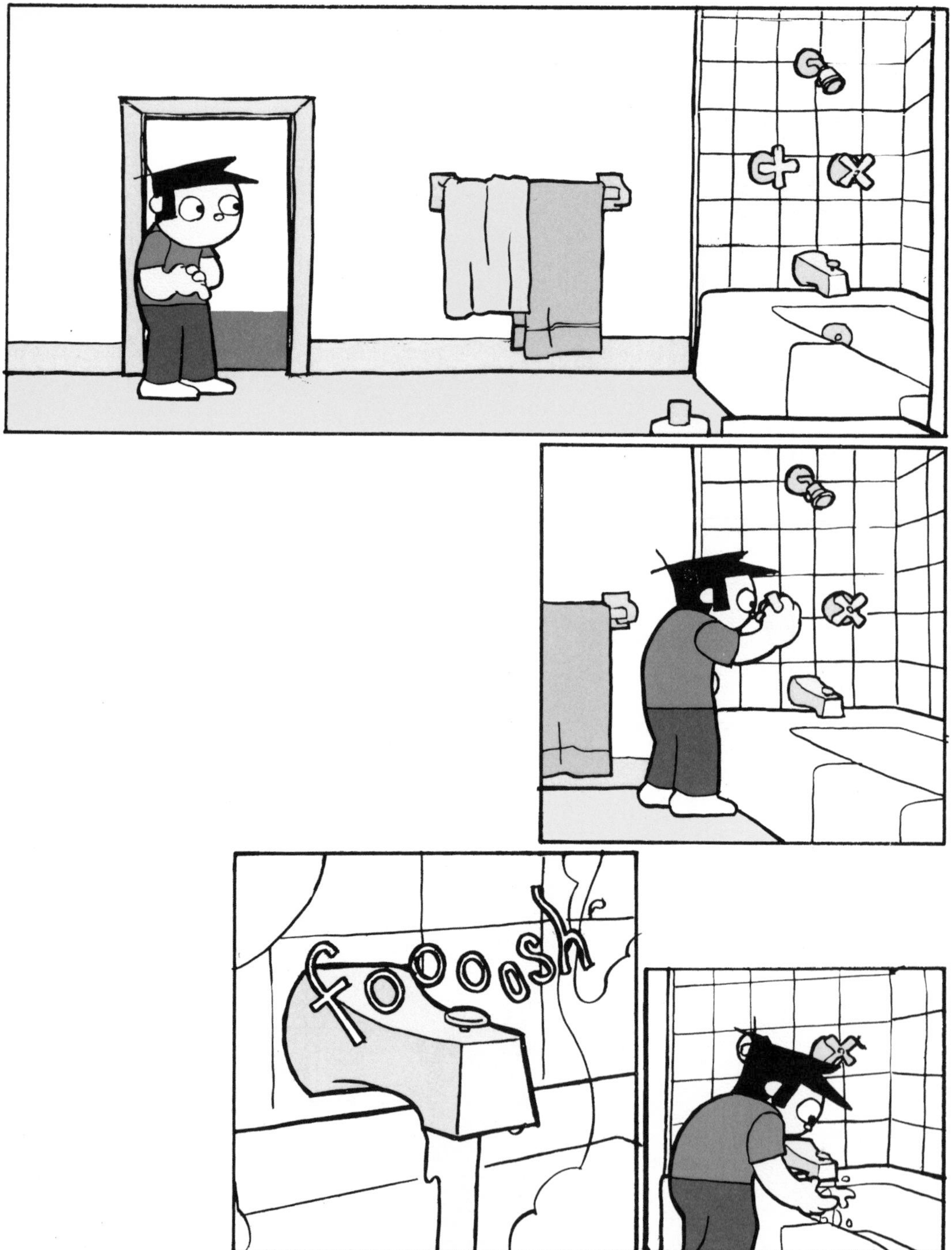
fooooshh

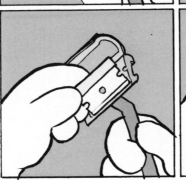

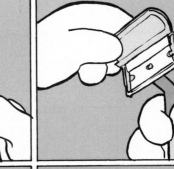

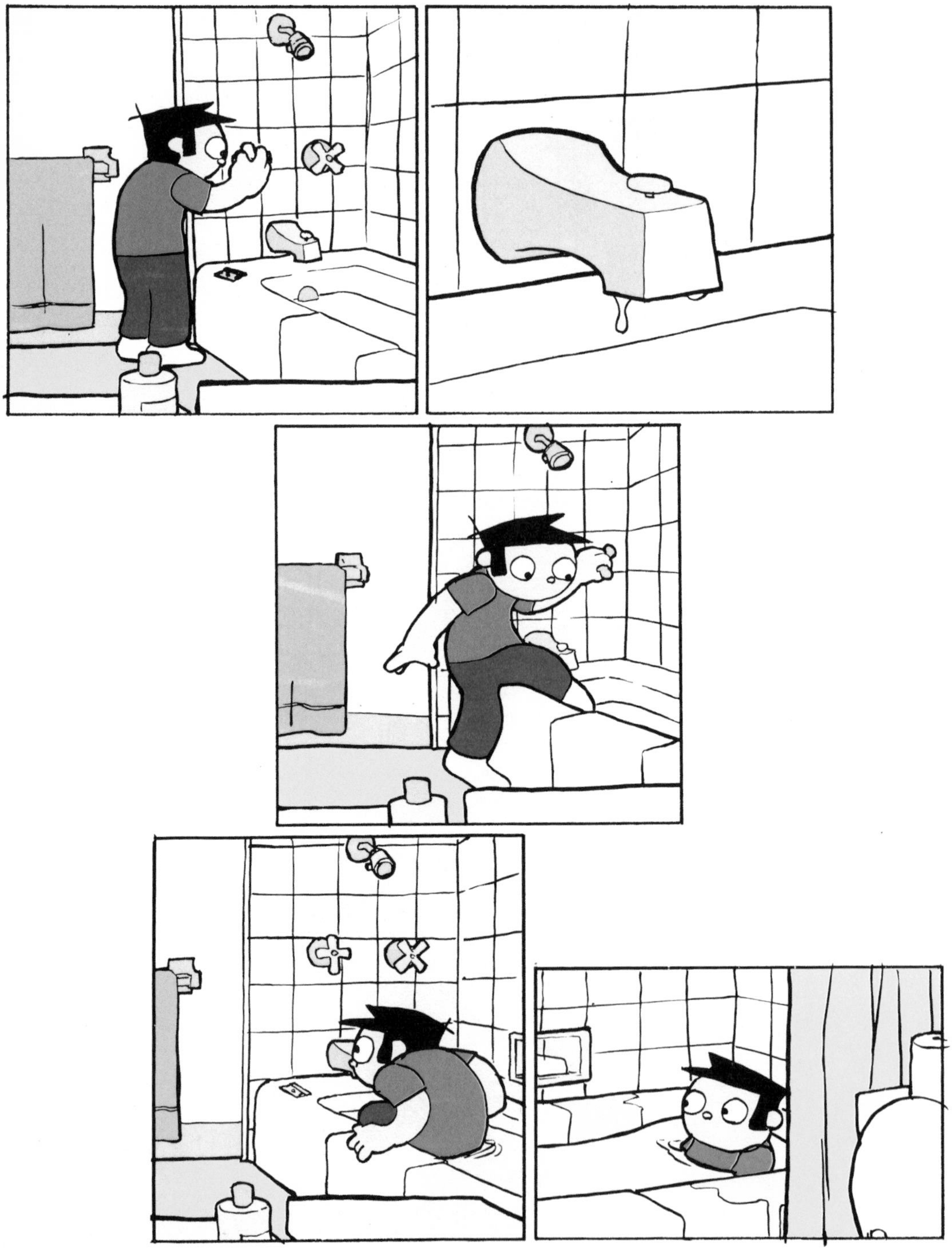

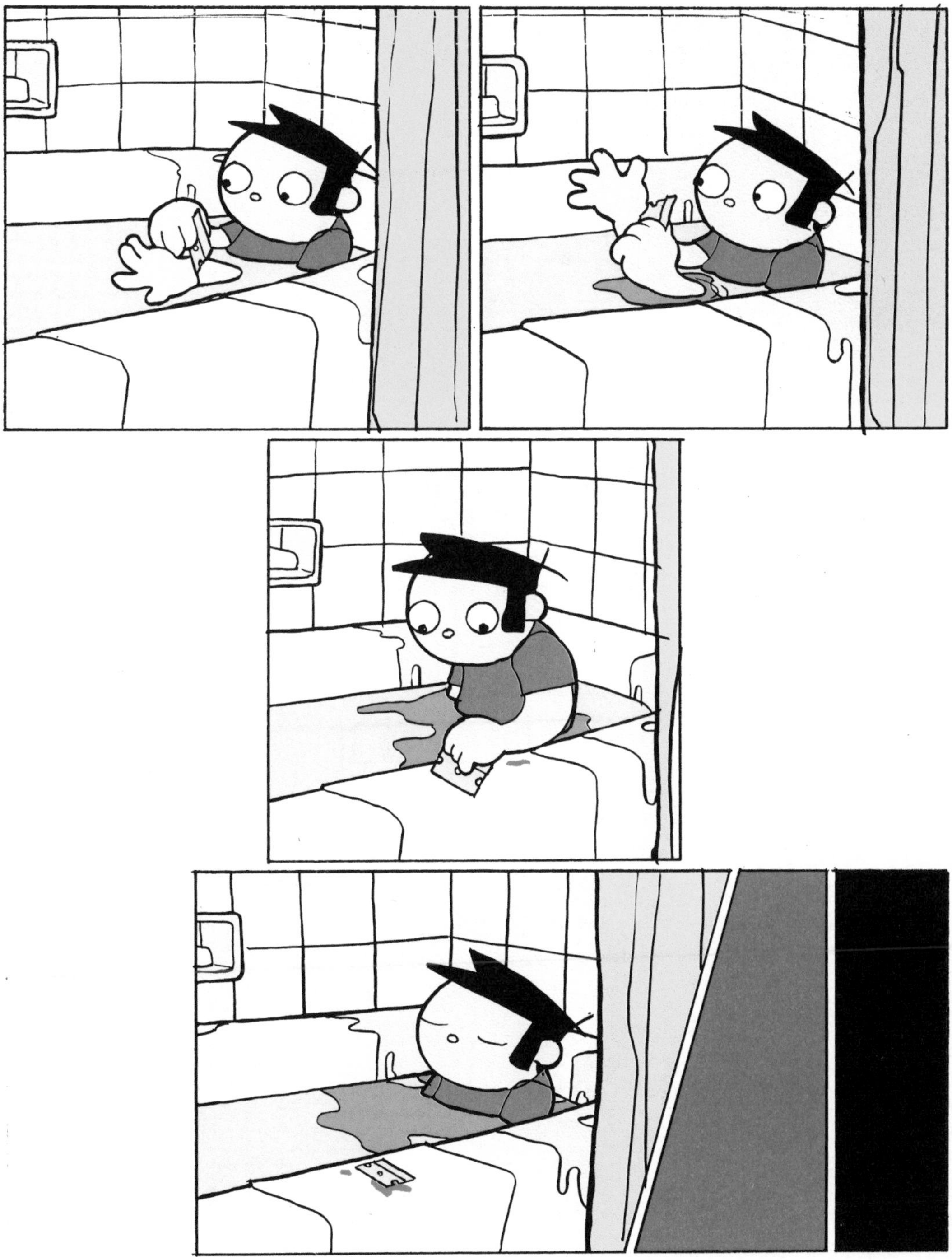

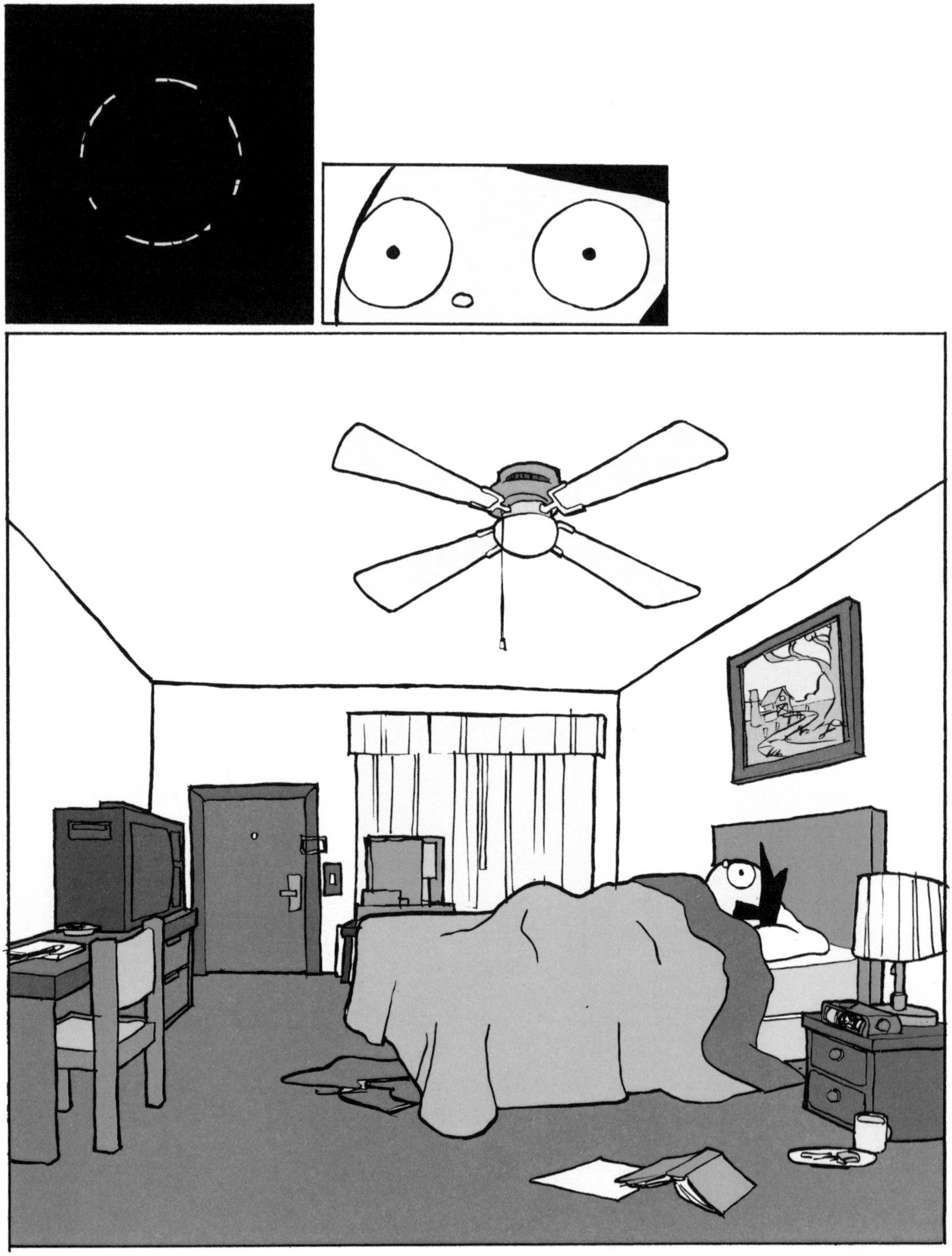

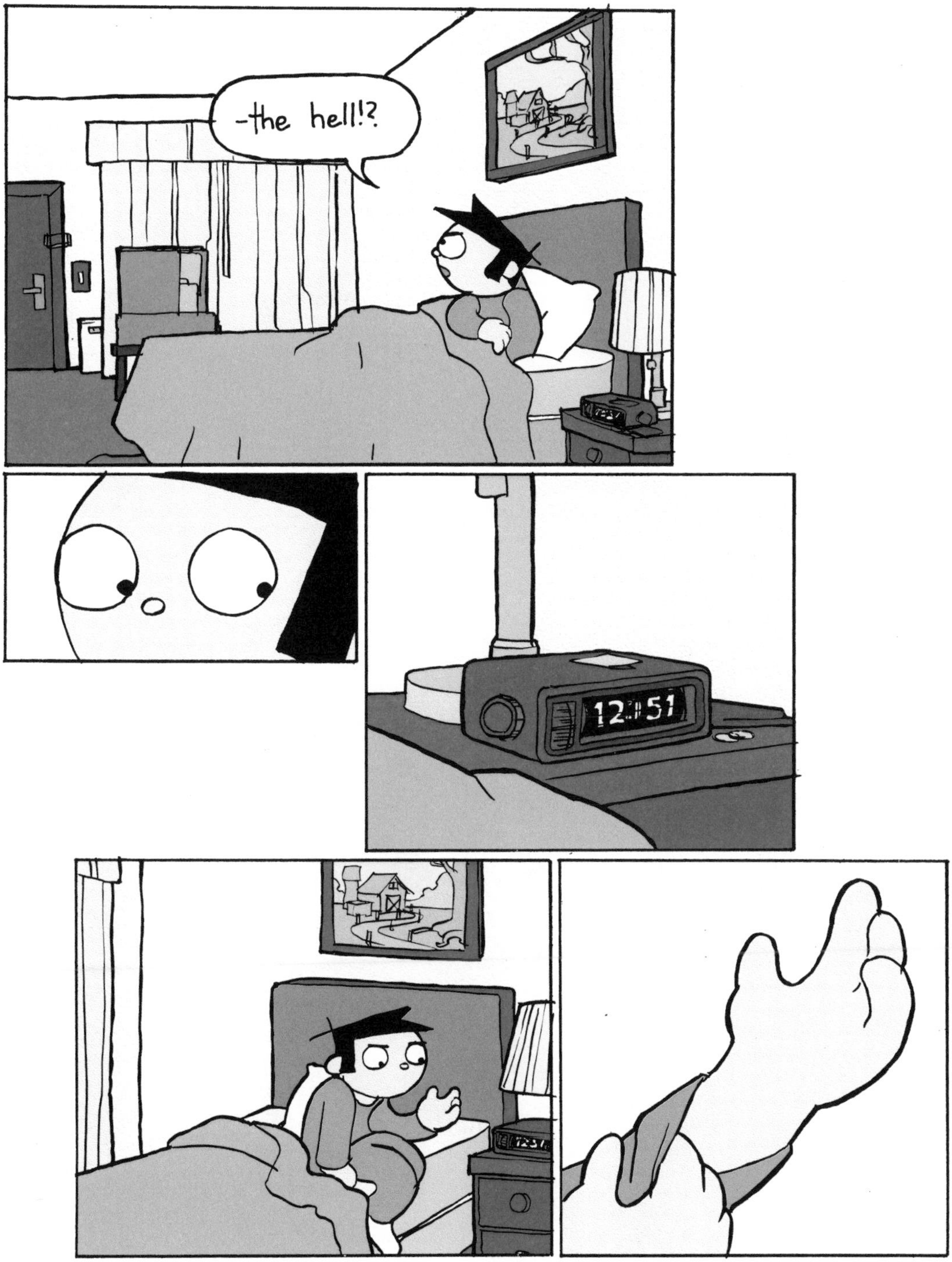
-the hell!?
12:51

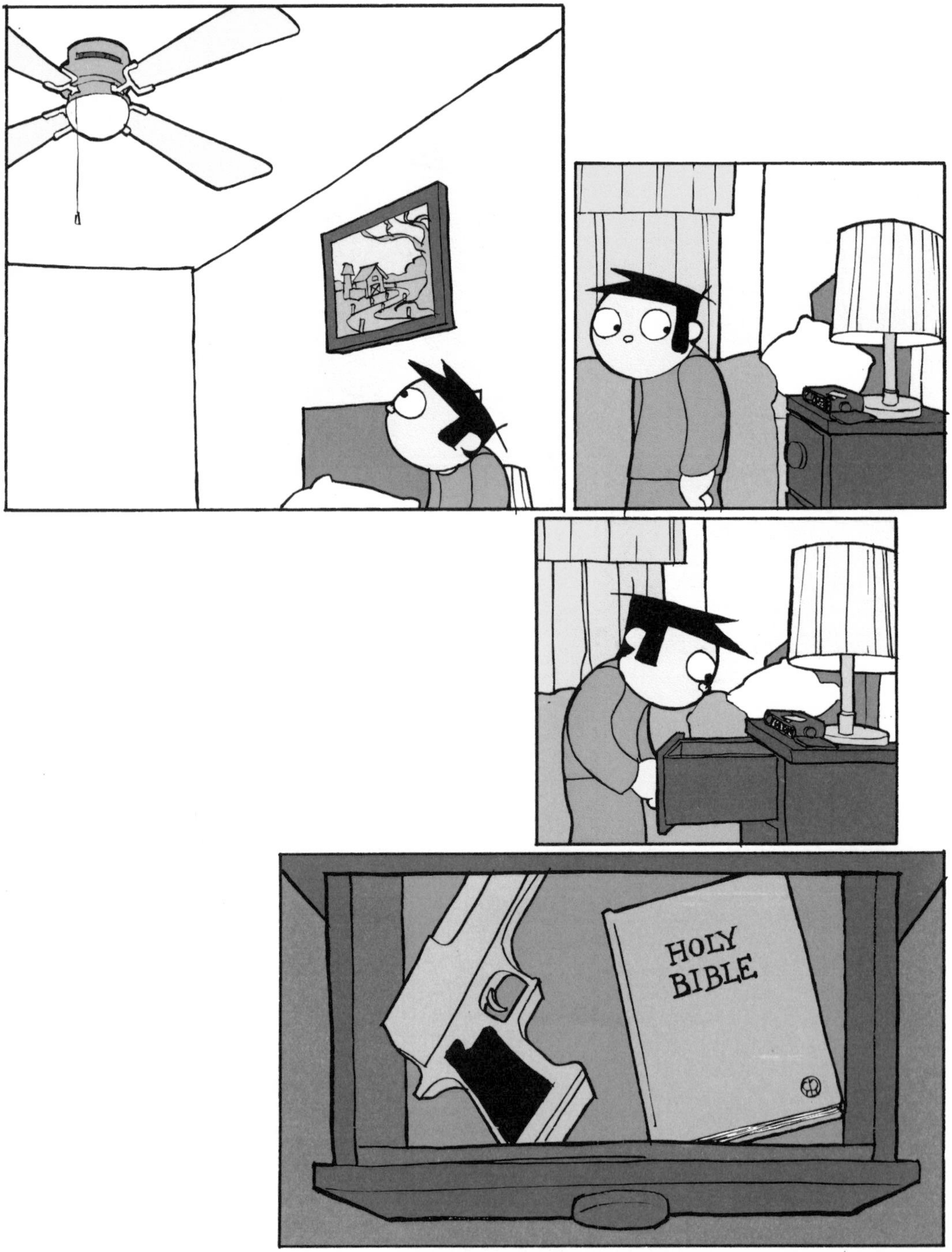
HOLY
BIBLE

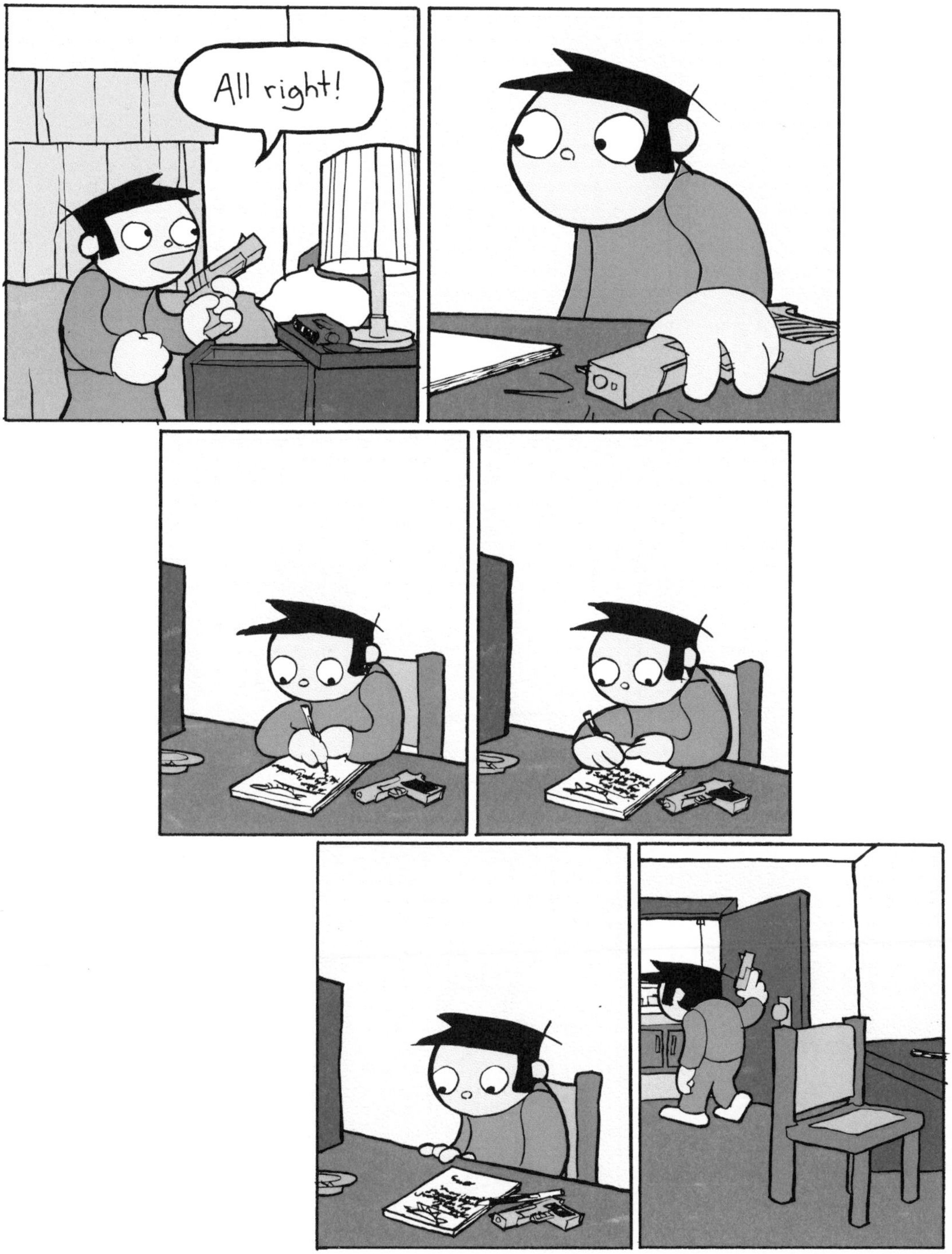
All right!

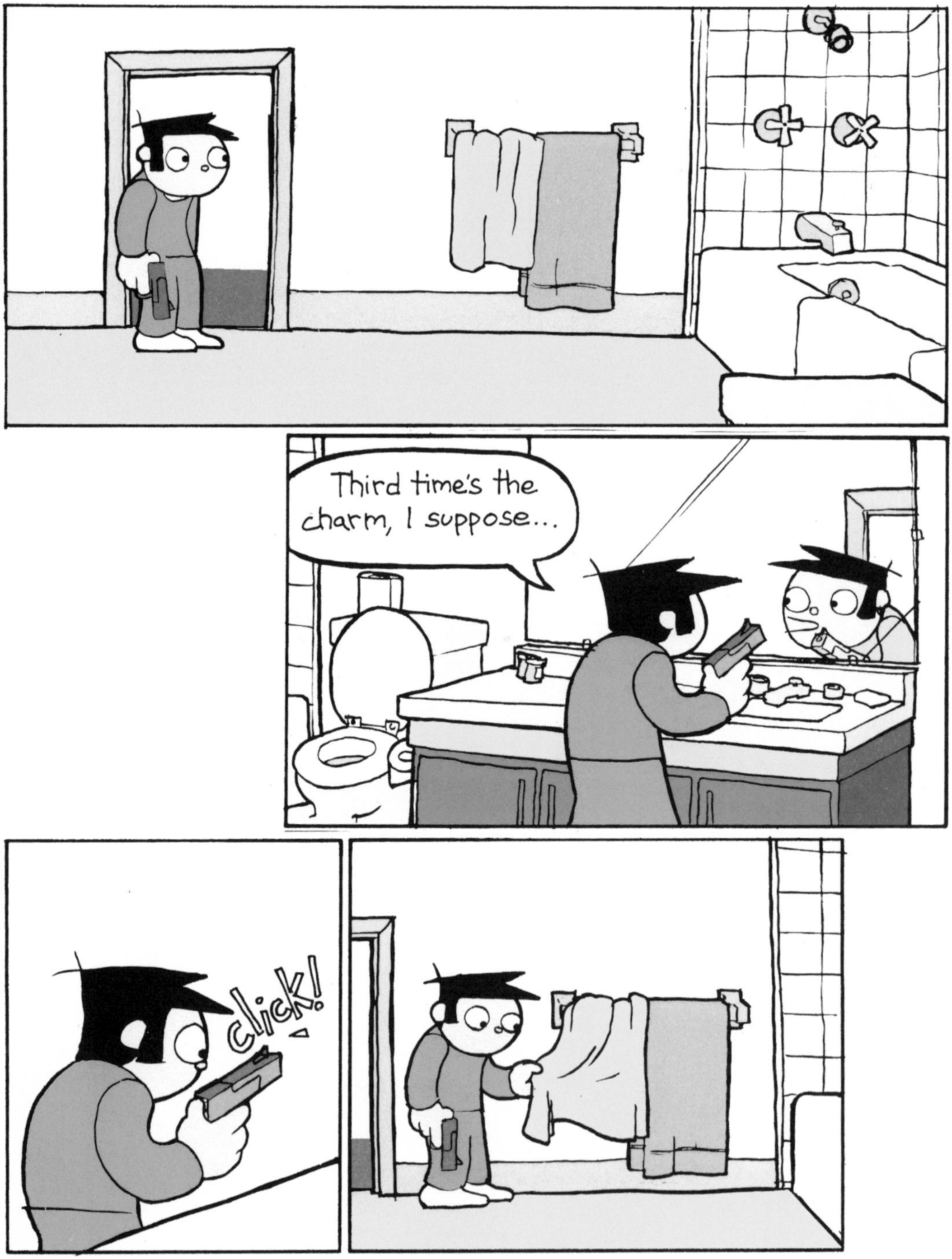
Third time's the charm, I suppose...
click!

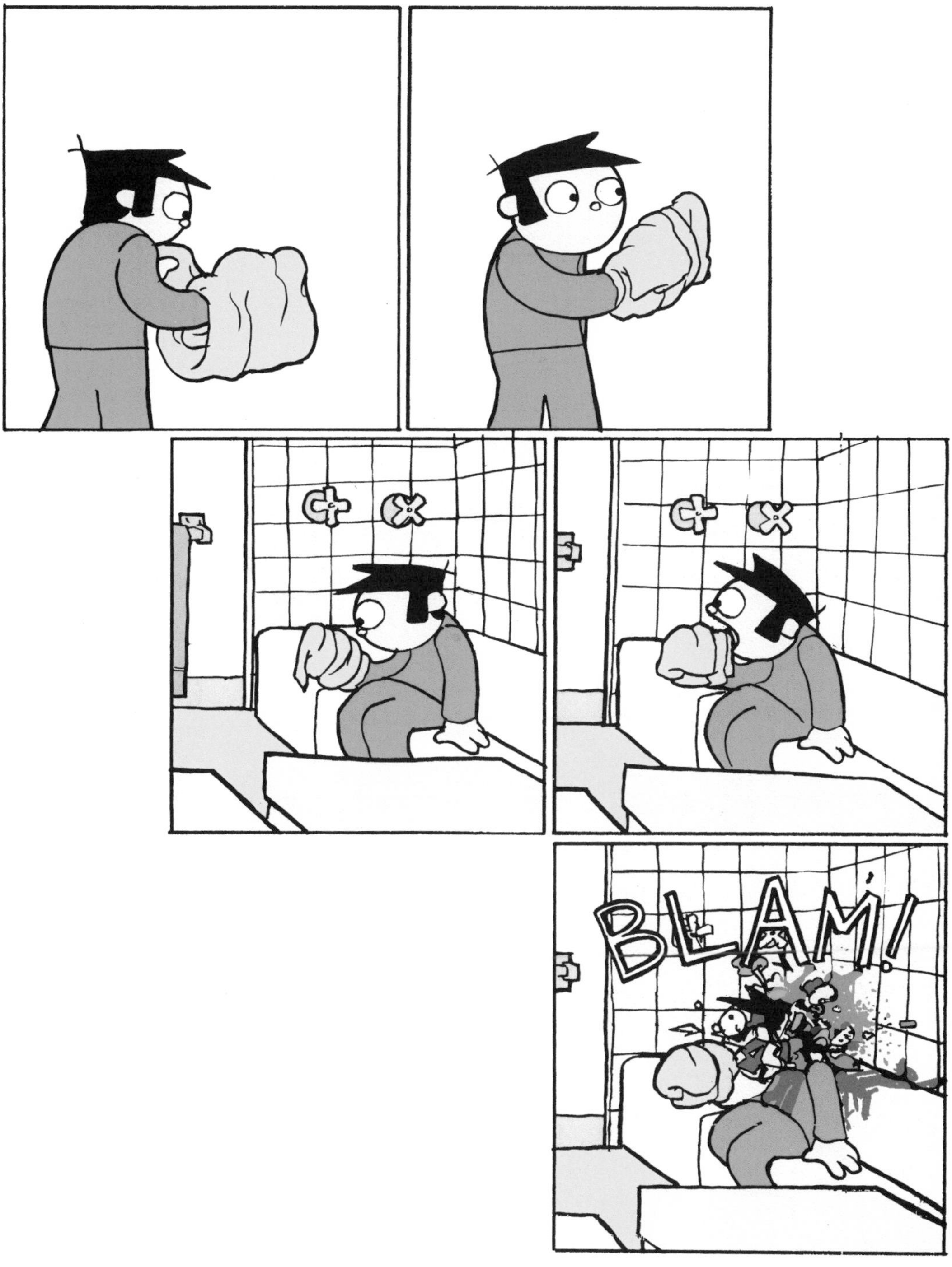
BLAM!

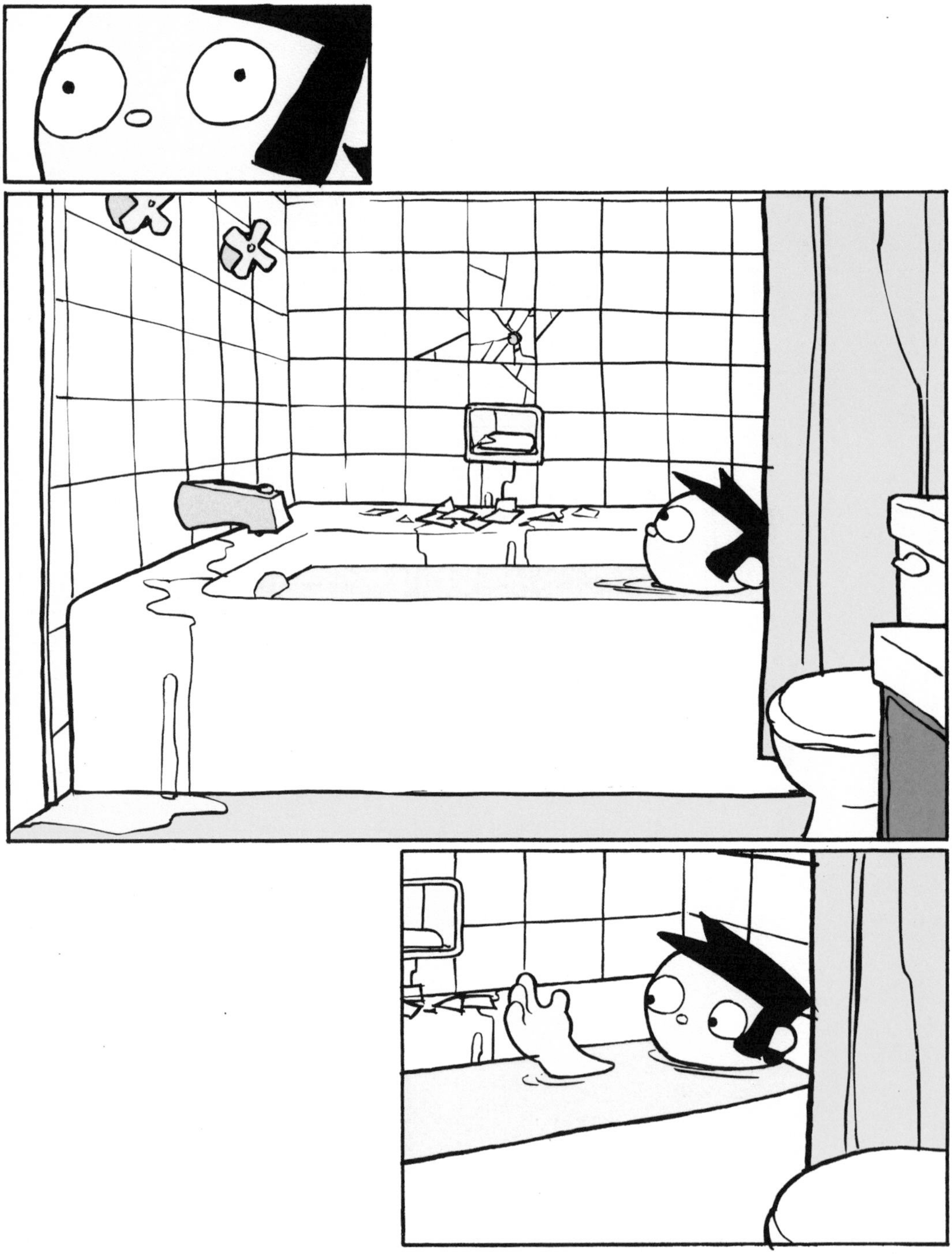

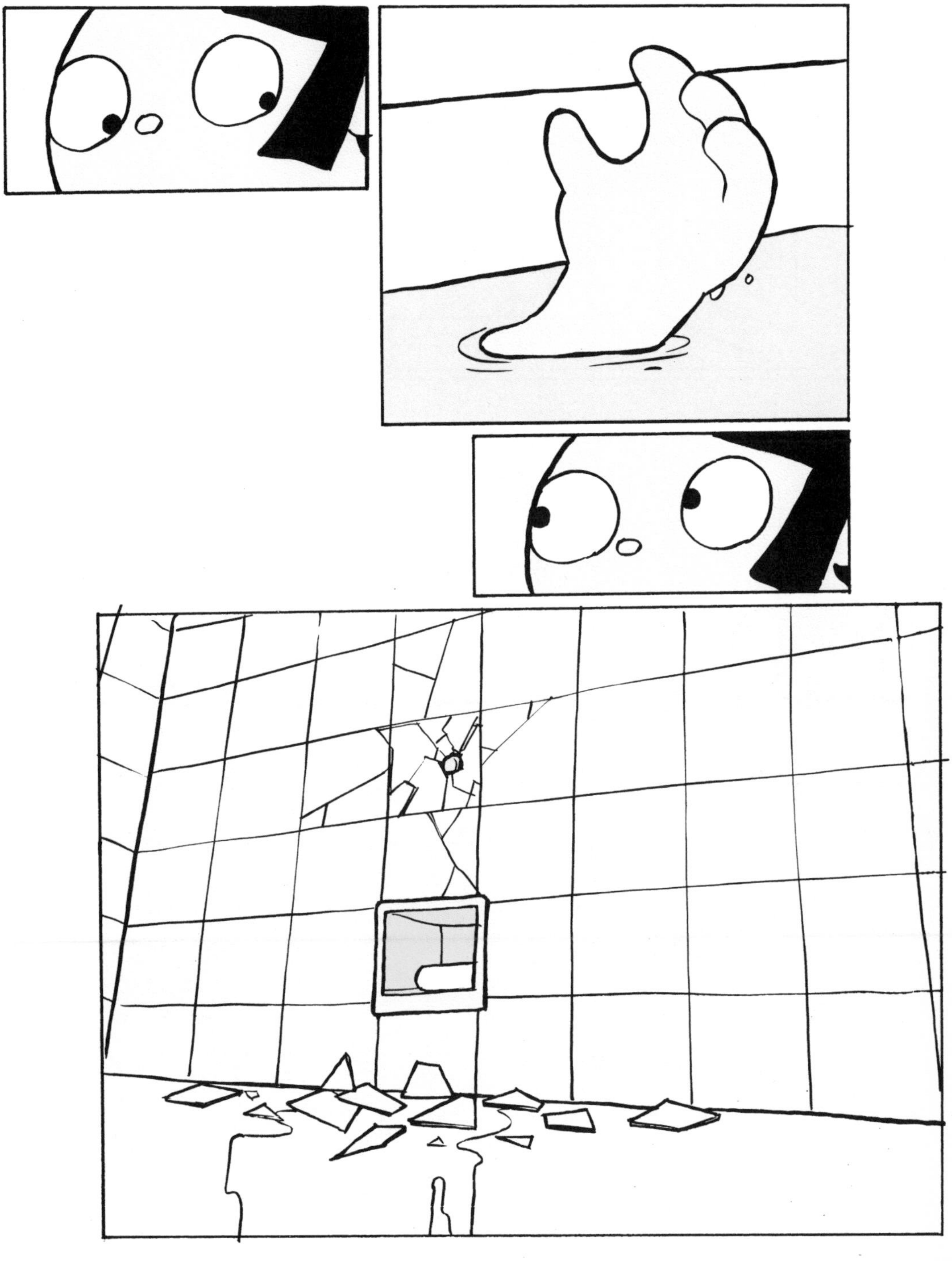

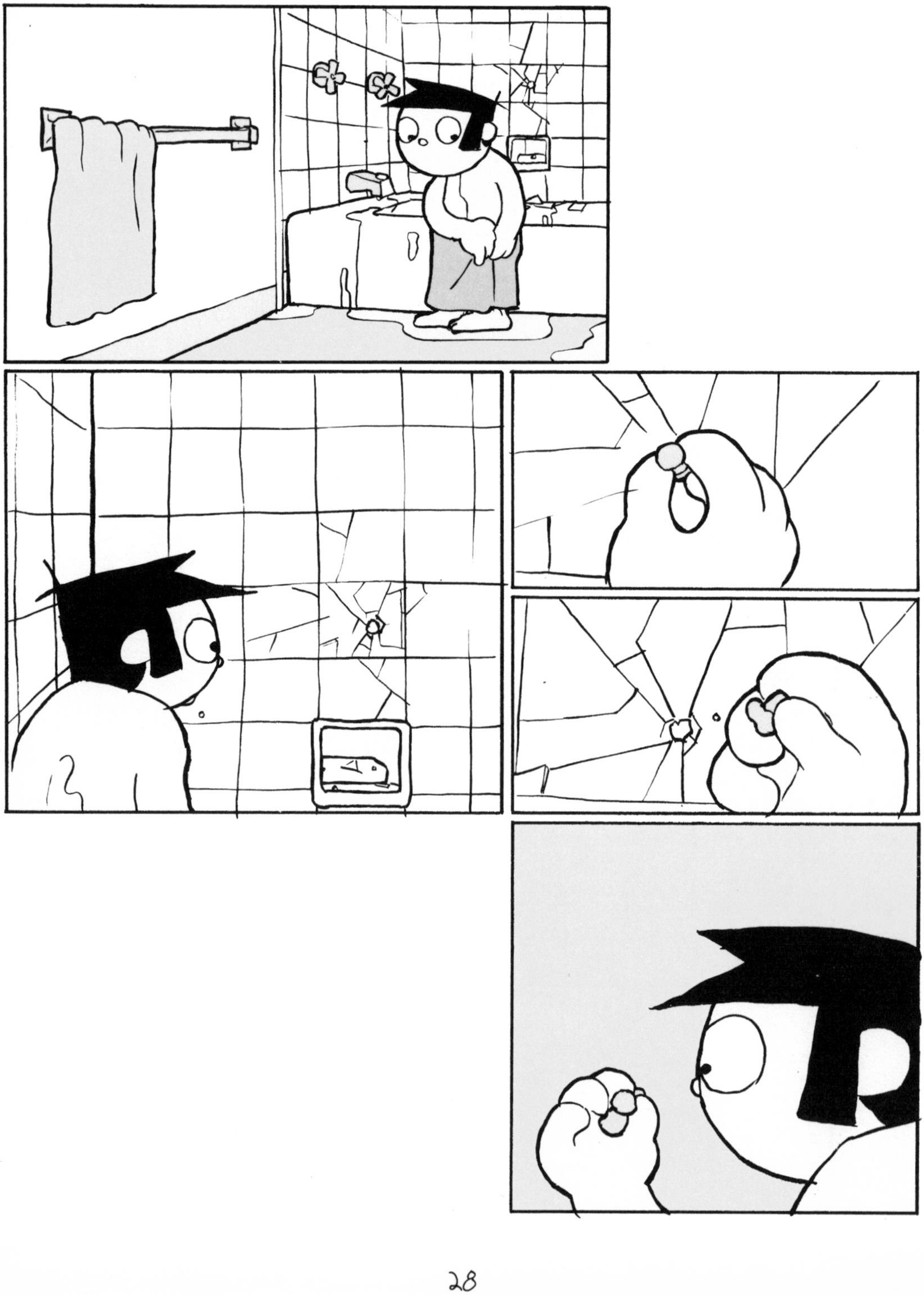

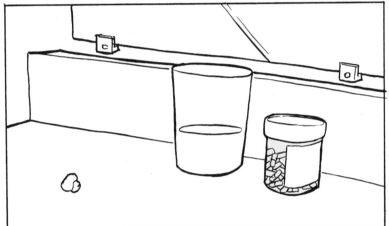

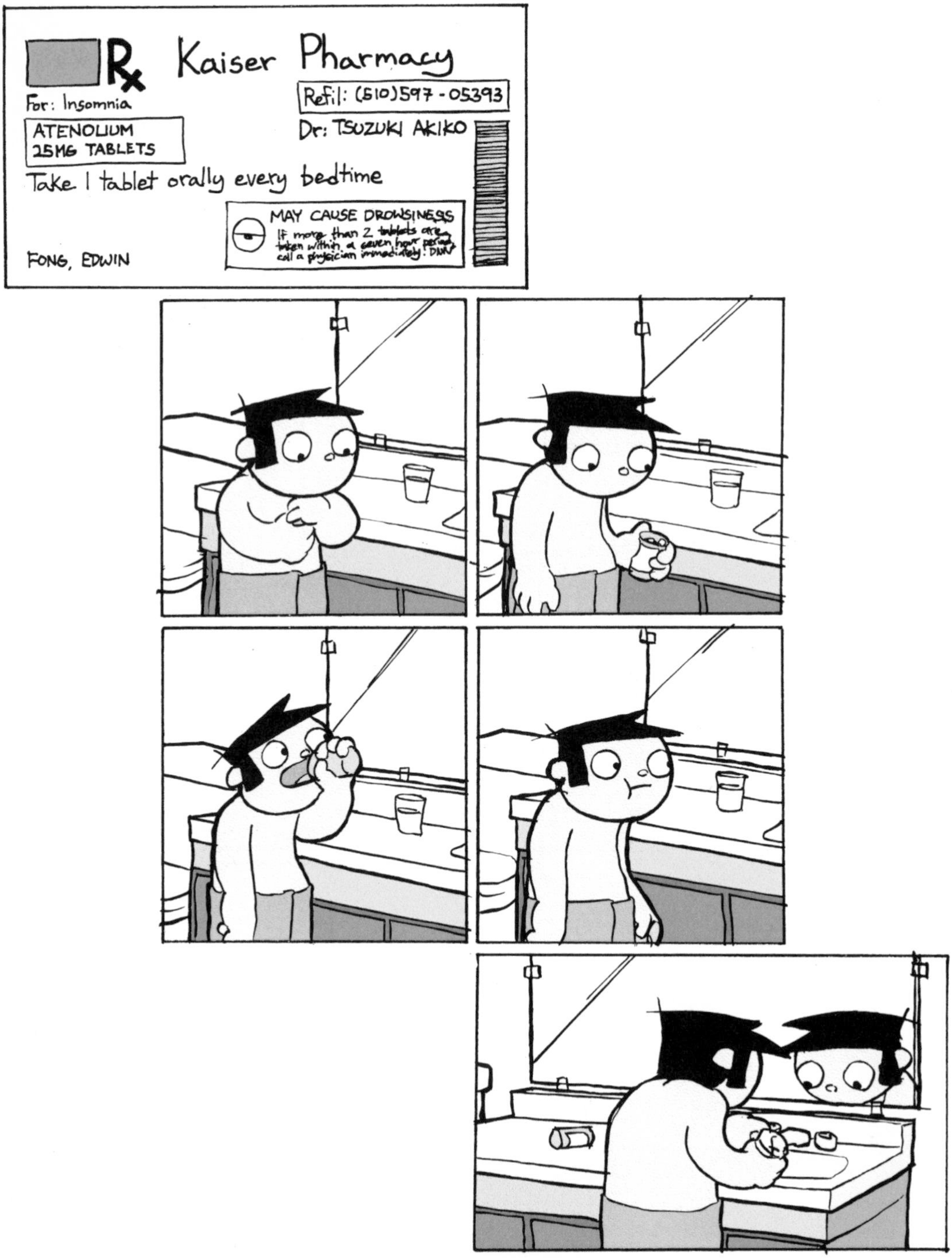

Rx Kaiser Pharmacy
For: Insomnia
Refil: (510)597-05393
ATENOLIUM
25MG TABLETS
Dr: TSUZUKI AKIKO
Take 1 tablet orally every bedtime
MAY CAUSE DROWSINESS
If more than 2 tablets are taken within a seven hour period call a physician immediately! DNN
FONG, EDWIN

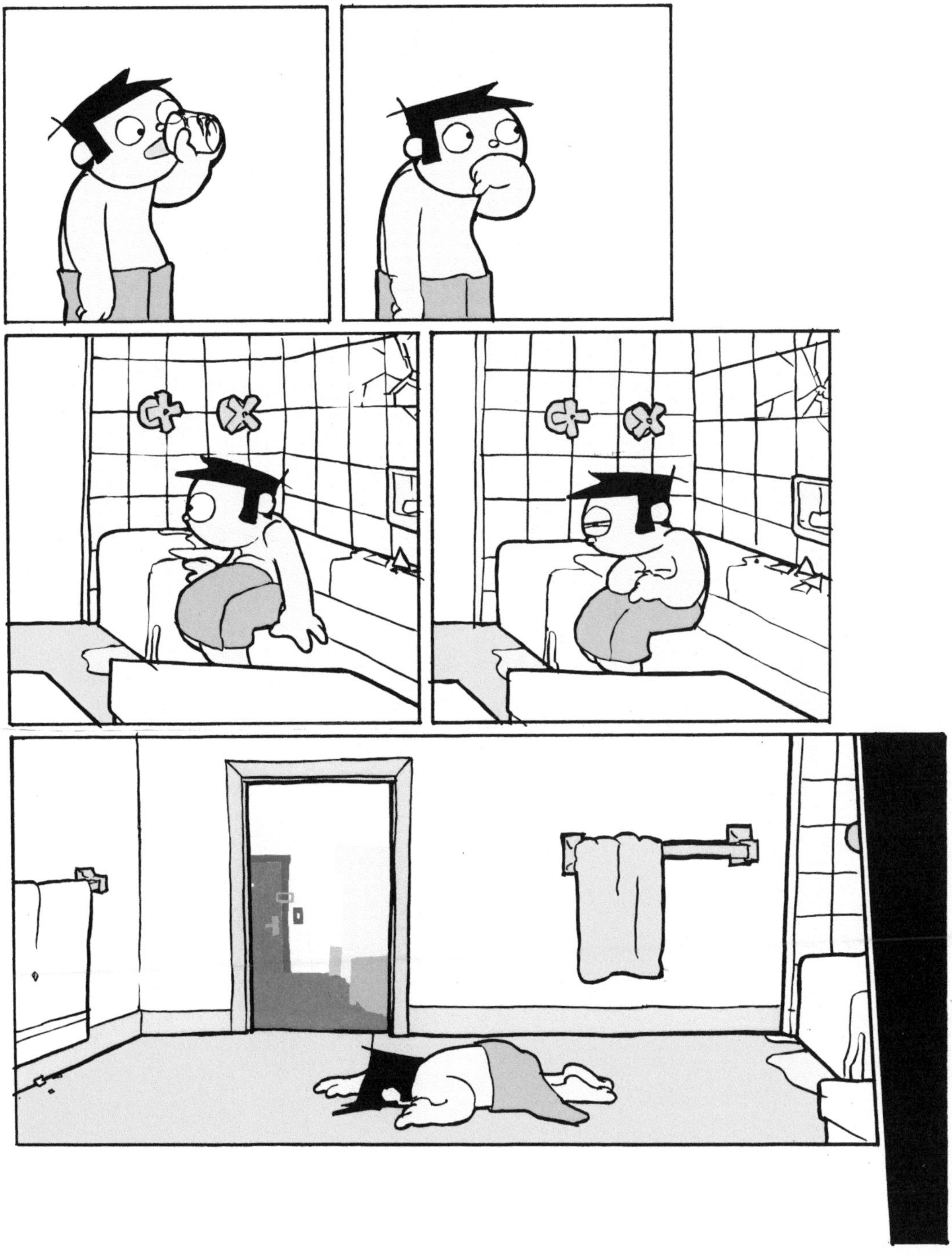

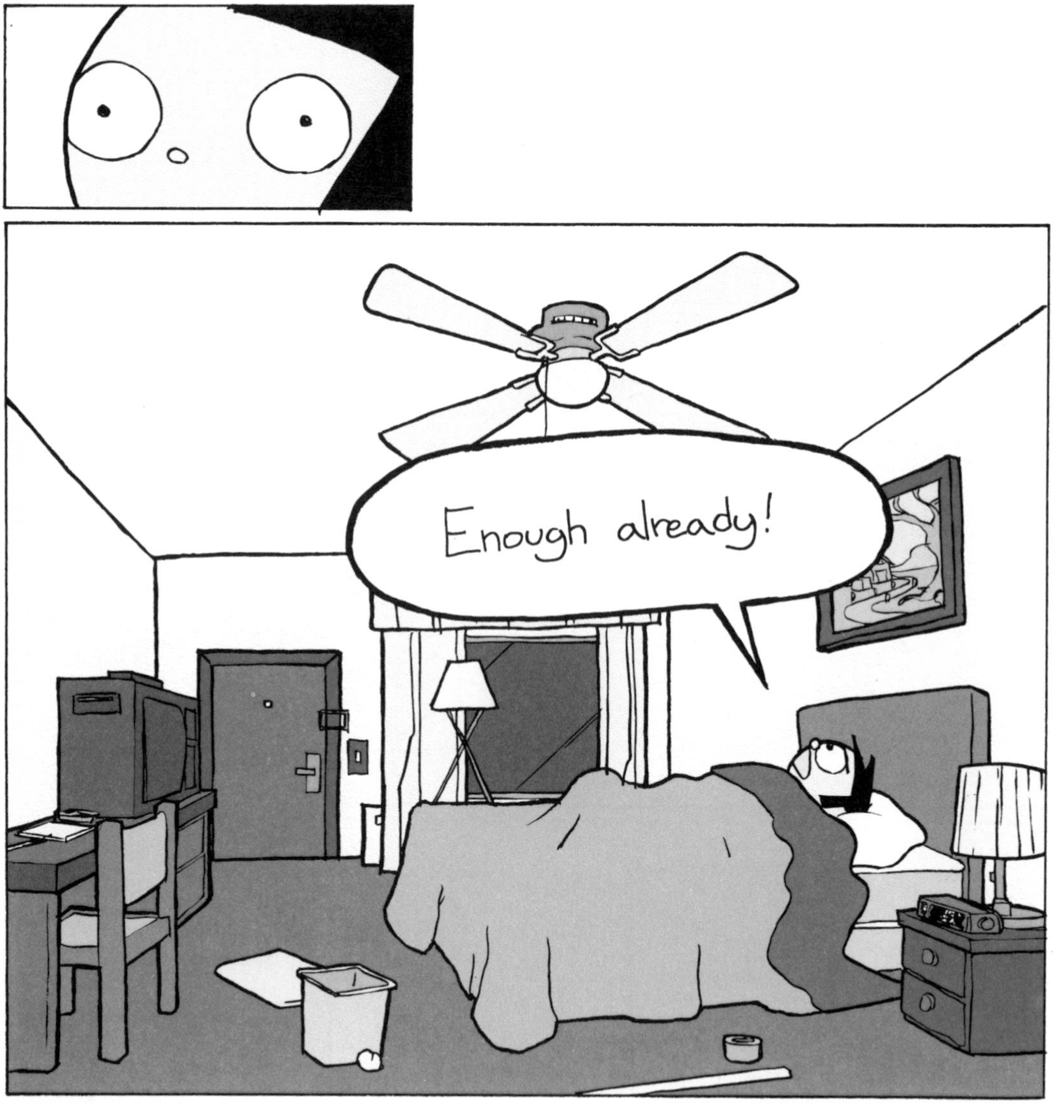
Enough already!

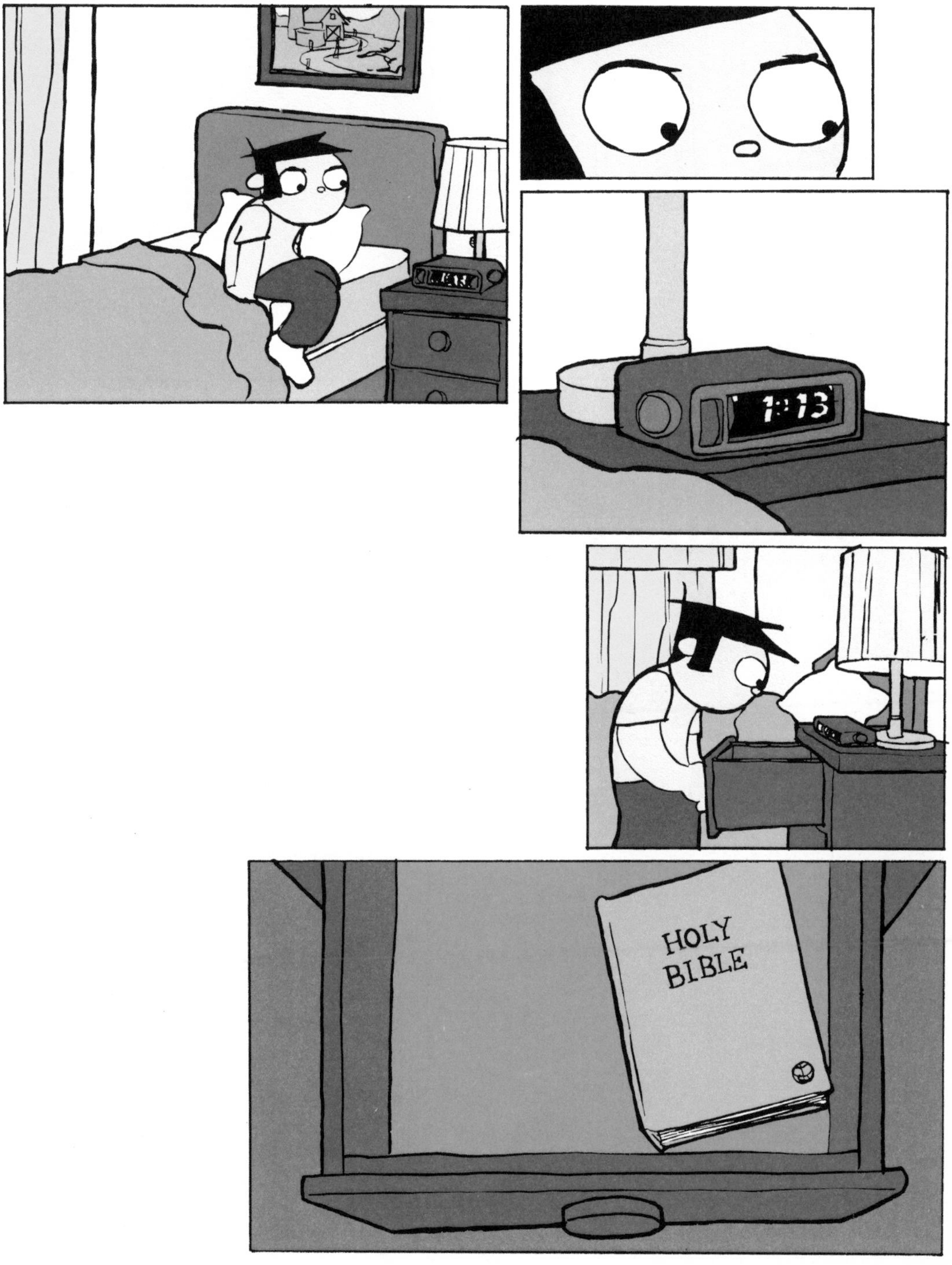
1:13
HOLY
BIBLE

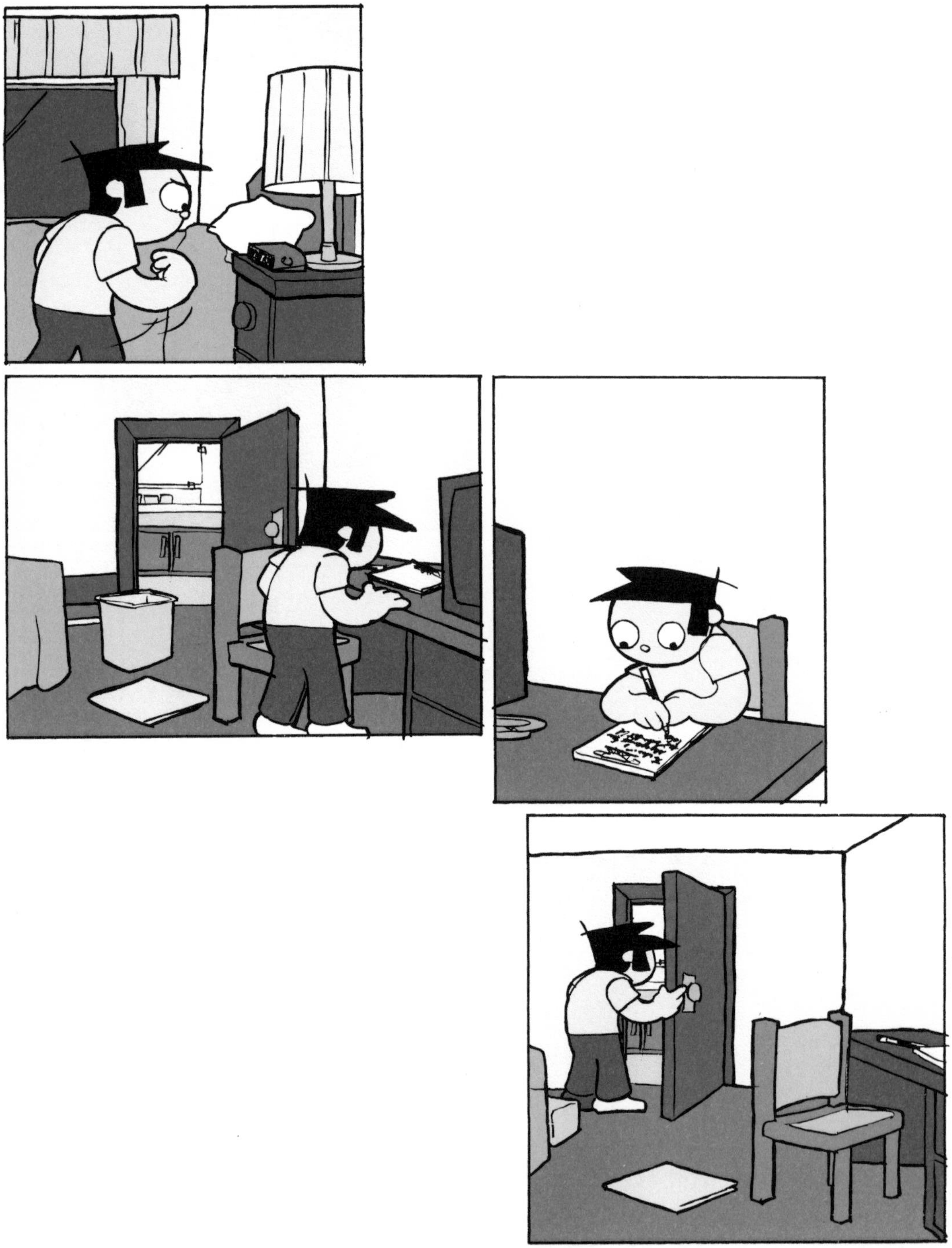

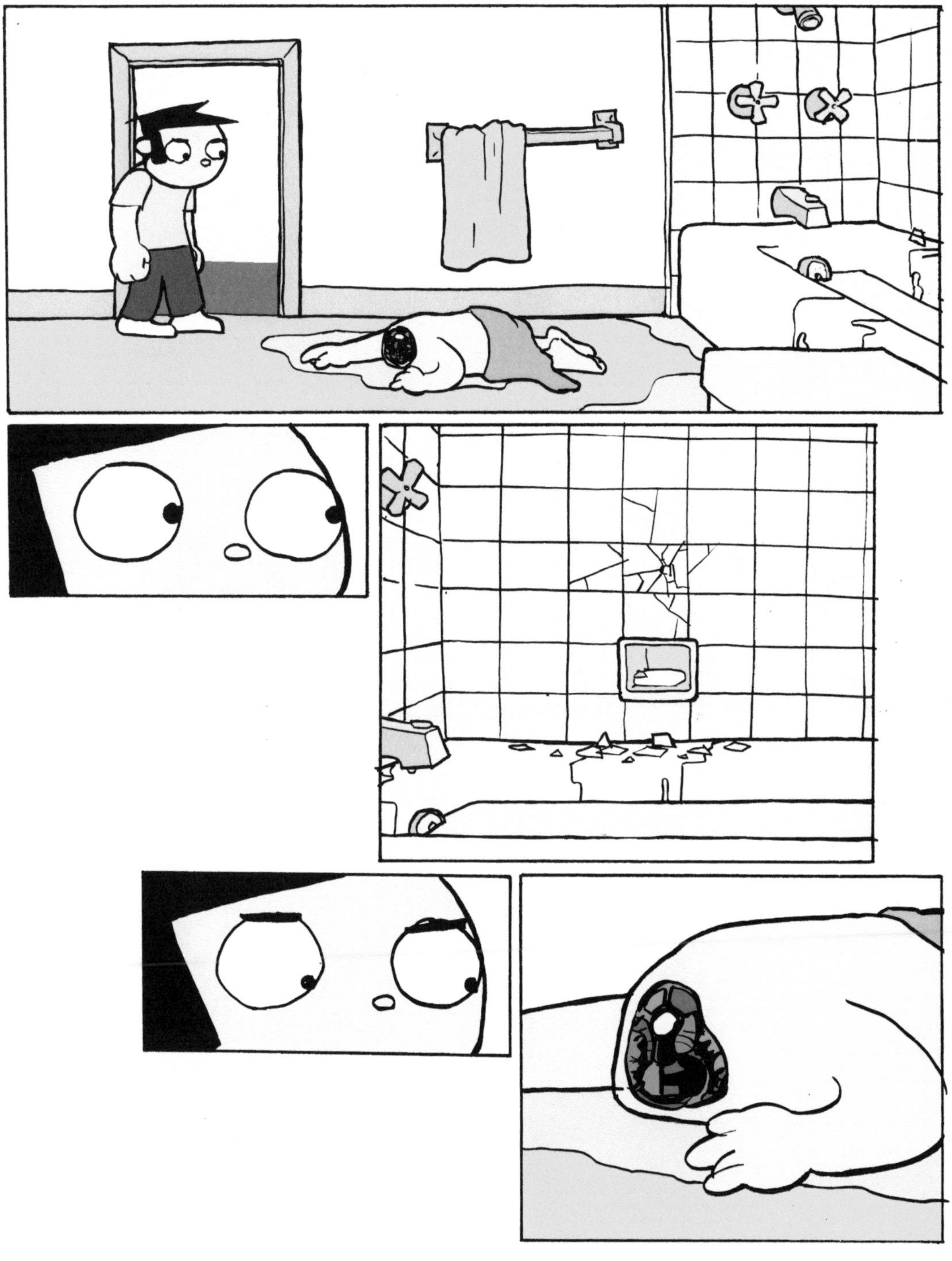

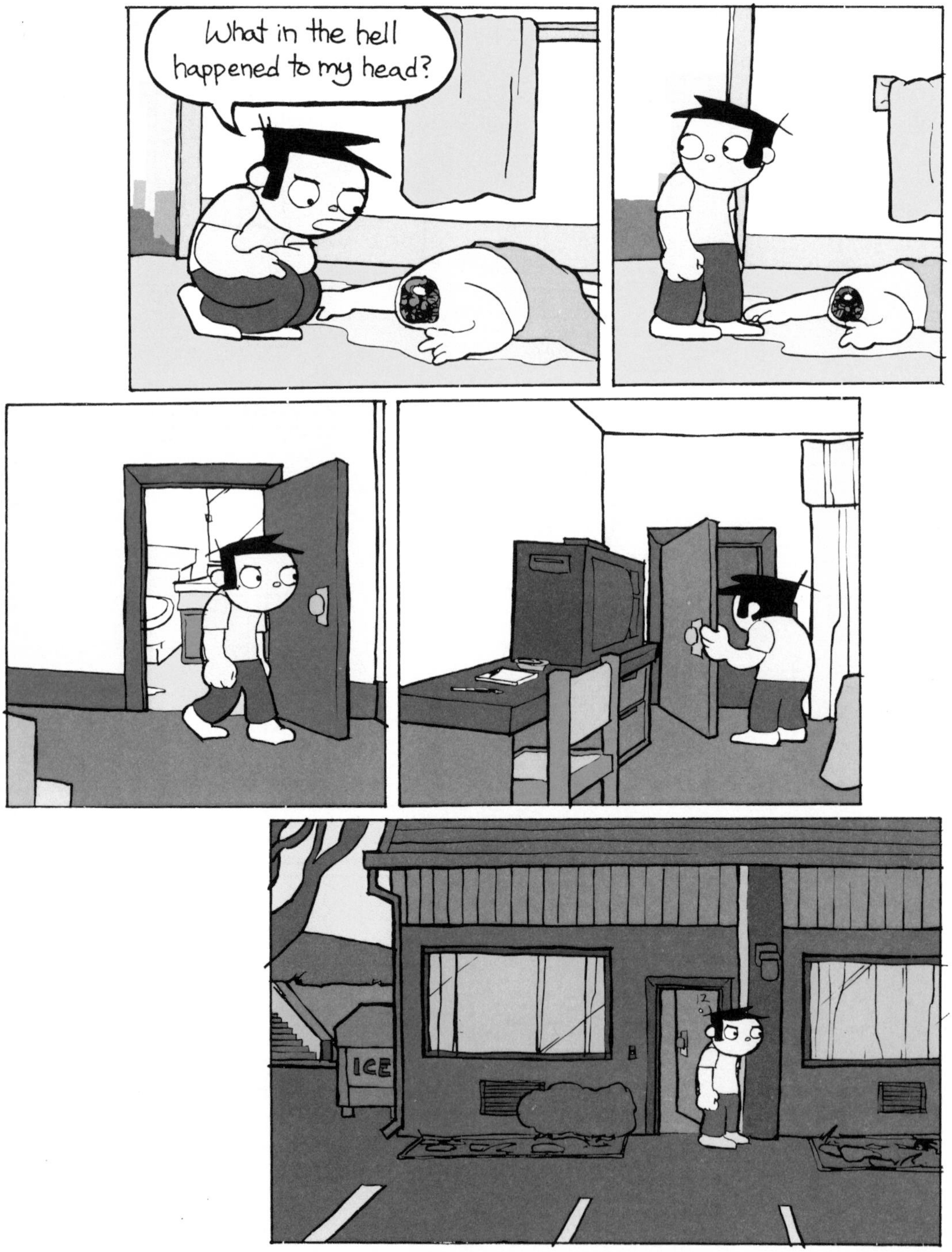
What in the hell happened to my head?
ICE

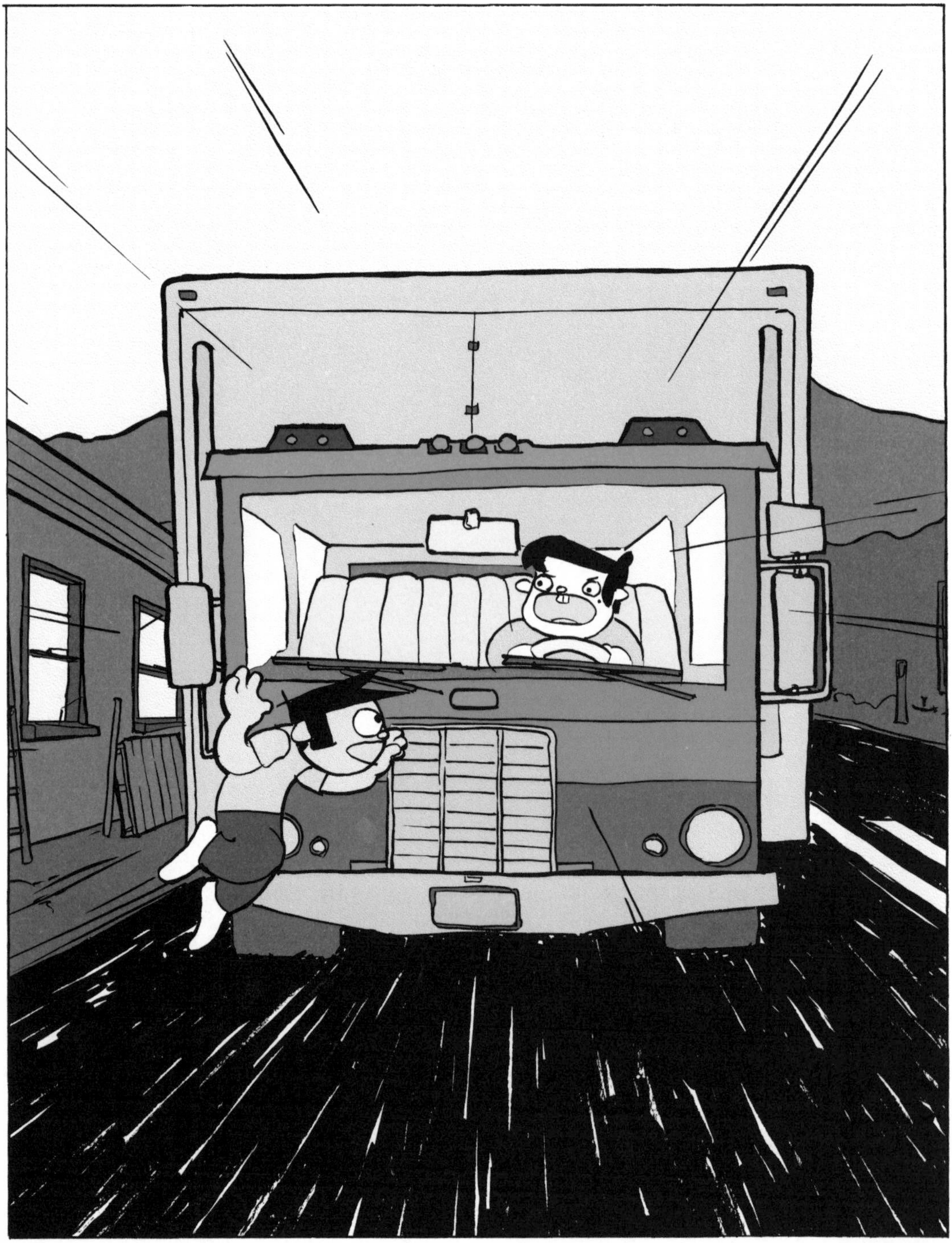

CHAPTER 2

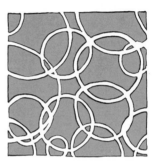
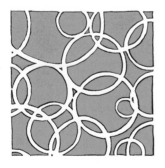
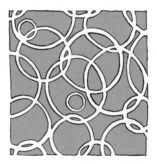

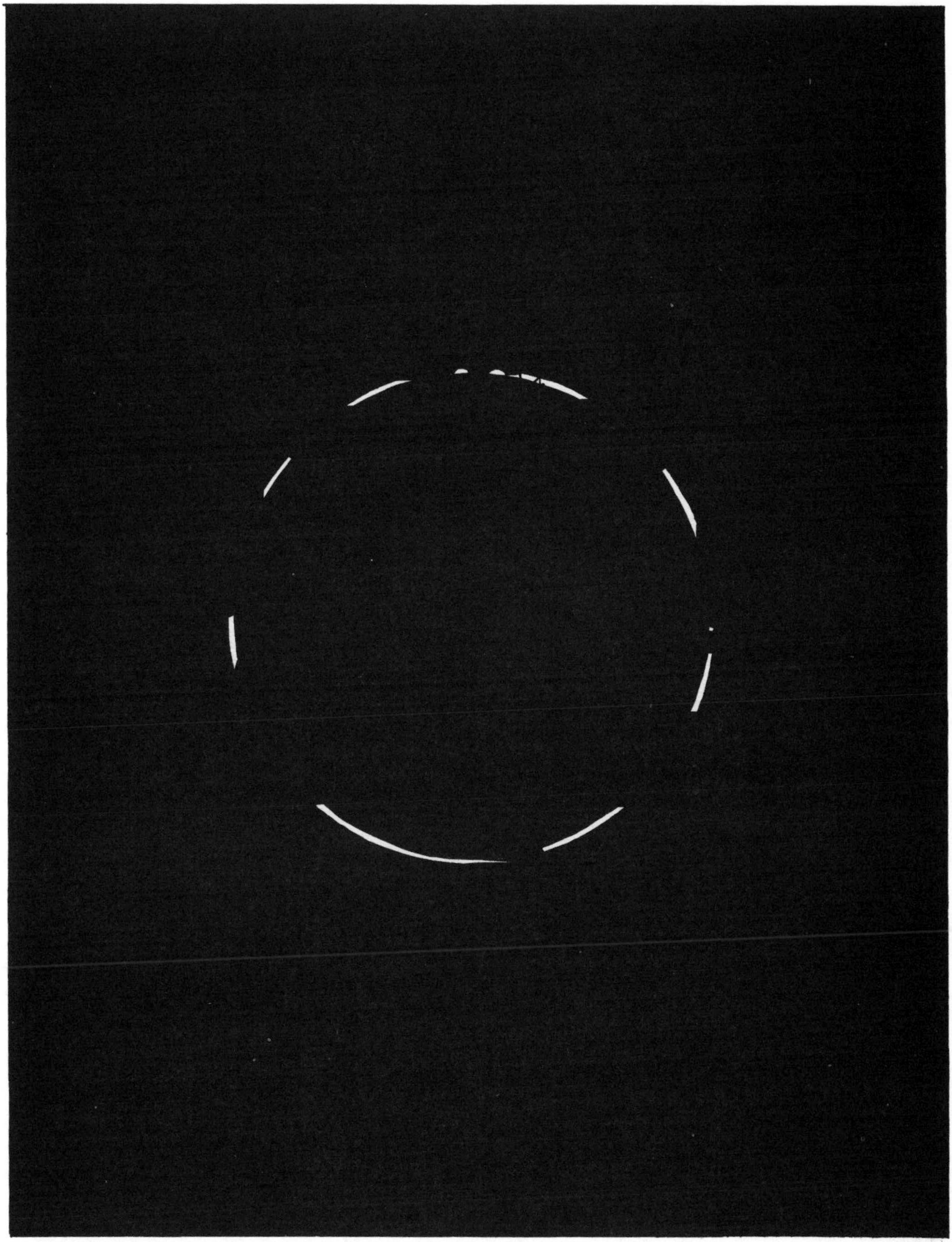

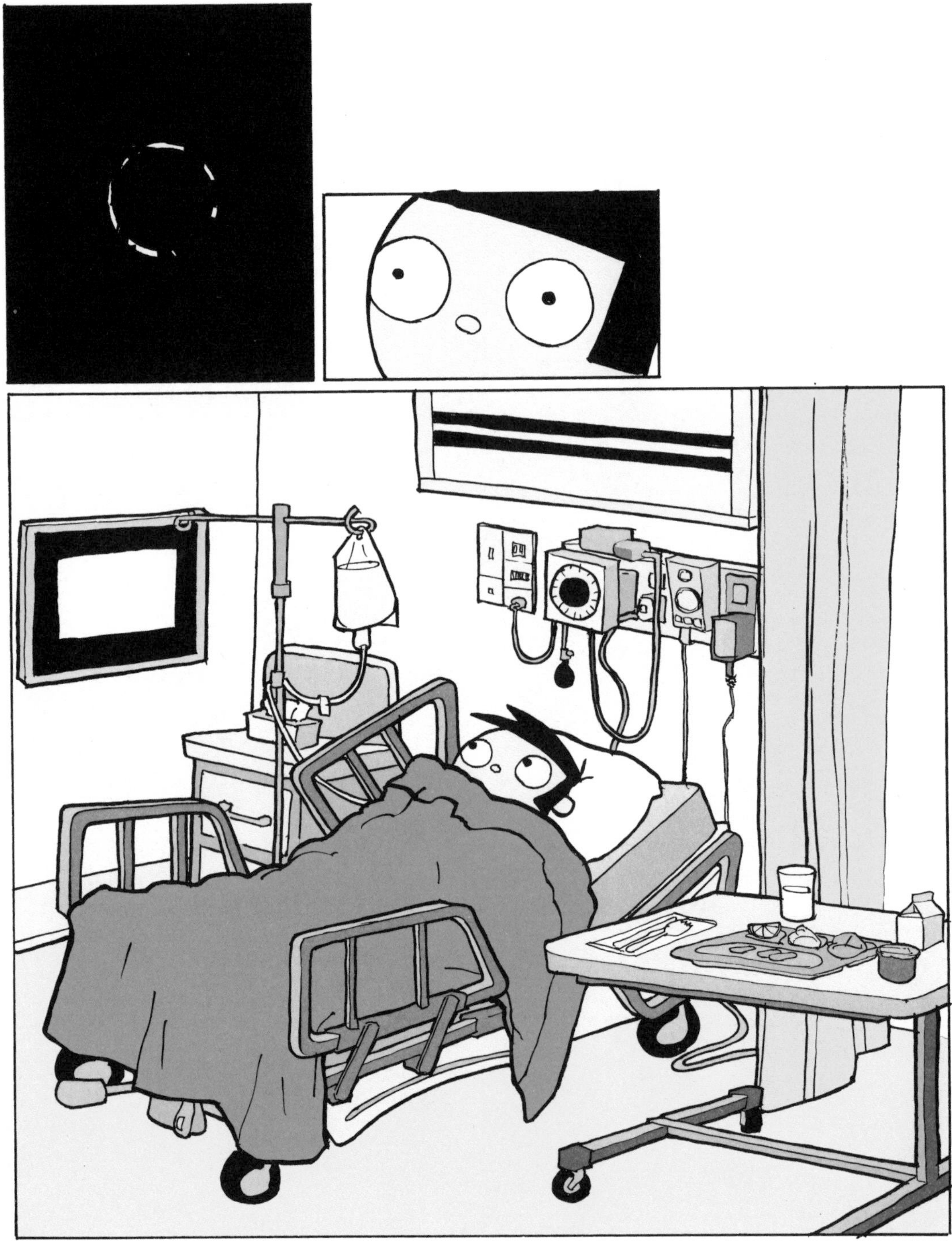

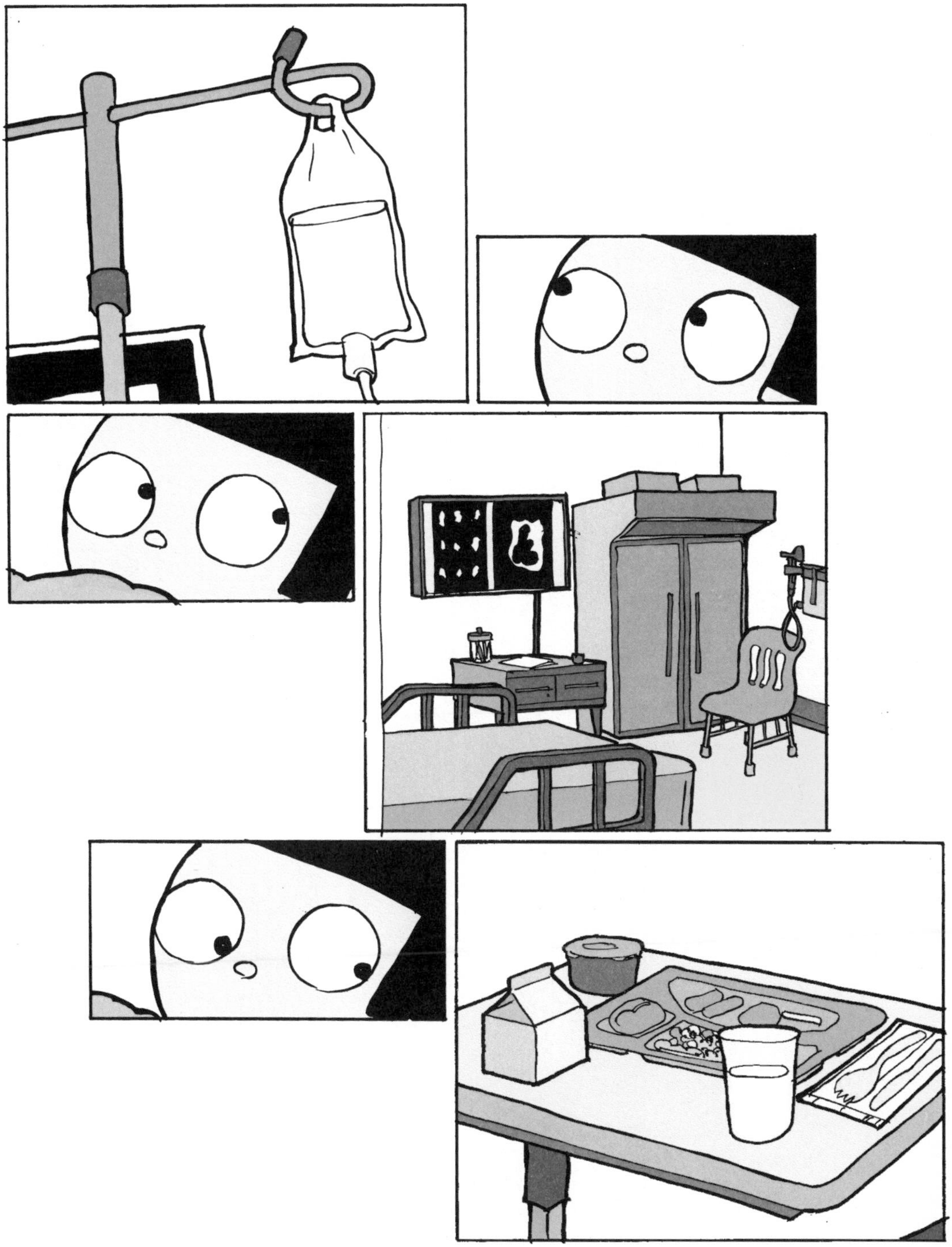

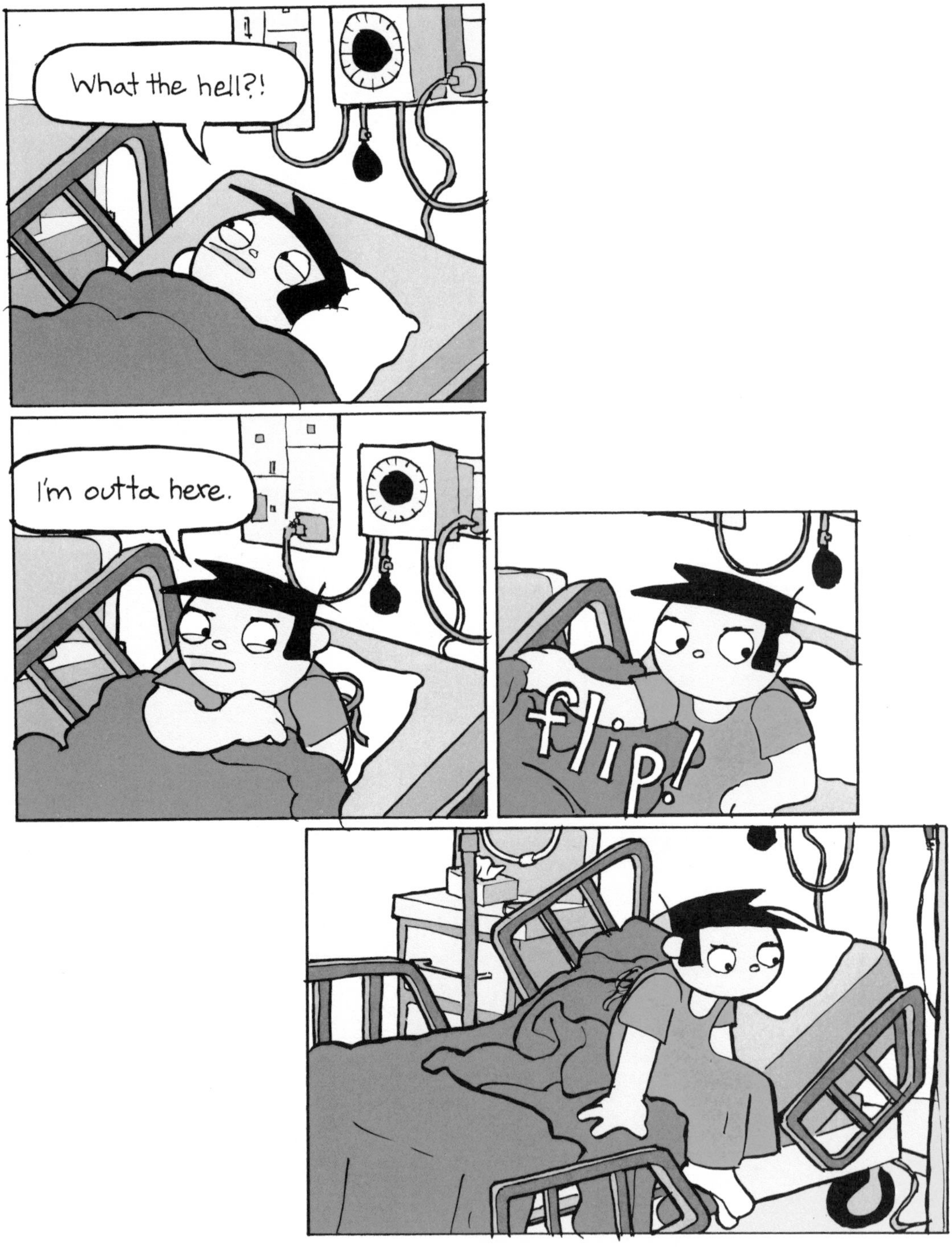
What the hell?!
I'm outta here.
flip!

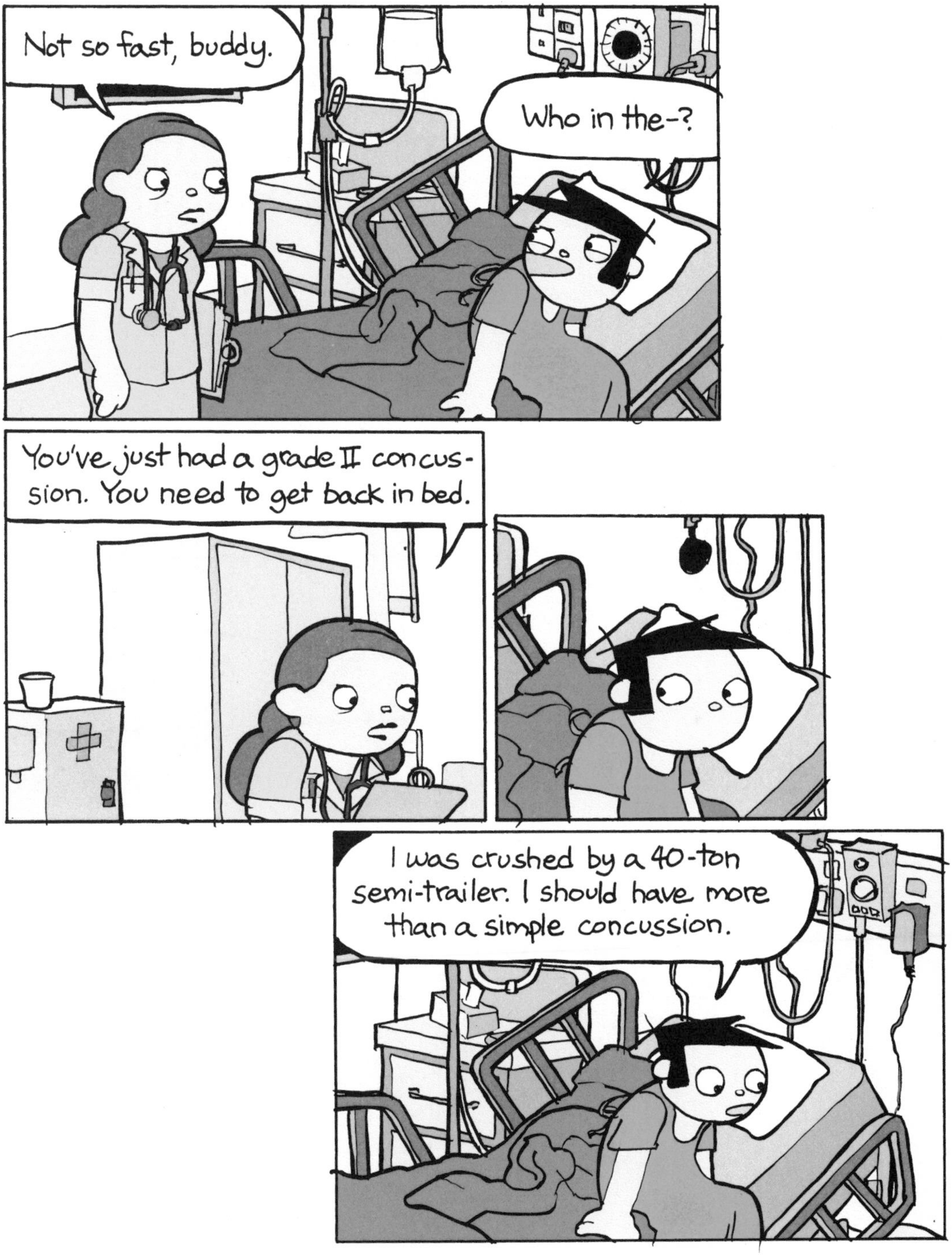
Not so fast, buddy.
Who in the-?
You've just had a grade II concussion. You need to get back in bed.
I was crushed by a 40-ton semi-trailer. I should have more than a simple concussion.

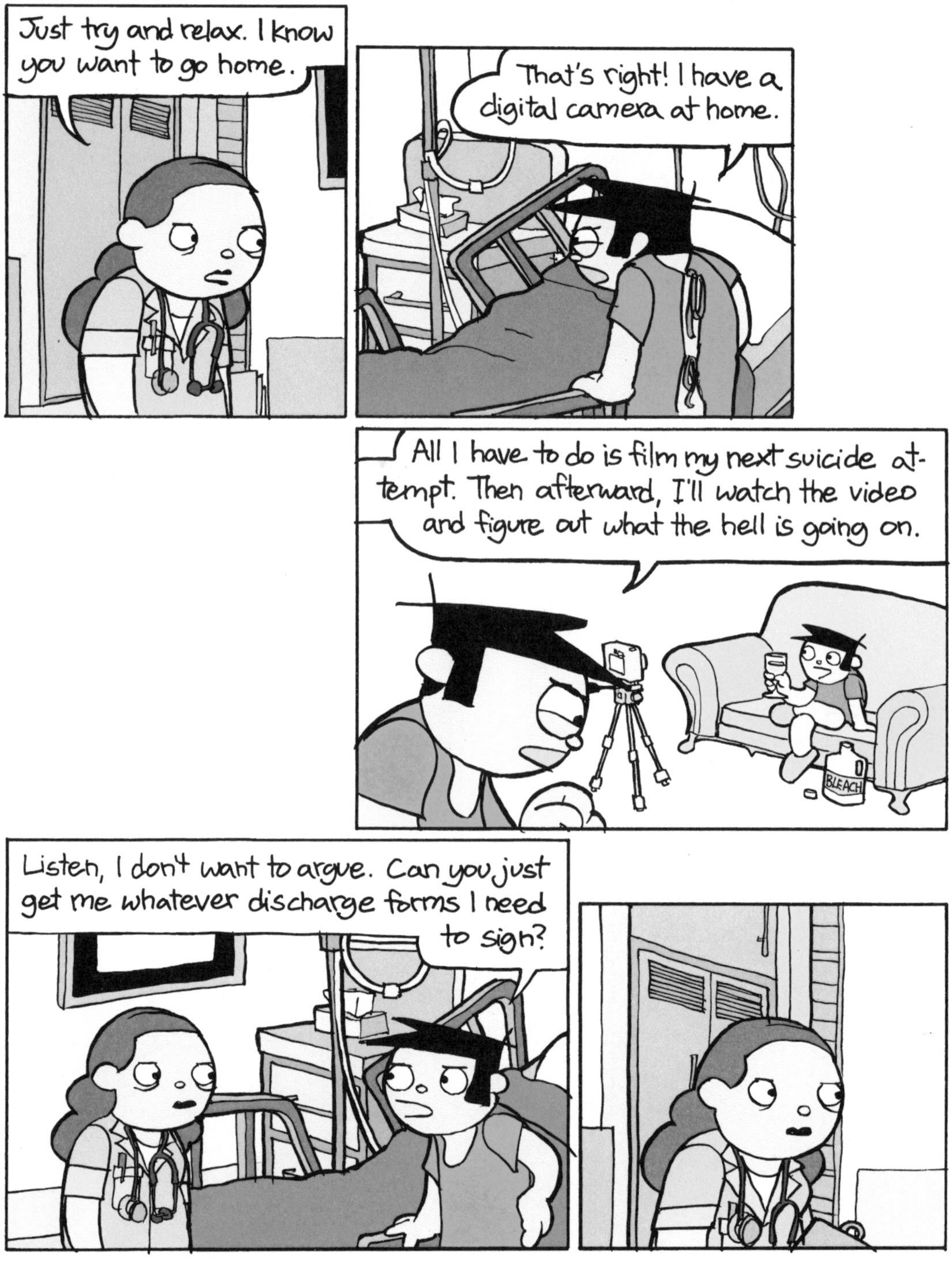
Just try and relax. I know you want to go home.
That's right! I have a digital camera at home.
All I have to do is film my next suicide attempt. Then afterward, I'll watch the video and figure out what the hell is going on.
BLEACH
Listen, I don't want to argue. Can you just get me whatever discharge forms I need to sign?

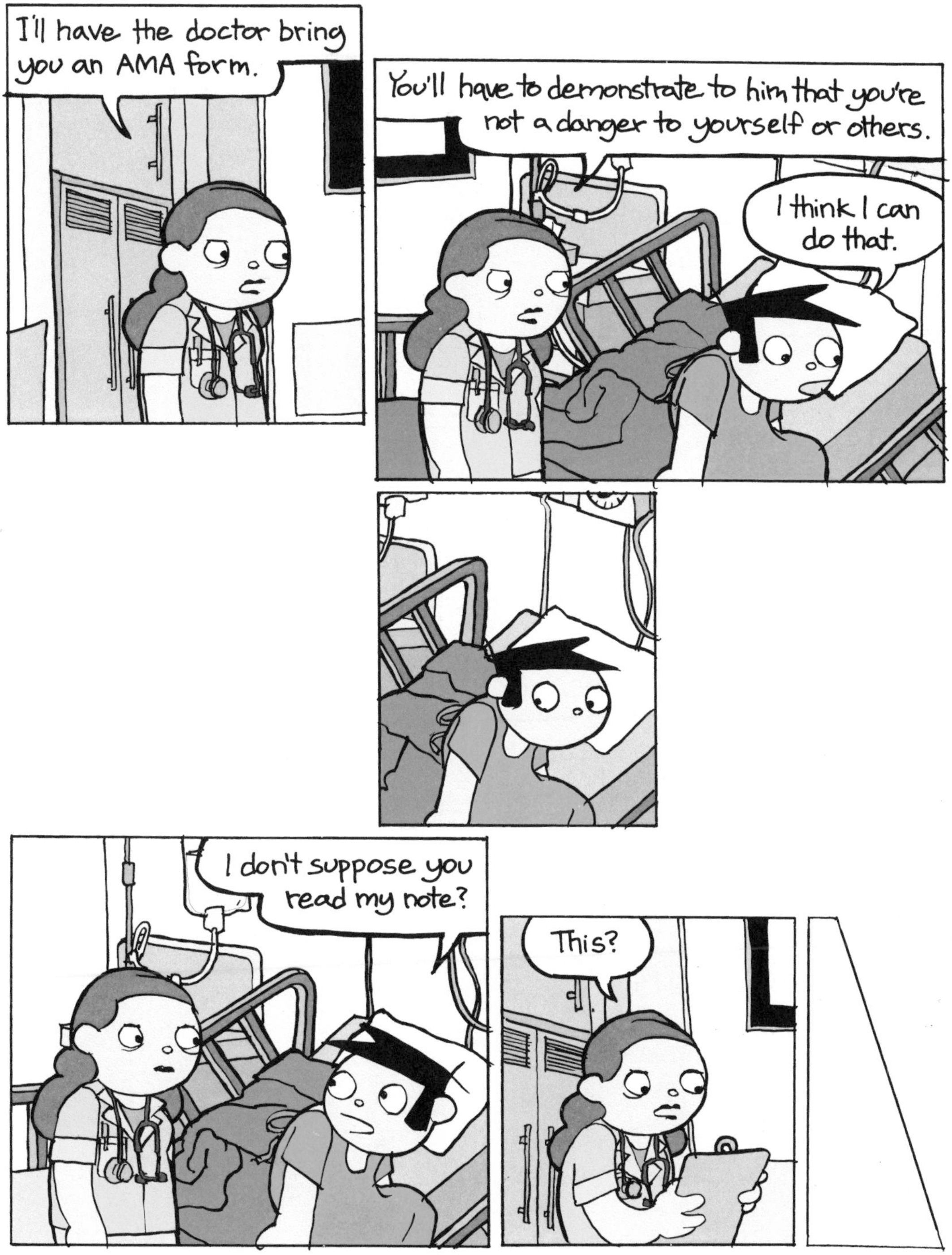
I'll have the doctor bring you an AMA form.
You'll have to demonstrate to him that you're not a danger to yourself or others.
I think I can do that.
I don't suppose you read my note?
This?

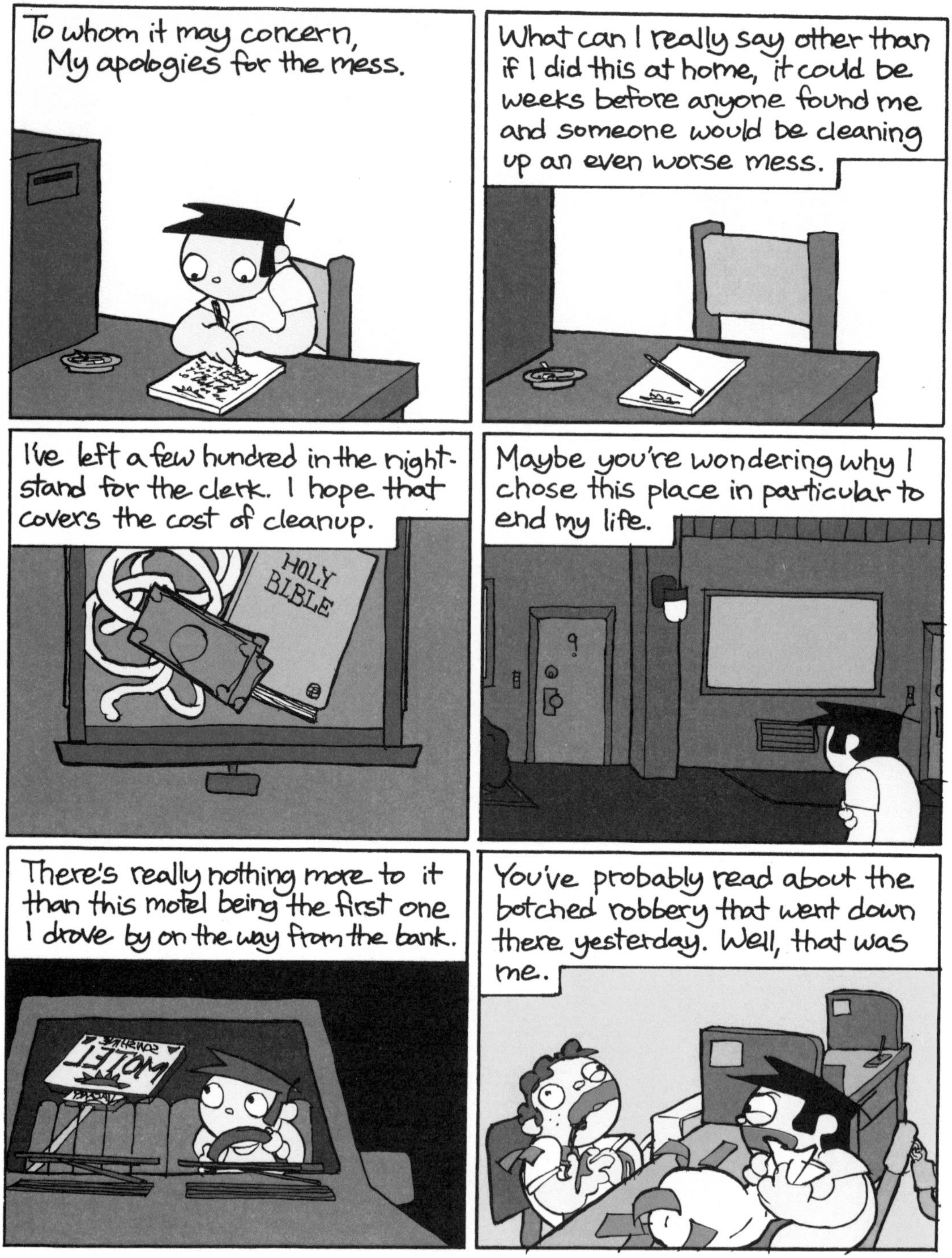
To whom it may concern,
My apologies for the mess.
What can I really say other than if I did this at home, it could be weeks before anyone found me and someone would be cleaning up an even worse mess.
I've left a few hundred in the night-stand for the clerk. I hope that covers the cost of cleanup.
HOLY BIBLE
Maybe you're wondering why I chose this place in particular to end my life.
There's really nothing more to it than this motel being the first one I drove by on the way from the bank.
You've probably read about the botched robbery that went down there yesterday. Well, that was me.

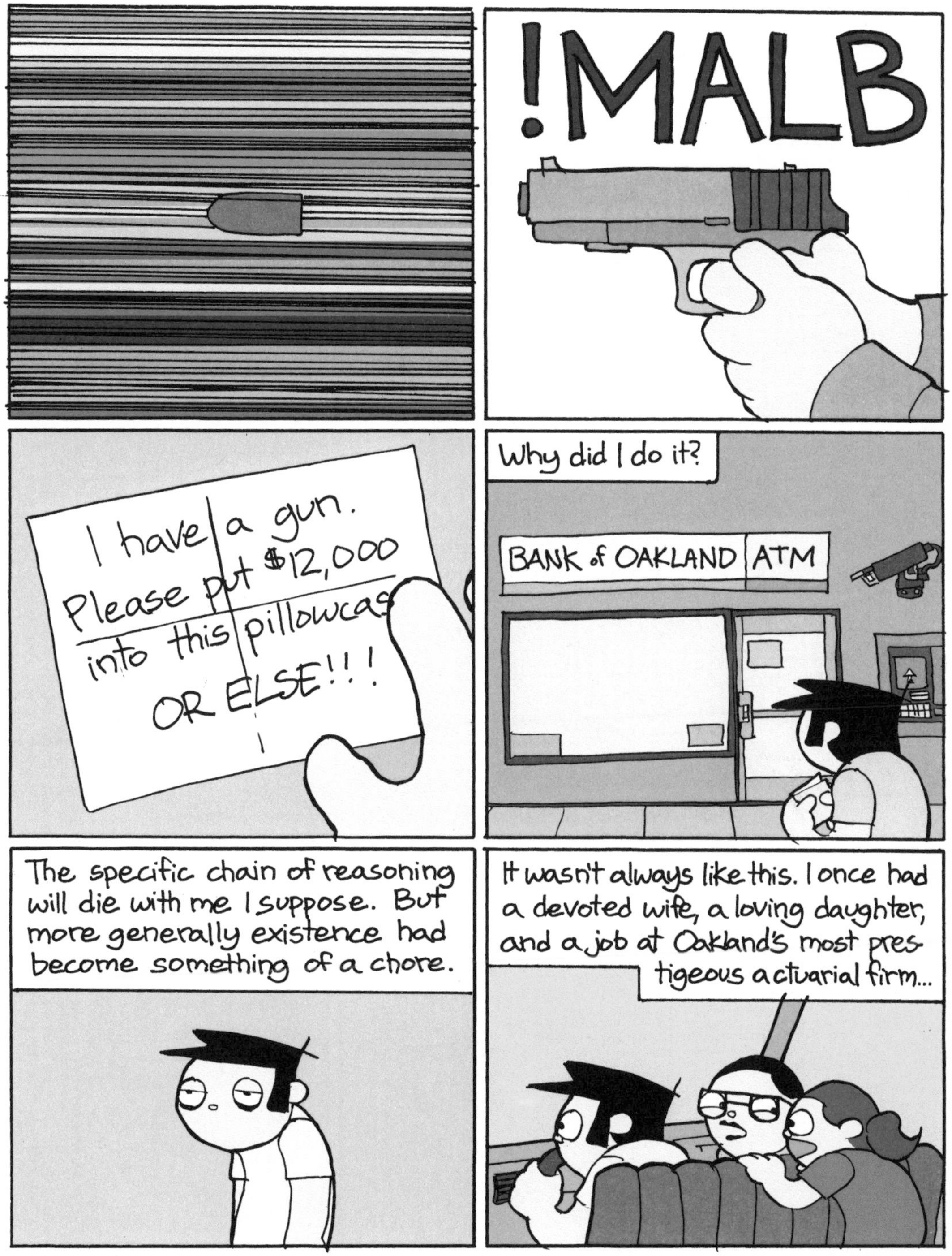
!MALB
I have a gun.
Please put $12,000
into this pillowcas
OR ELSE!!!
Why did I do it?
BANK of OAKLAND
ATM
The specific chain of reasoning will die with me I suppose. But more generally existence had become something of a chore.
It wasn't always like this. I once had a devoted wife, a loving daughter, and a job at Oakland's most prestigeous actuarial firm...

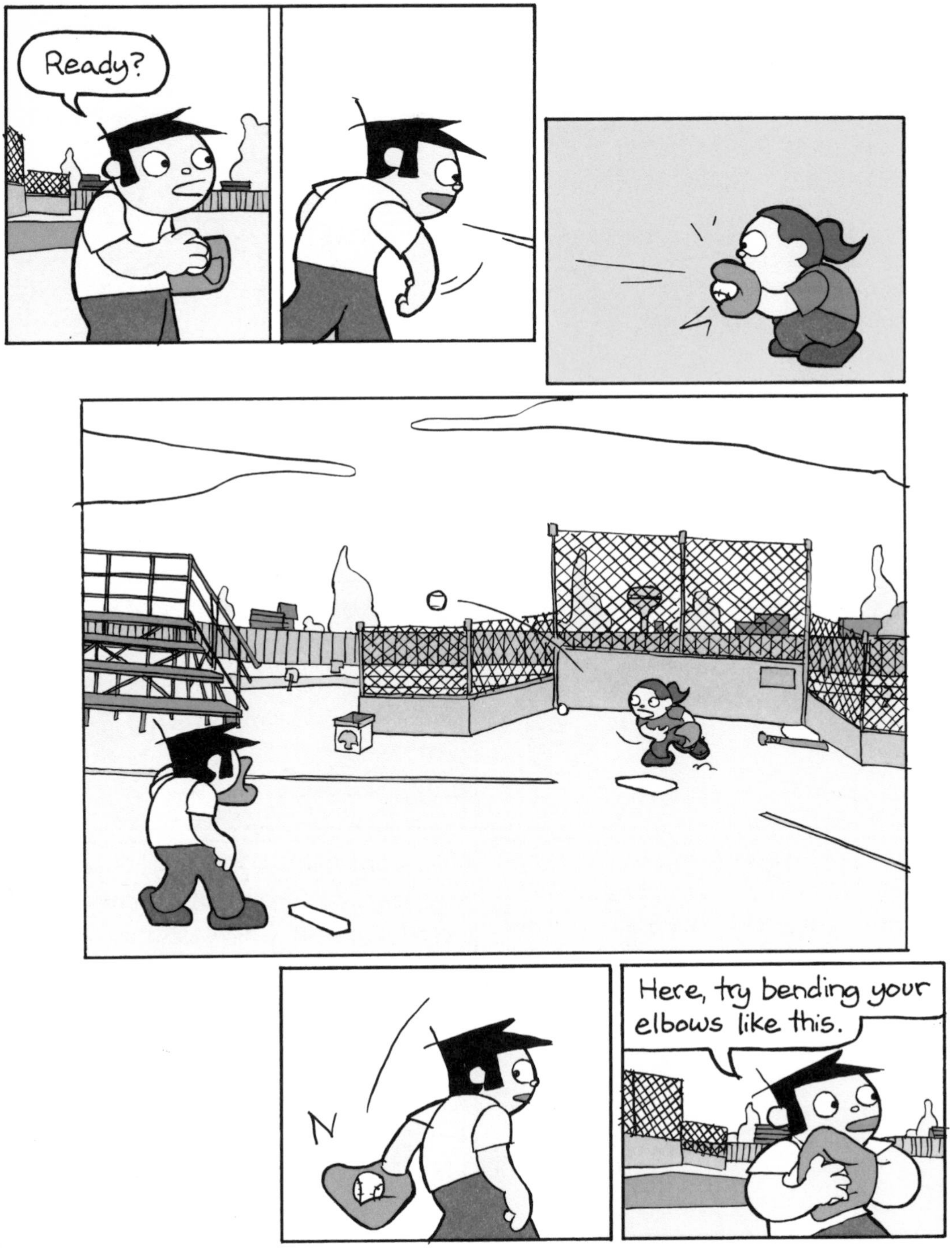
Ready?
N
Here, try bending your elbows like this.

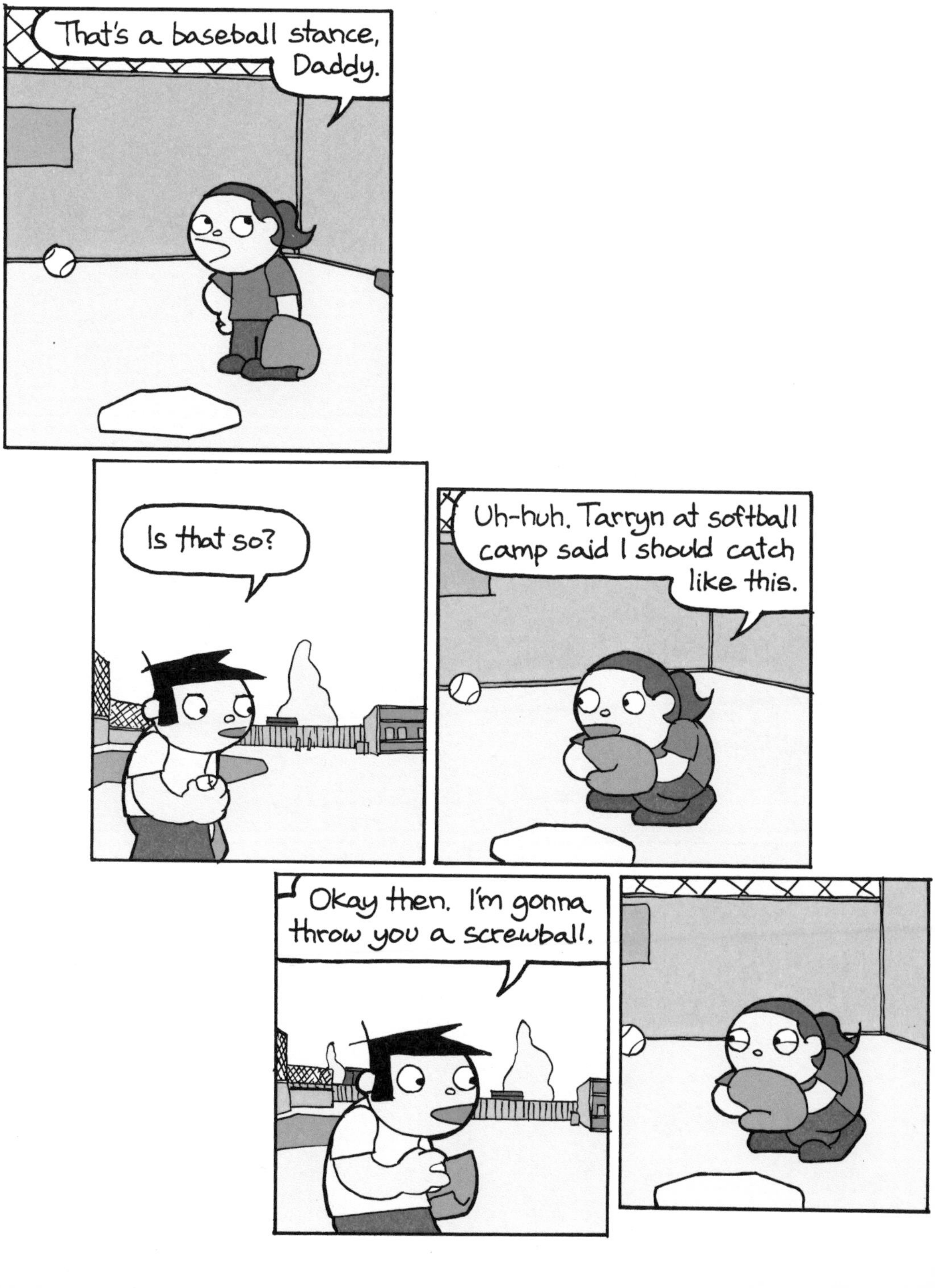
That's a baseball stance, Daddy.
Is that so?
Uh-huh. Tarryn at softball camp said I should catch like this.
Okay then. I'm gonna throw you a screwball.

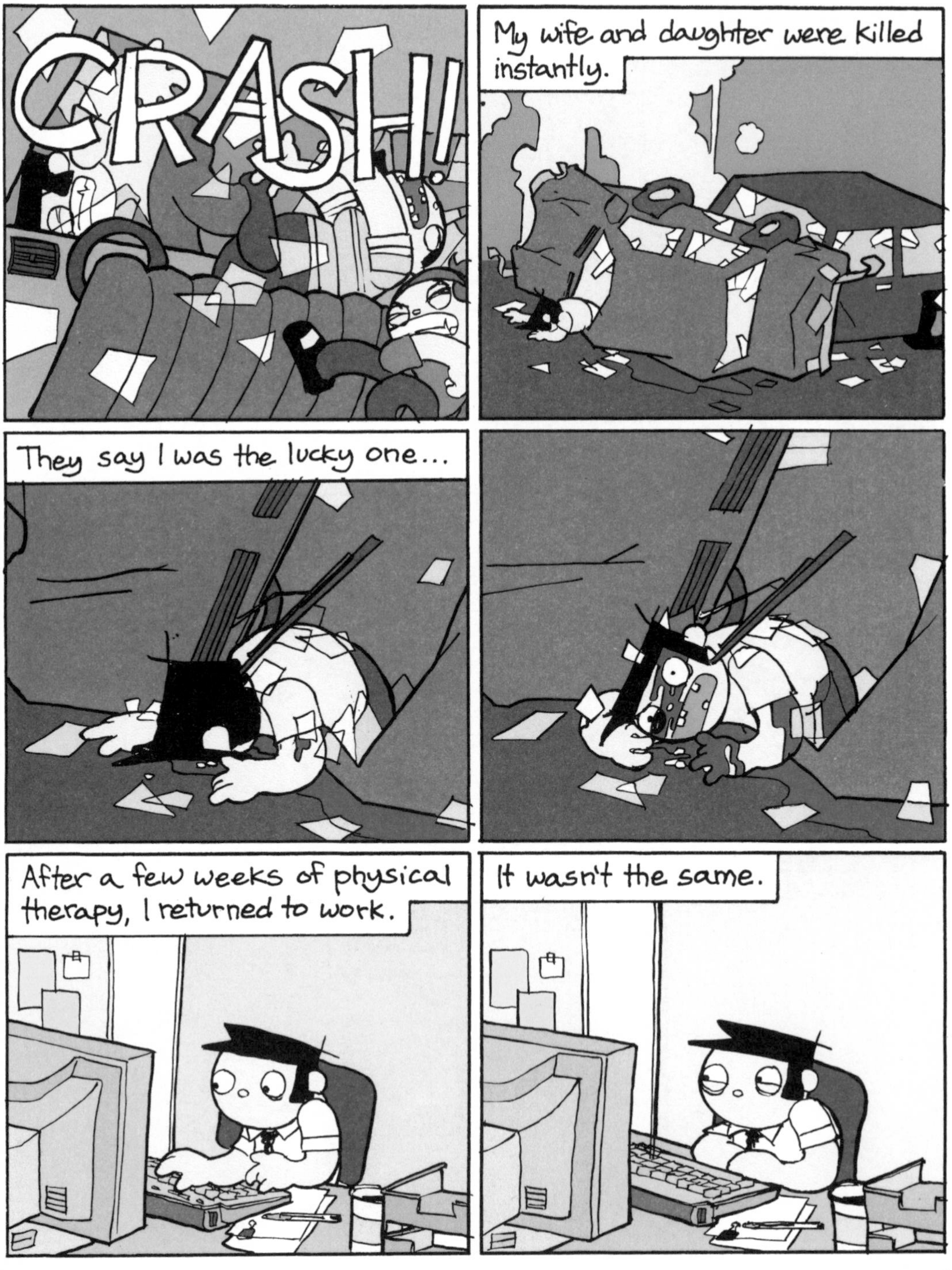
CRASH!!
My wife and daughter were killed instantly.
They say I was the lucky one...
After a few weeks of physical therapy, I returned to work.
It wasn't the same.

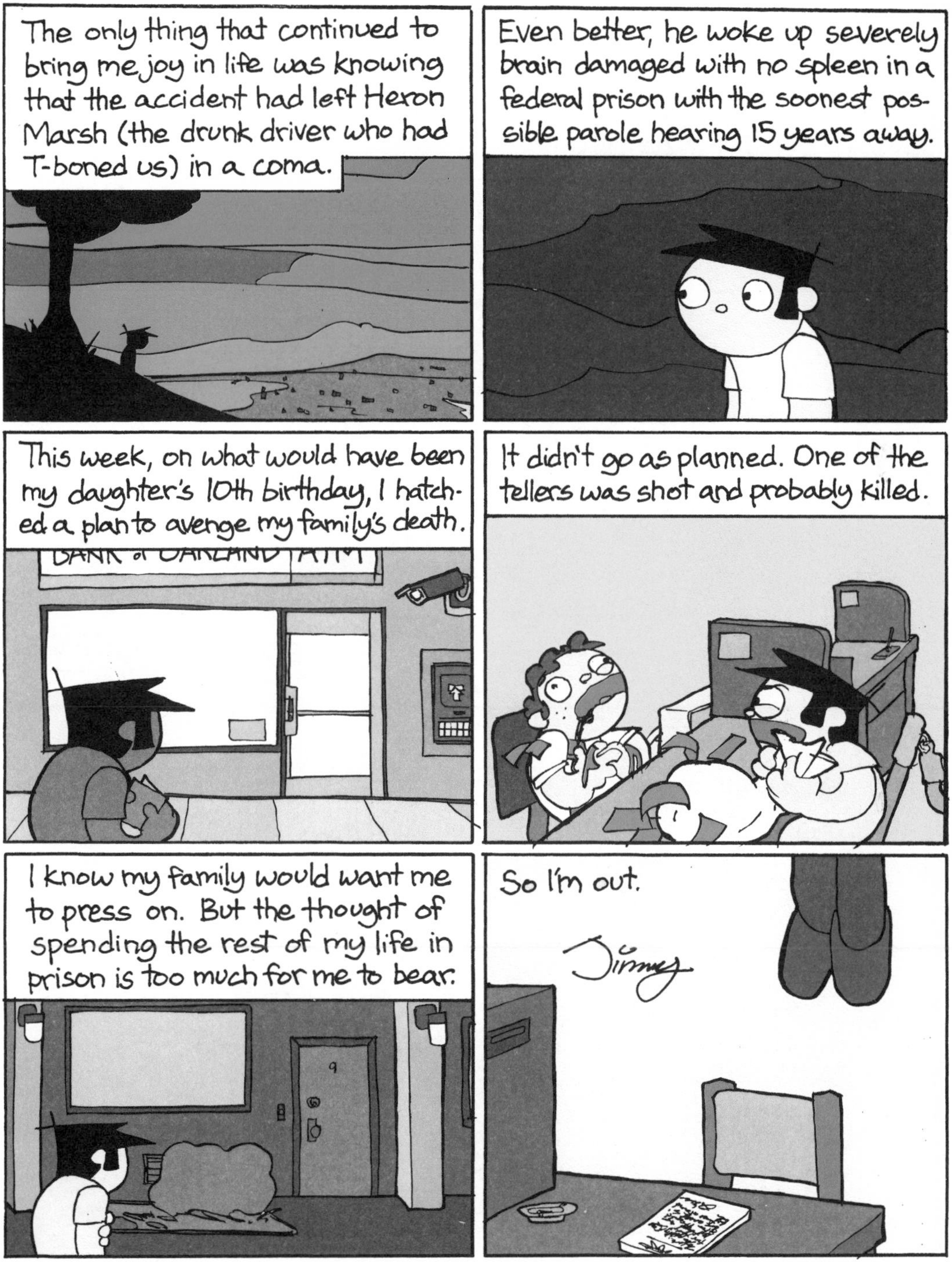

The only thing that continued to bring me joy in life was knowing that the accident had left Heron Marsh (the drunk driver who had T-boned us) in a coma.
Even better, he woke up severely brain damaged with no spleen in a federal prison with the soonest possible parole hearing 15 years away.
This week, on what would have been my daughter's 10th birthday, I hatched a plan to avenge my family's death.
It didn't go as planned. One of the tellers was shot and probably killed.
I know my family would want me to press on. But the thought of spending the rest of my life in prison is too much for me to bear.
So I'm out.
Jimmy

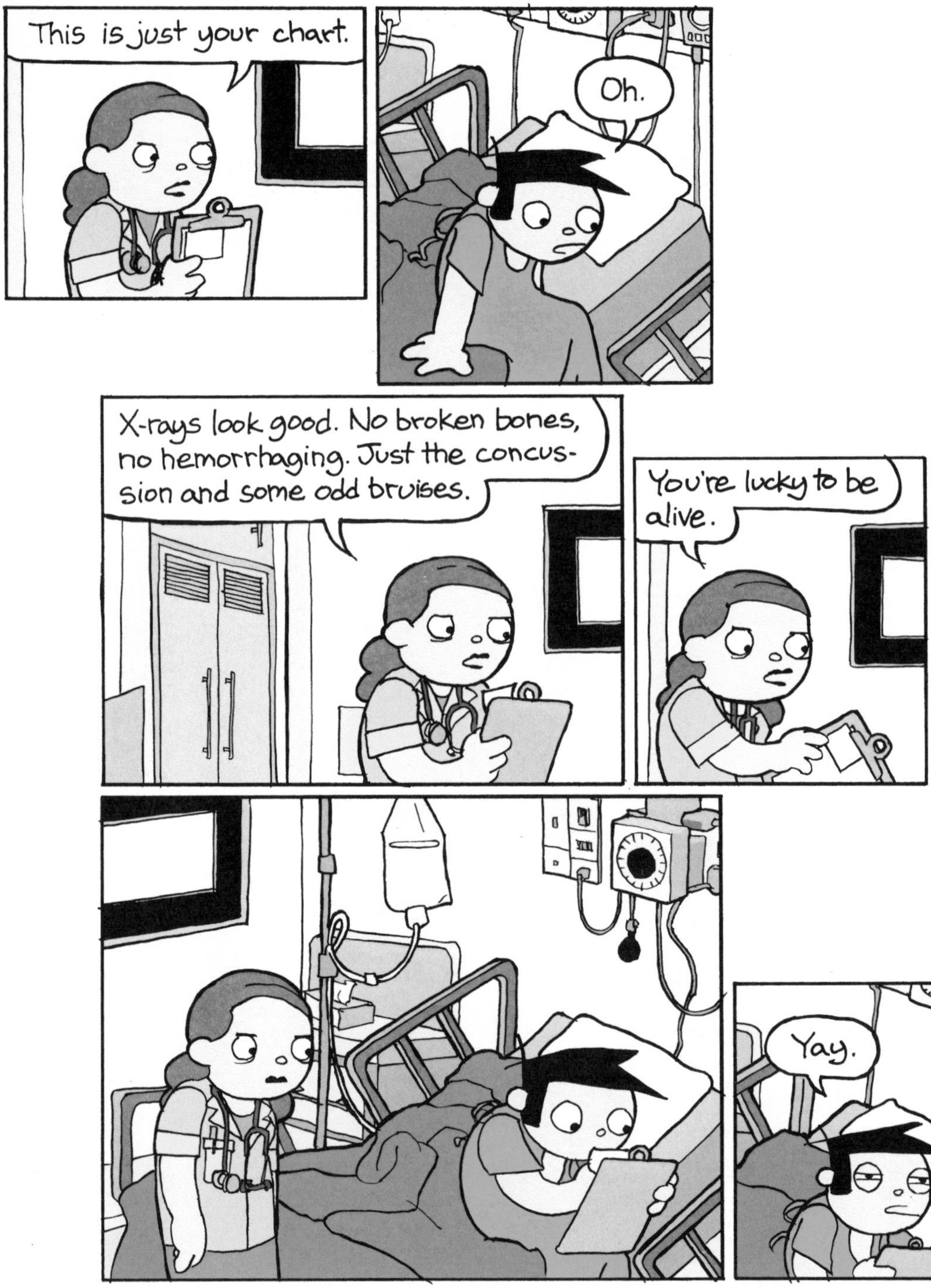
This is just your chart.
Oh.
X-rays look good. No broken bones, no hemorrhaging. Just the concussion and some odd bruises.
You're lucky to be alive.
Yay.

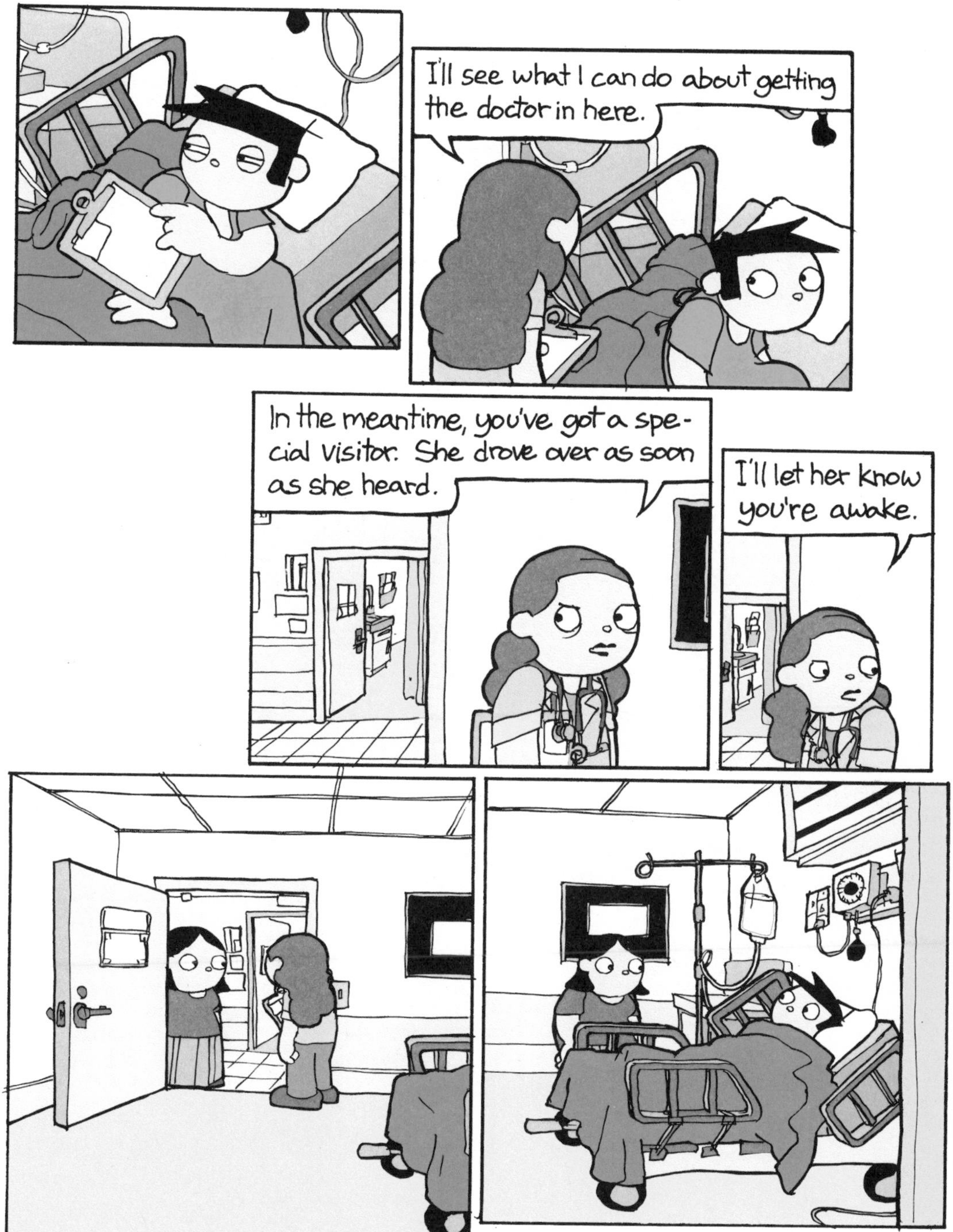
I'll see what I can do about getting the doctor in here.
In the meantime, you've got a special visitor. She drove over as soon as she heard.
I'll let her know you're awake.

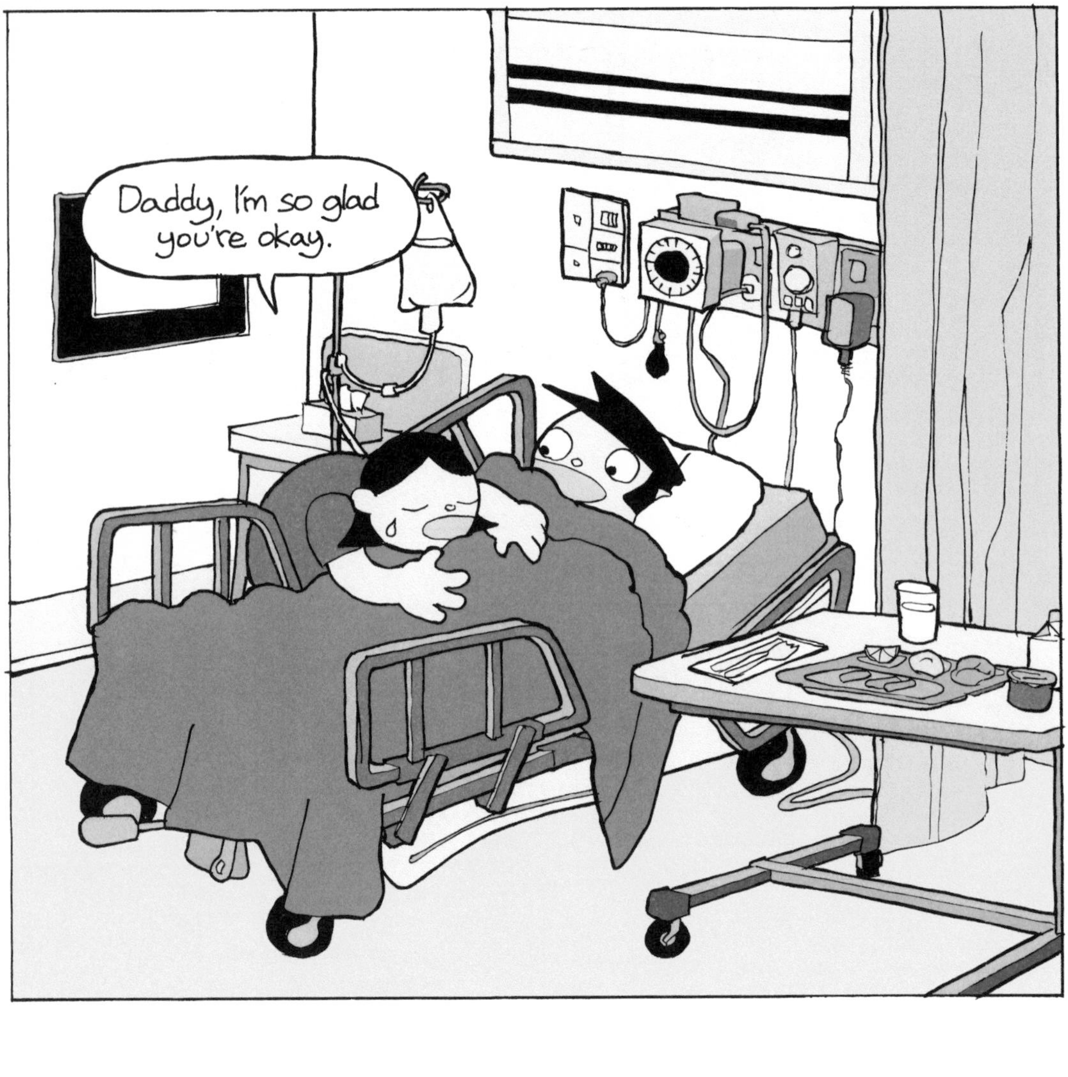
Daddy, I'm so glad you're okay.

CHAPTER 3

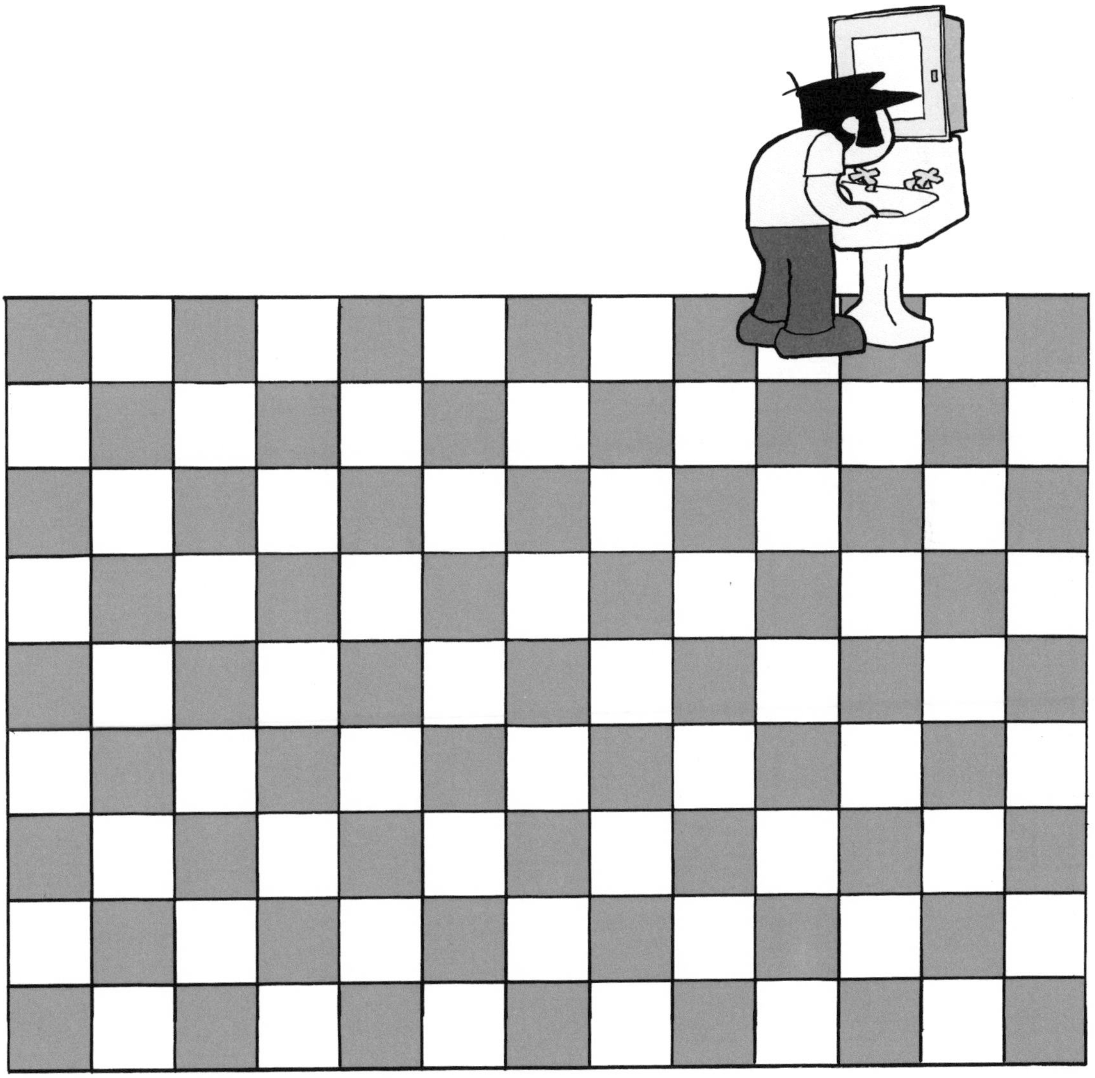

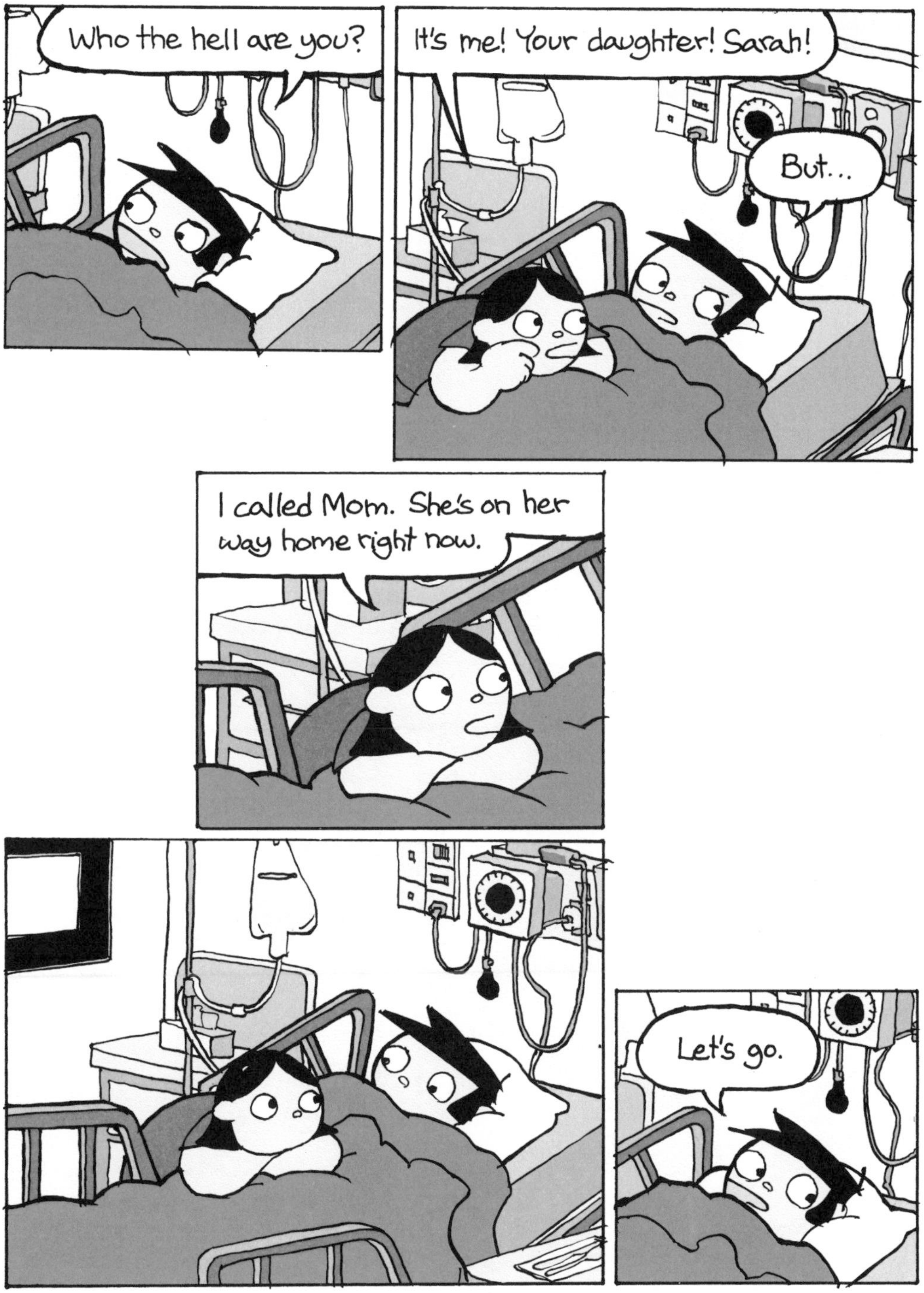
Who the hell are you?
It's me! Your daughter! Sarah!
But...
I called Mom. She's on her way home right now.
Let's go.

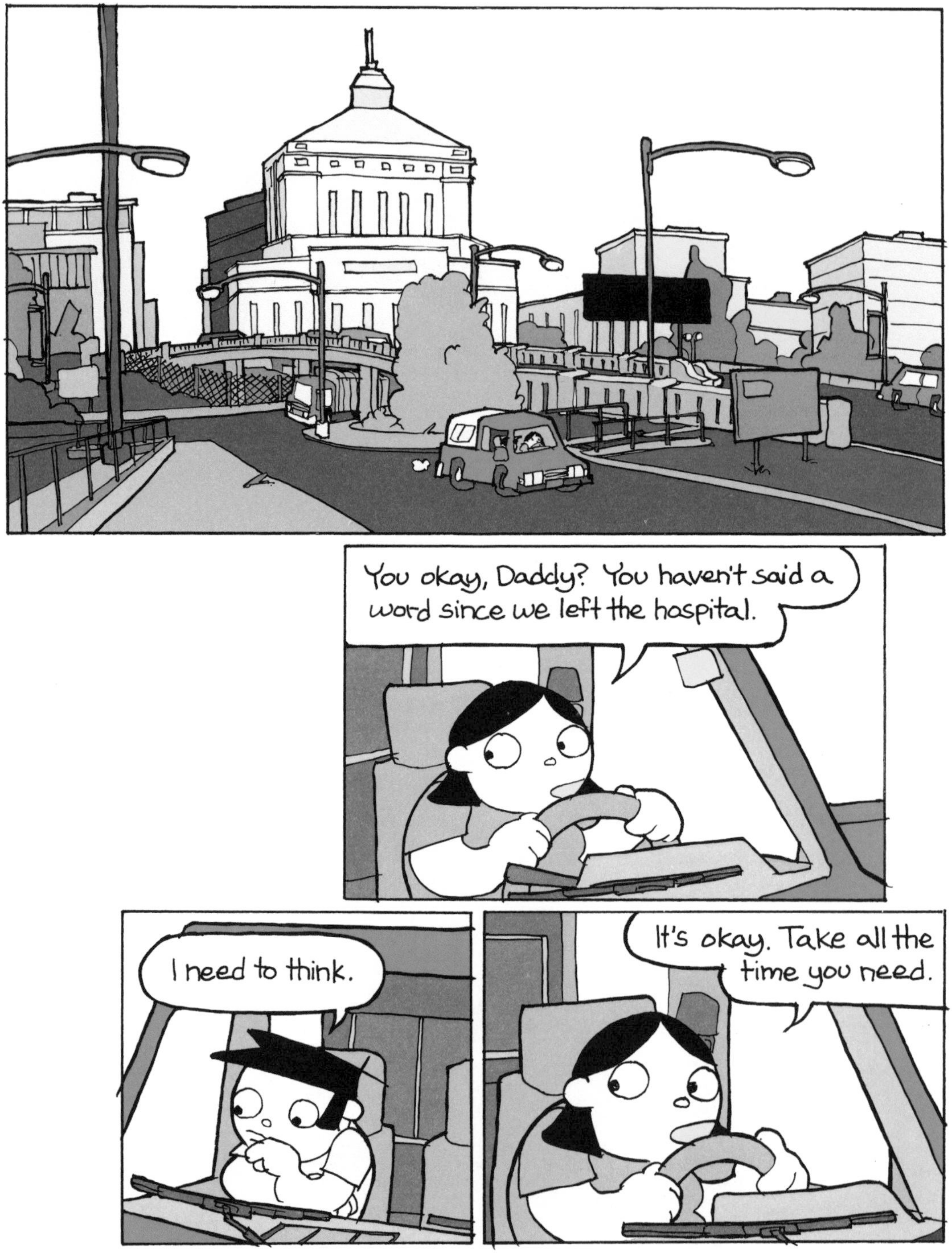
You okay, Daddy? You haven't said a word since we left the hospital.
I need to think.
It's okay. Take all the time you need.

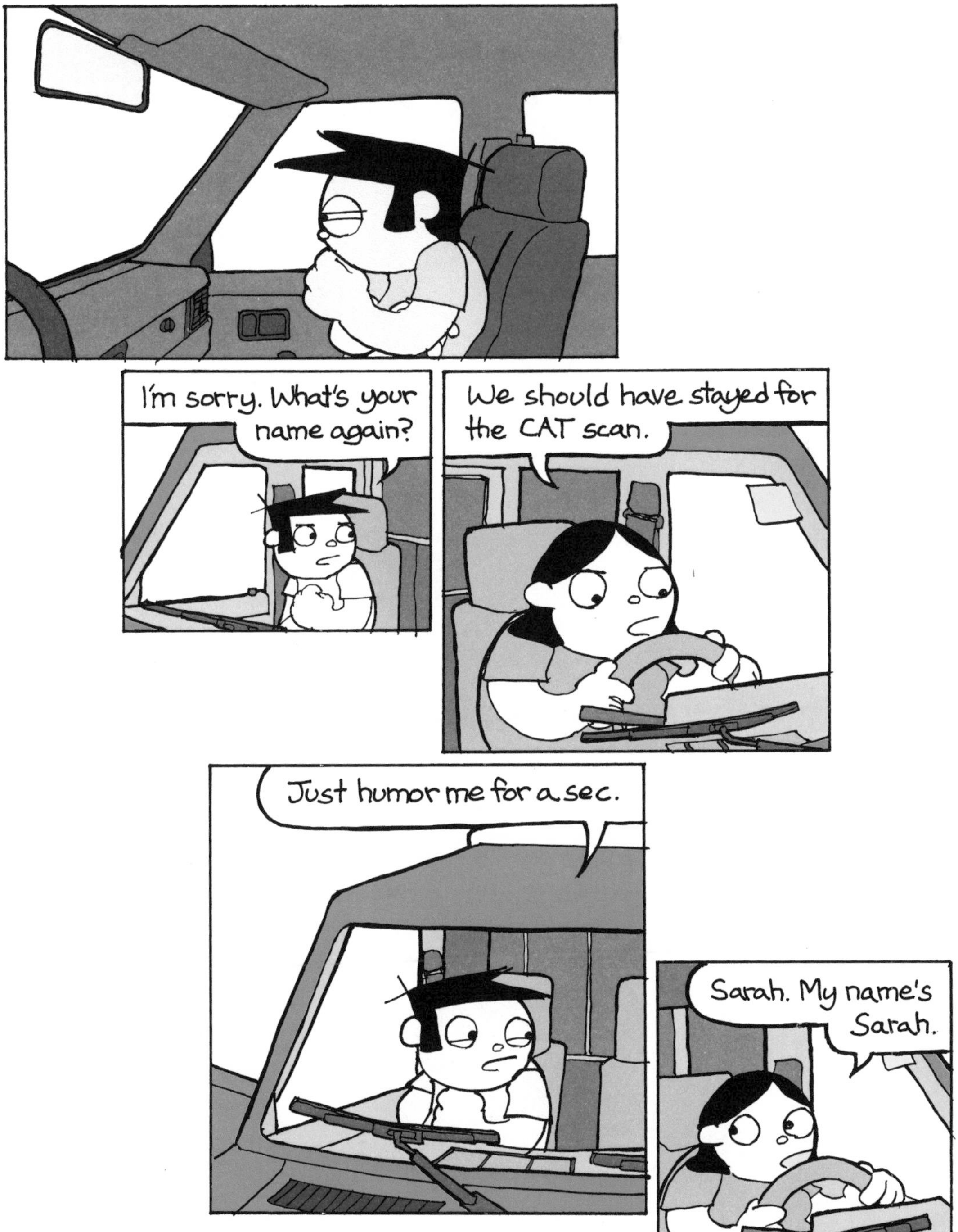
I'm sorry. What's your name again?
We should have stayed for the CAT scan.
Just humor me for a sec.
Sarah. My name's Sarah.

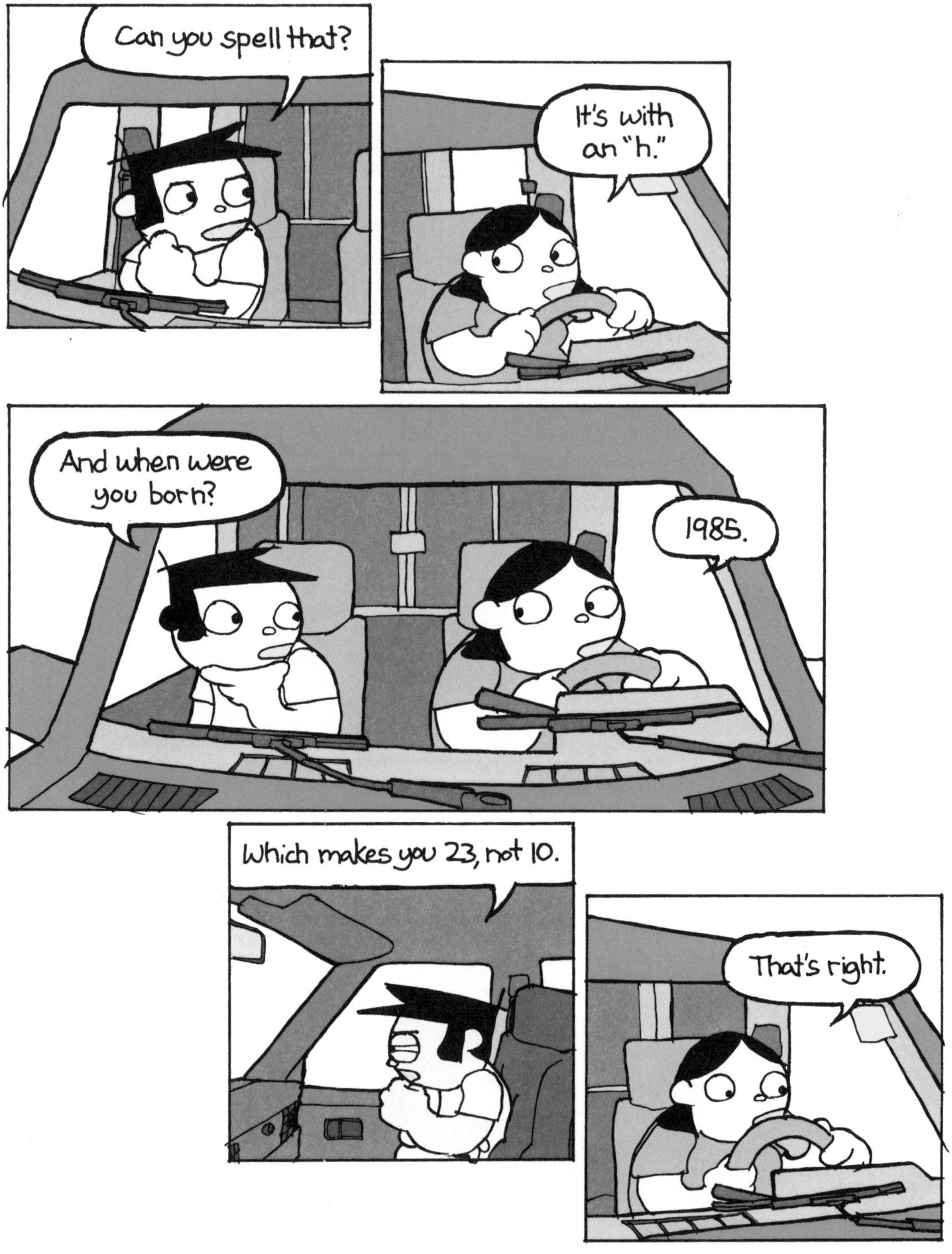
Can you spell that?
It's with an "h."
And when were you born?
1985.
Which makes you 23, not 10.
That's right.

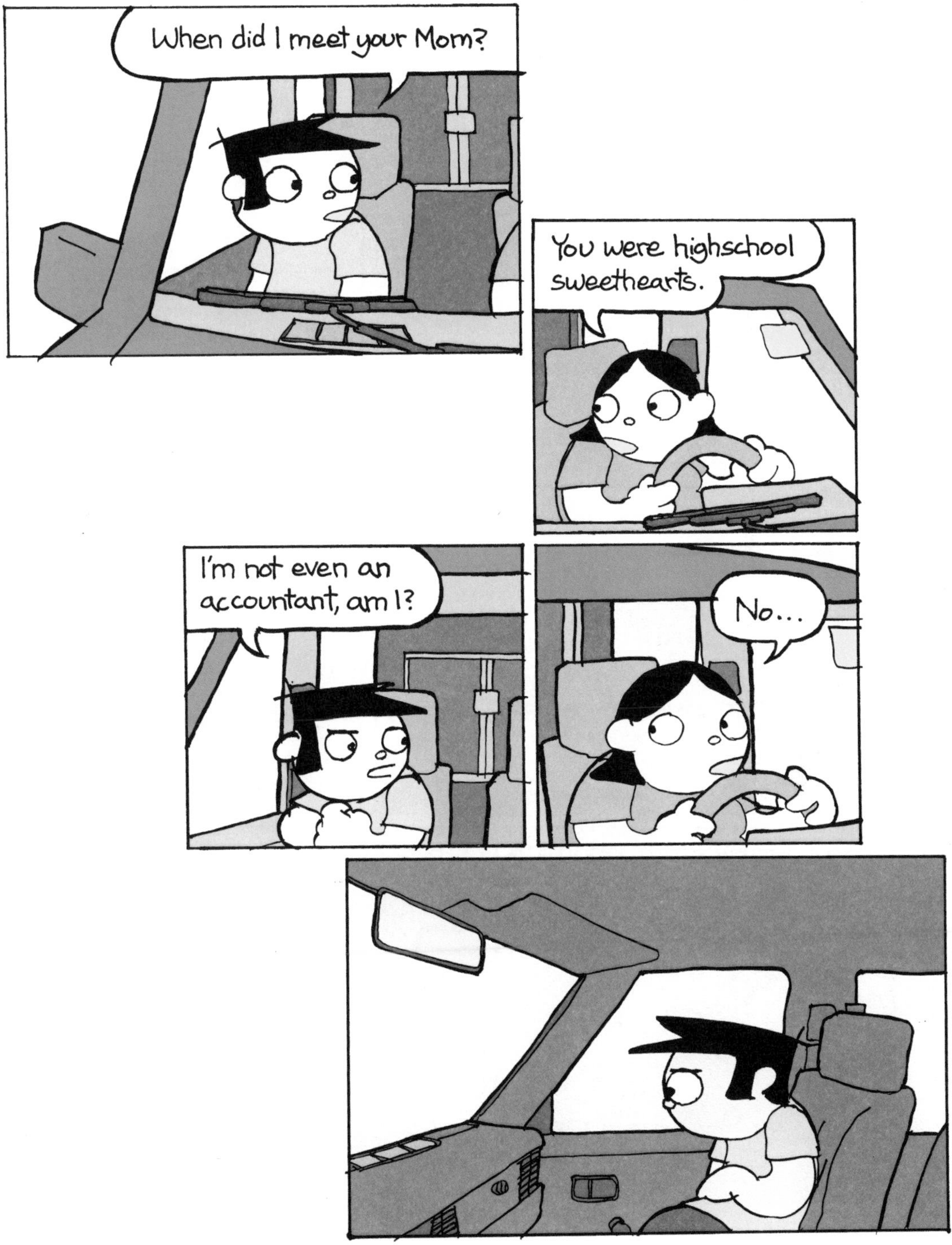
When did I meet your Mom?
You were highschool sweethearts.
I'm not even an accountant, am I?
No...

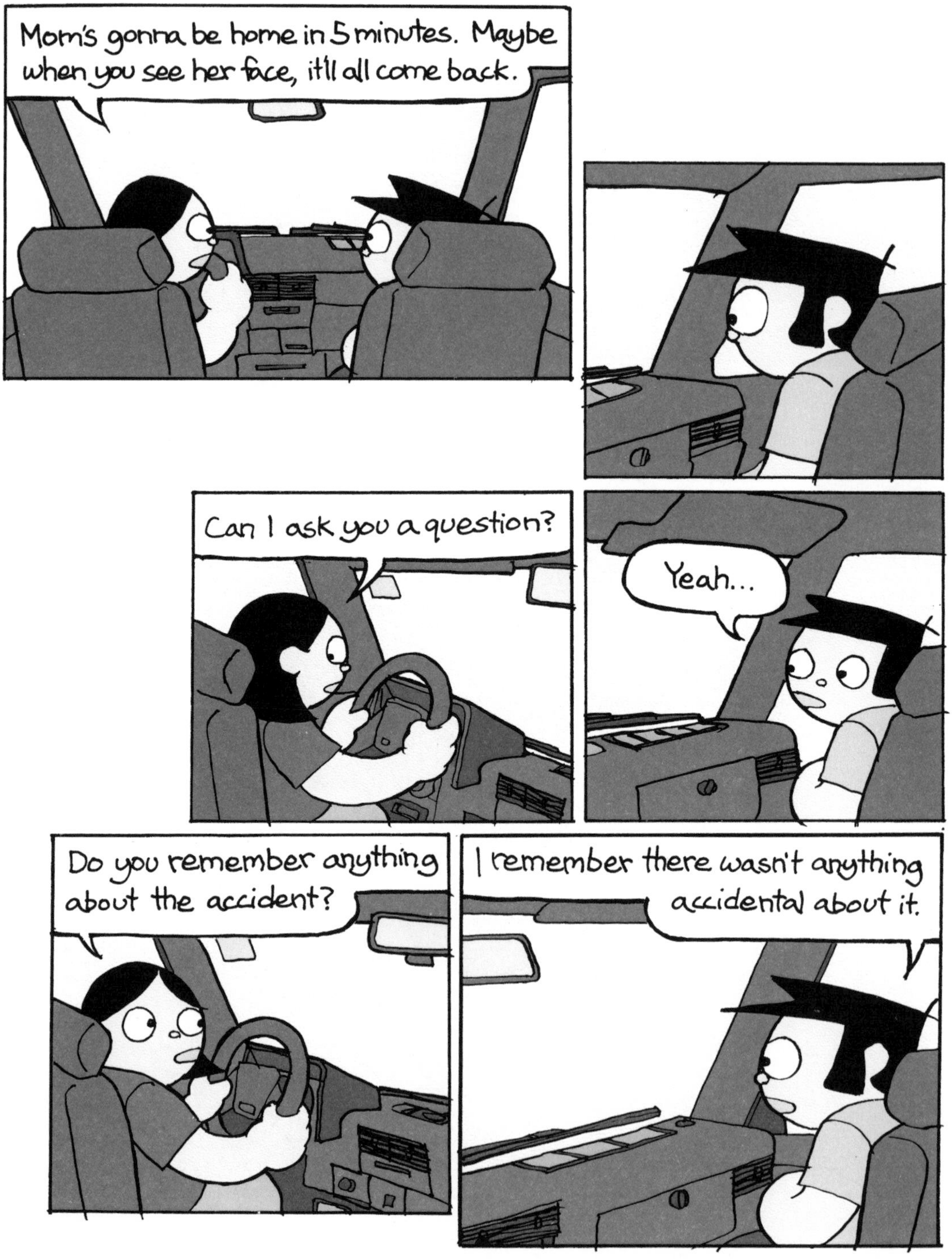
Mom's gonna be home in 5 minutes. Maybe when you see her face, it'll all come back.
Can I ask you a question?
Yeah...
Do you remember anything about the accident?
I remember there wasn't anything accidental about it.

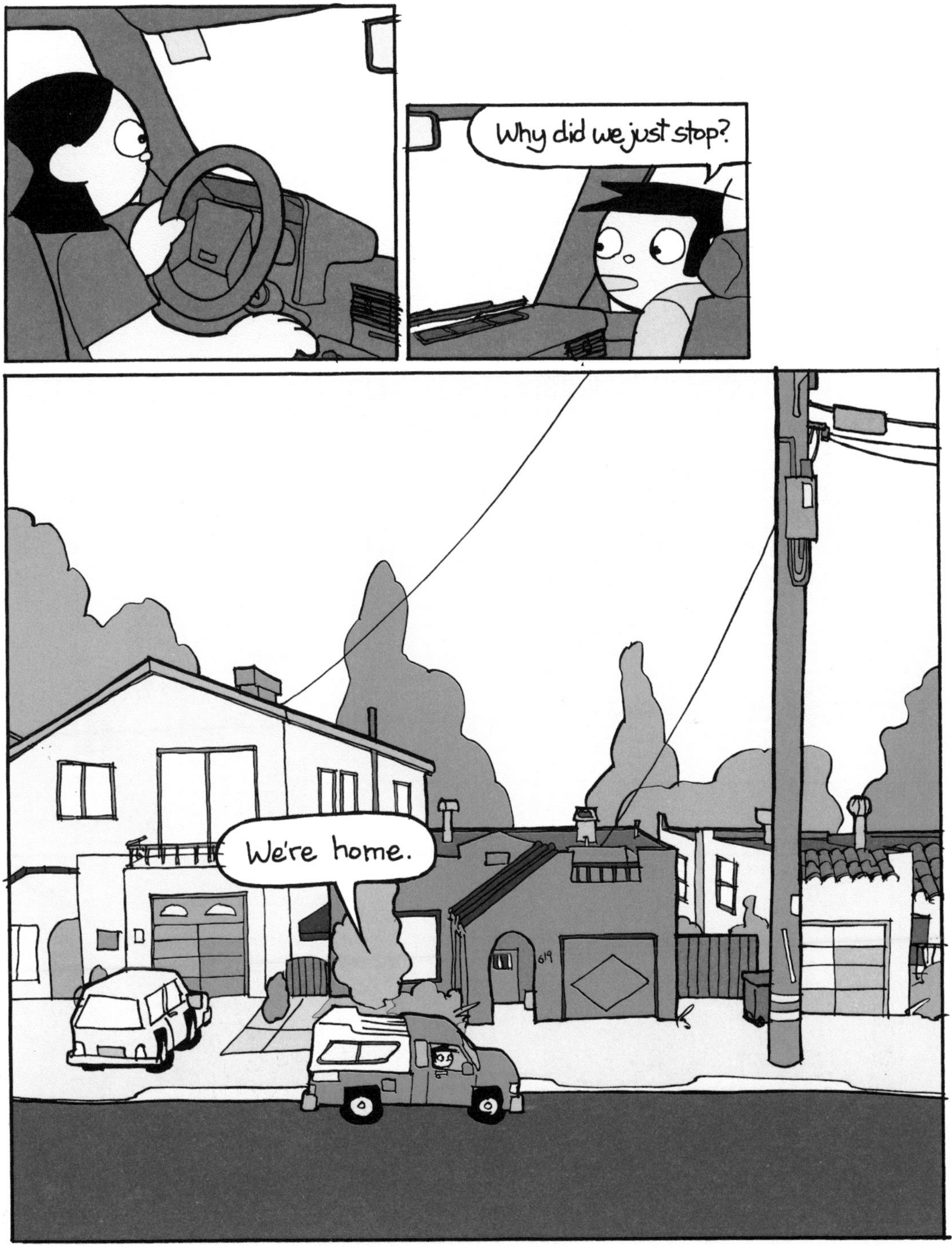
Why did we just stop?
We're home.

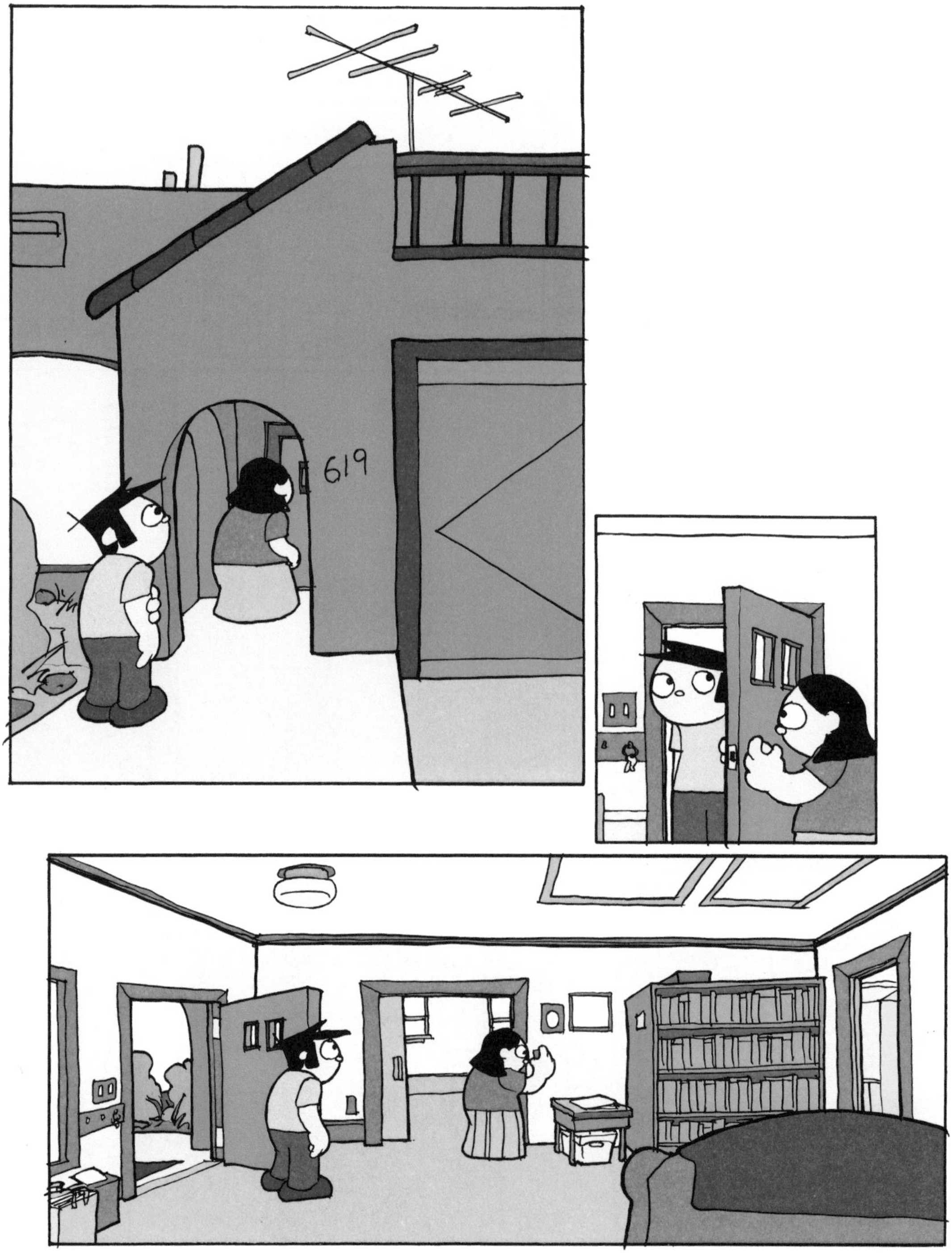
619

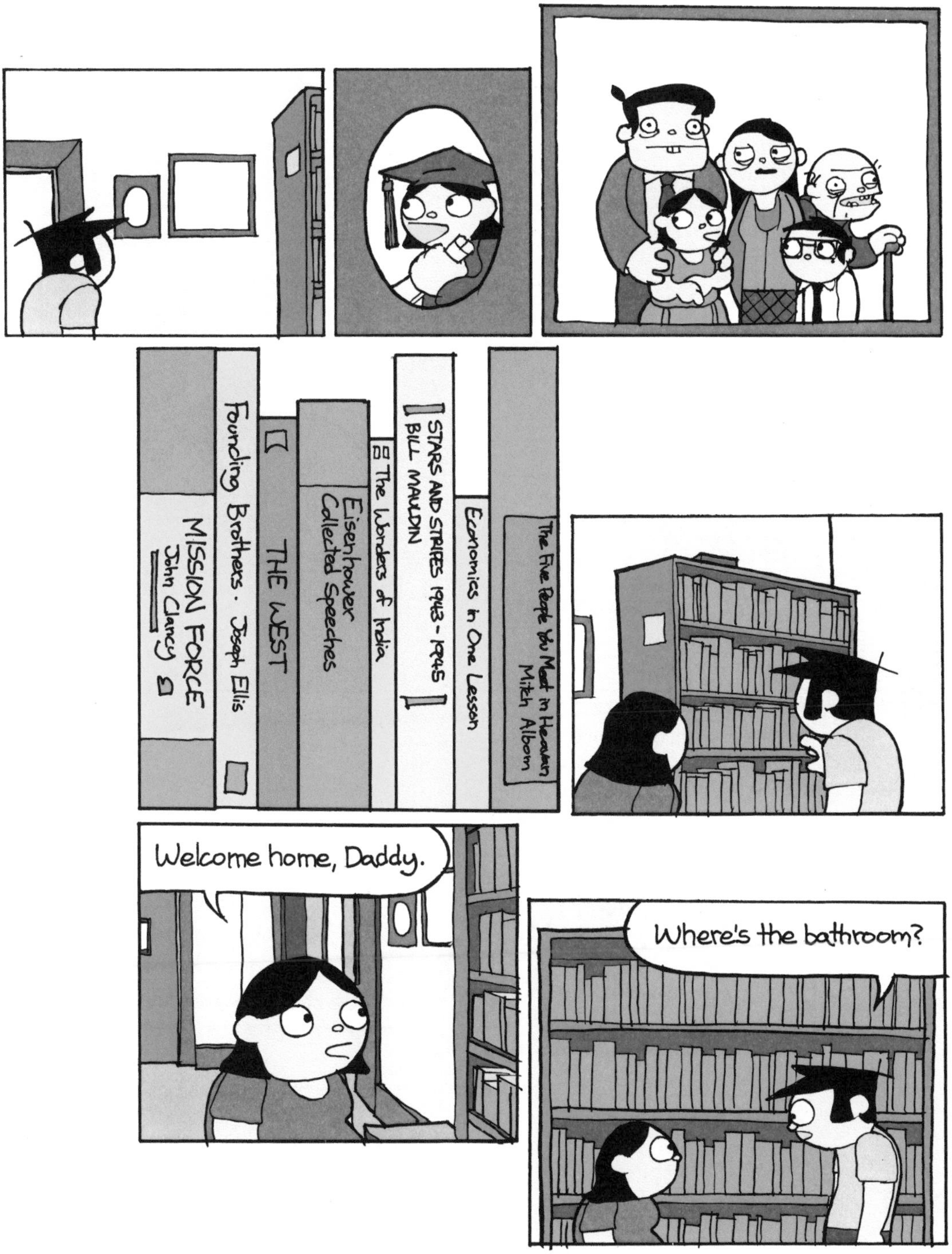
MISSION FORCE
John Clancy
Founding Brothers · Joseph Ellis
THE WEST
Eisenhower
Collected Speeches
The Wonders of India
STARS AND STRIPES 1943 - 1945
BILL MAULDIN
Economics in One Lesson
The Five People You Meet in Heaven
Mitch Albom
Welcome home, Daddy.
Where's the bathroom?

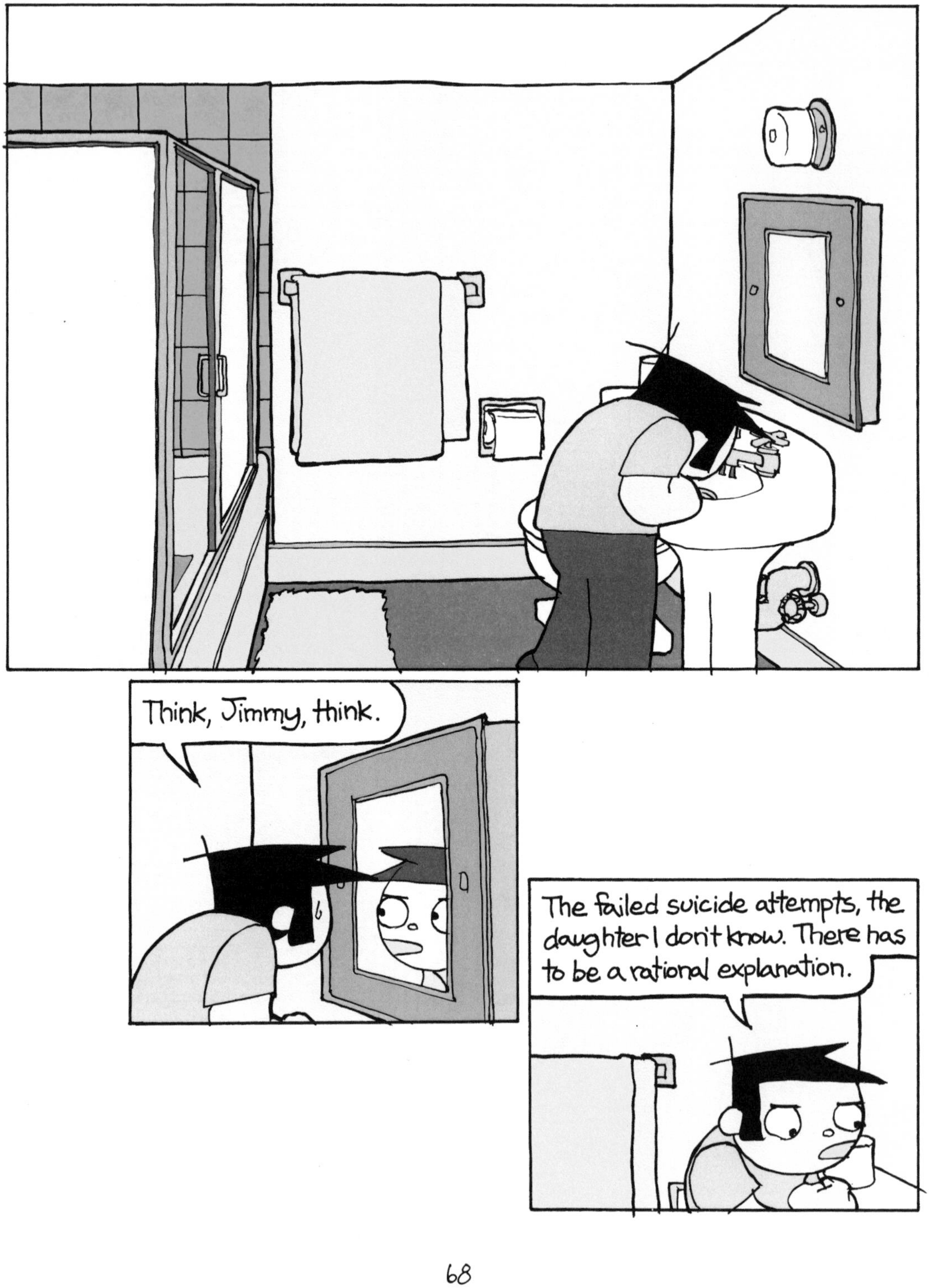
Think, Jimmy, think.
The failed suicide attempts, the daughter I don't know. There has to be a rational explanation.

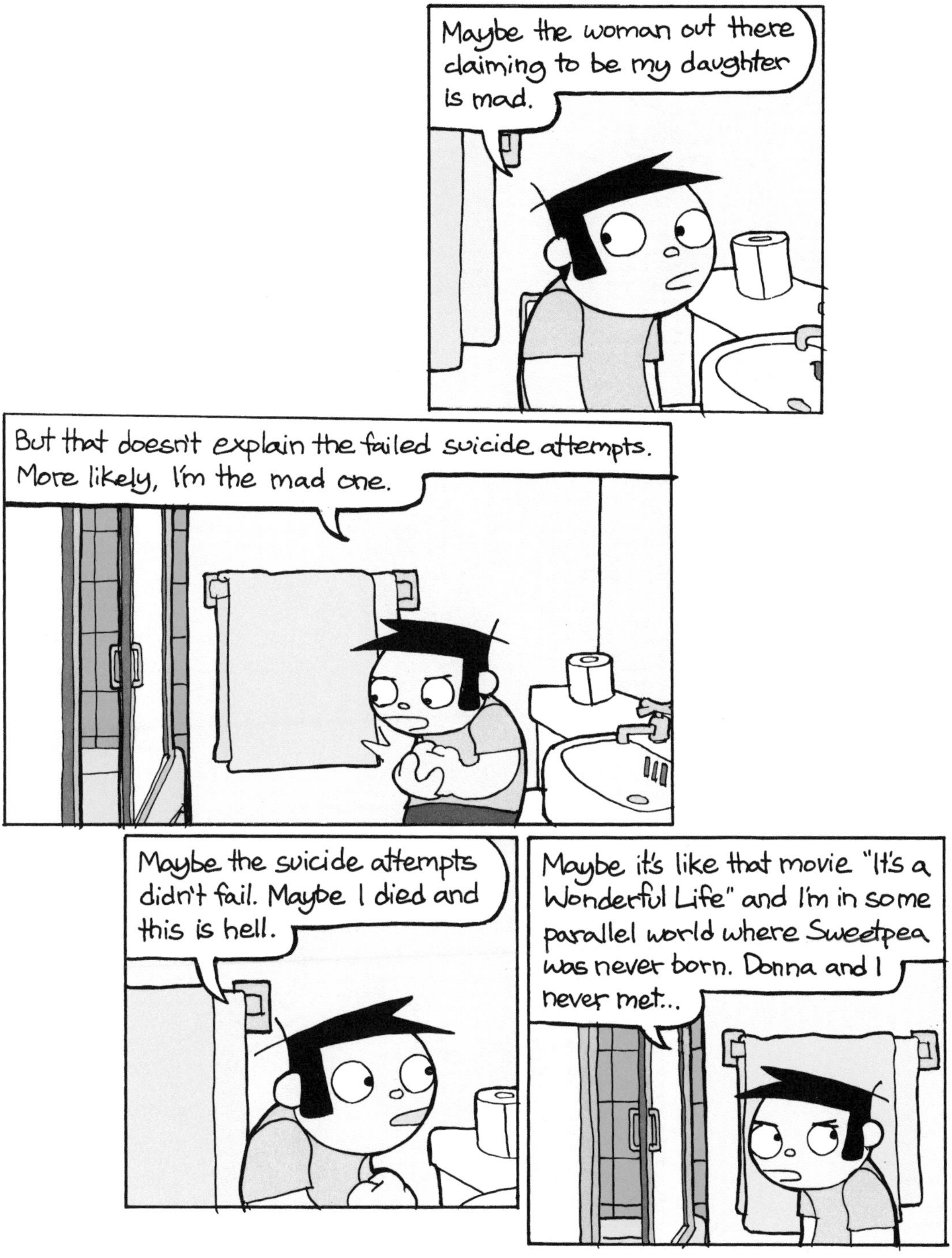

Maybe the woman out there claiming to be my daughter is mad.
But that doesn't explain the failed suicide attempts. More likely, I'm the mad one.
Maybe the suicide attempts didn't fail. Maybe I died and this is hell.
Maybe it's like that movie "It's a Wonderful Life" and I'm in some parallel world where Sweetpea was never born. Donna and I never met...

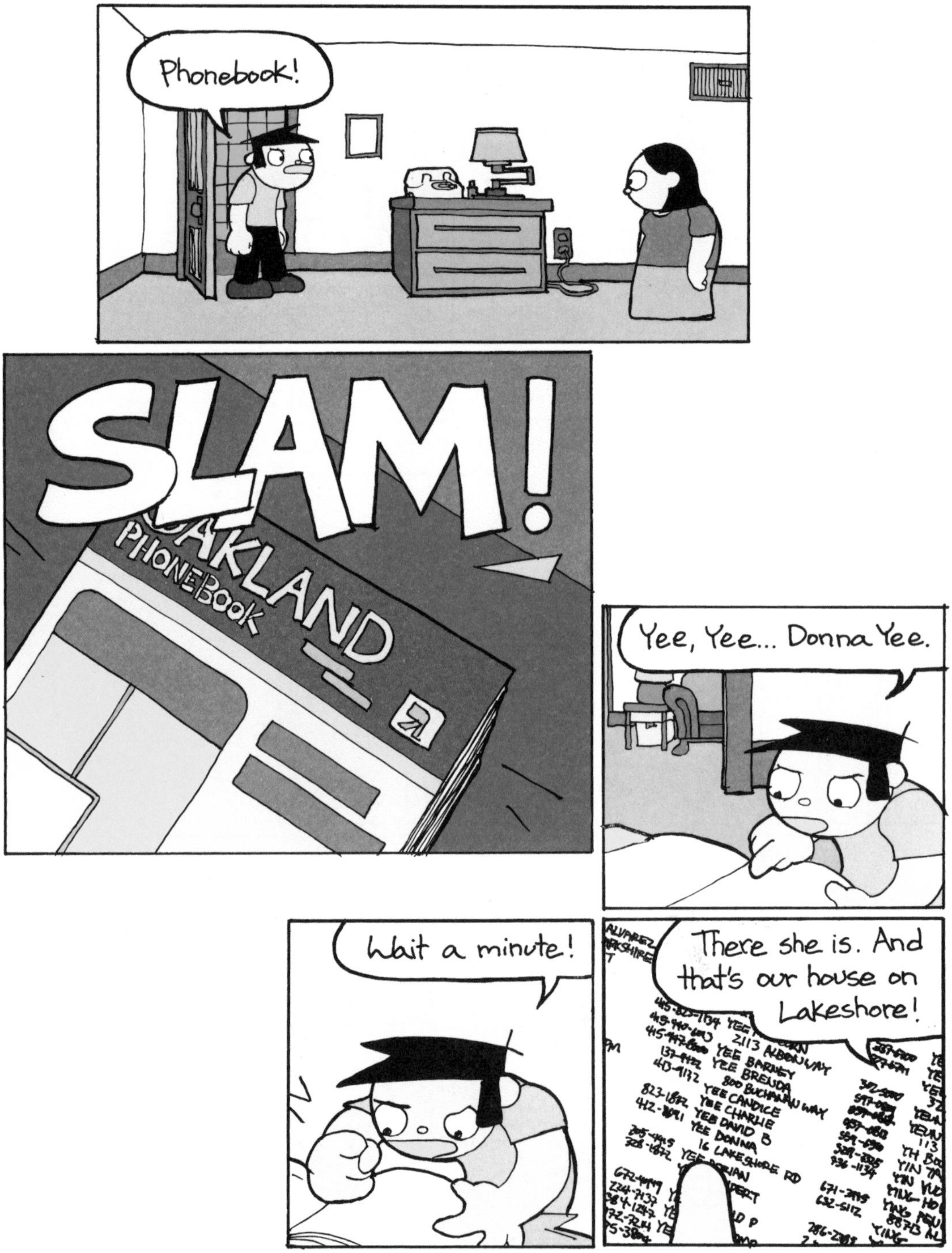
Phonebook!
SLAM!
OAKLAND PHONEBOOK
Yee, Yee... Donna Yee.
Wait a minute!
There she is. And that's our house on Lakeshore!

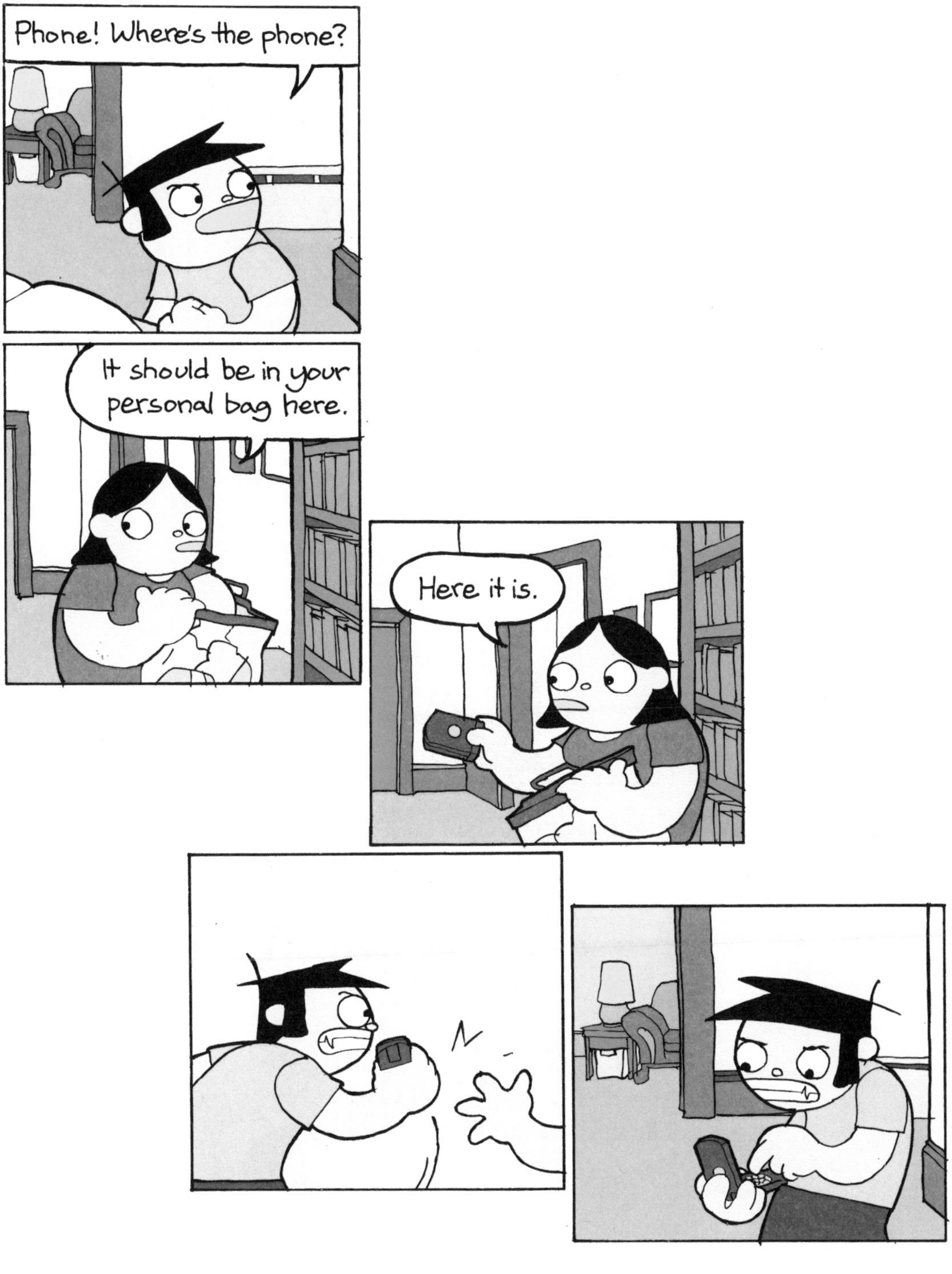
Phone! Where's the phone?
It should be in your personal bag here.
Here it is.

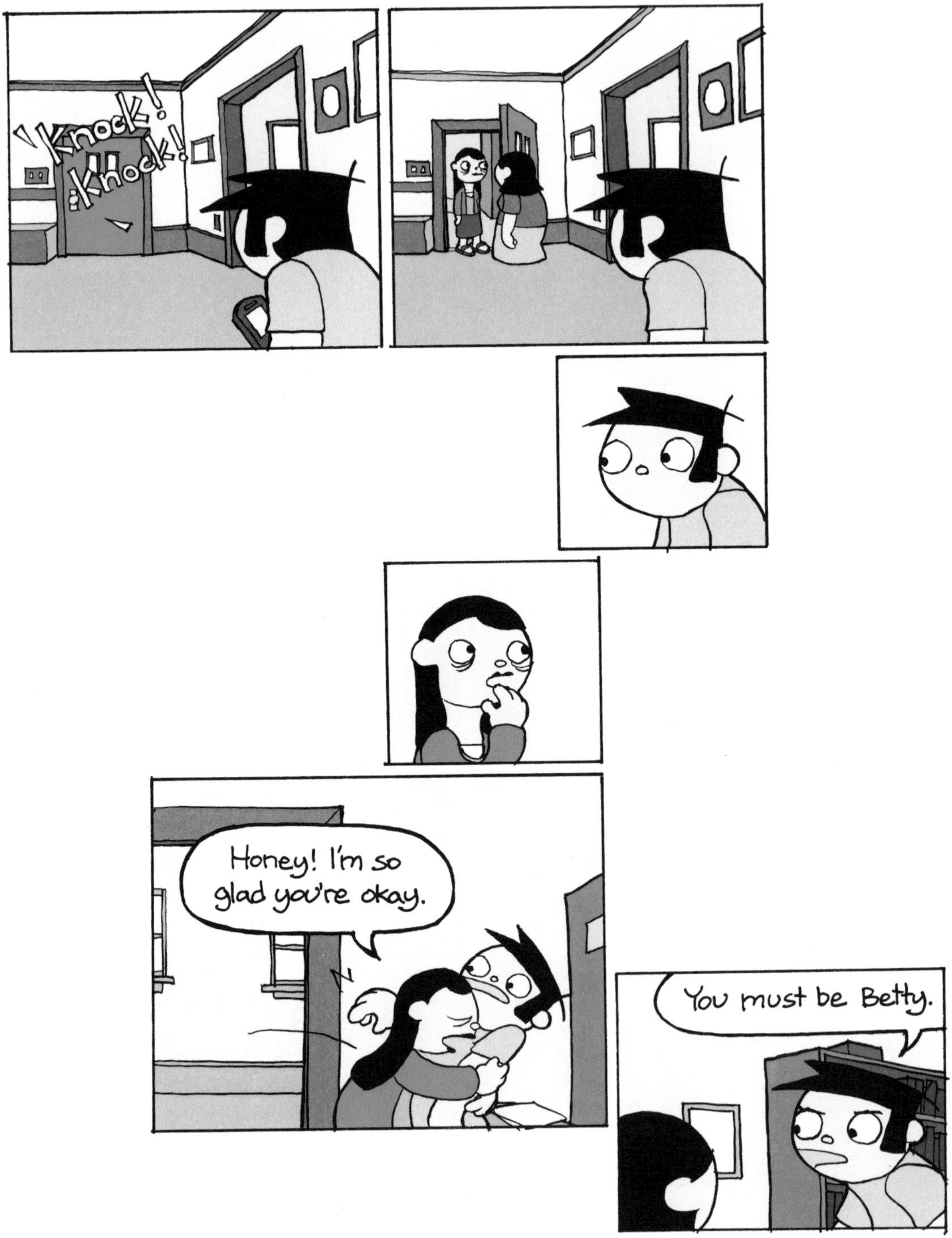
Knock!
Knock!
Honey! I'm so glad you're okay.
You must be Betty.

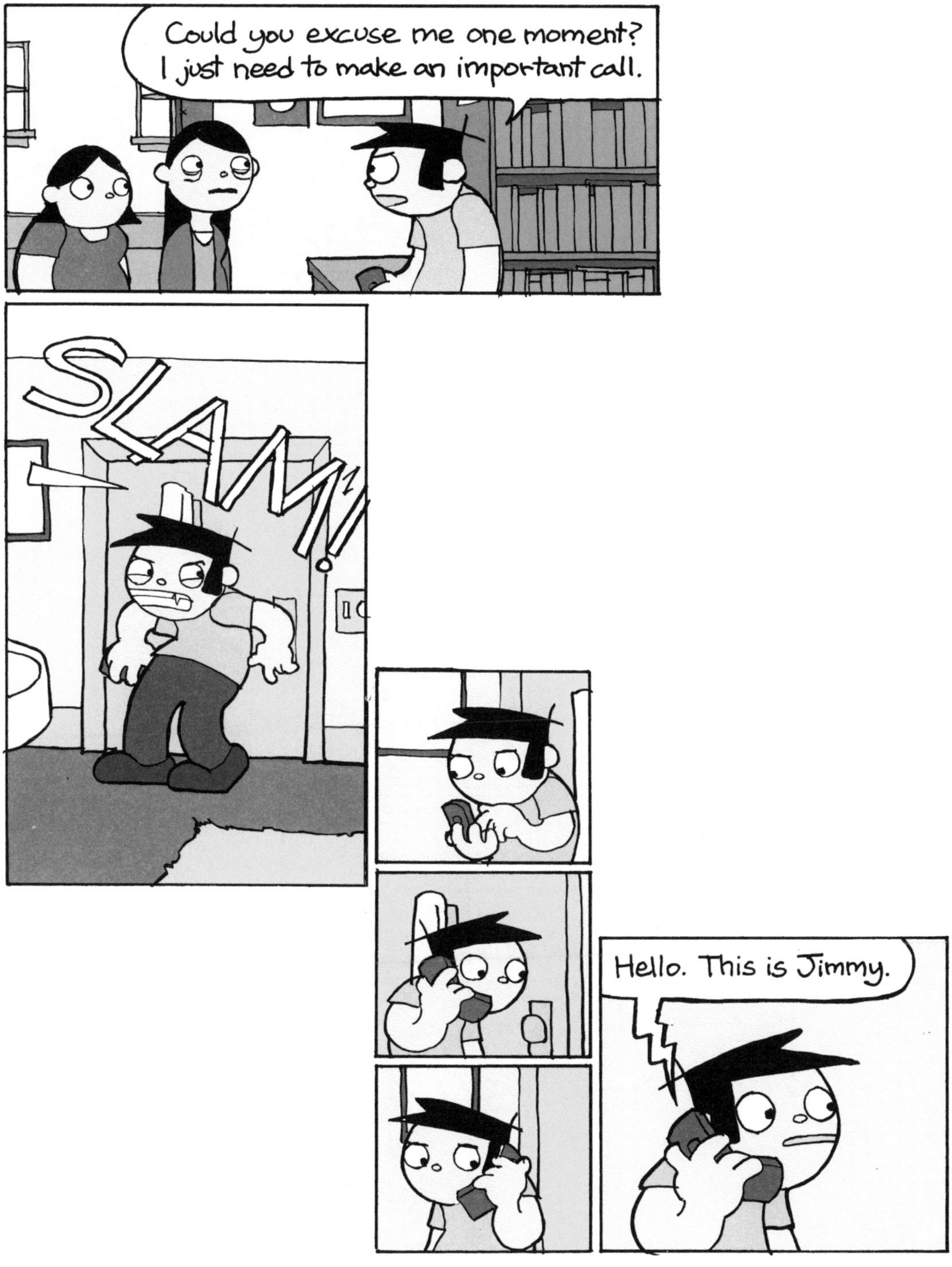
Could you excuse me one moment? I just need to make an important call.
SLAM!
Hello. This is Jimmy.

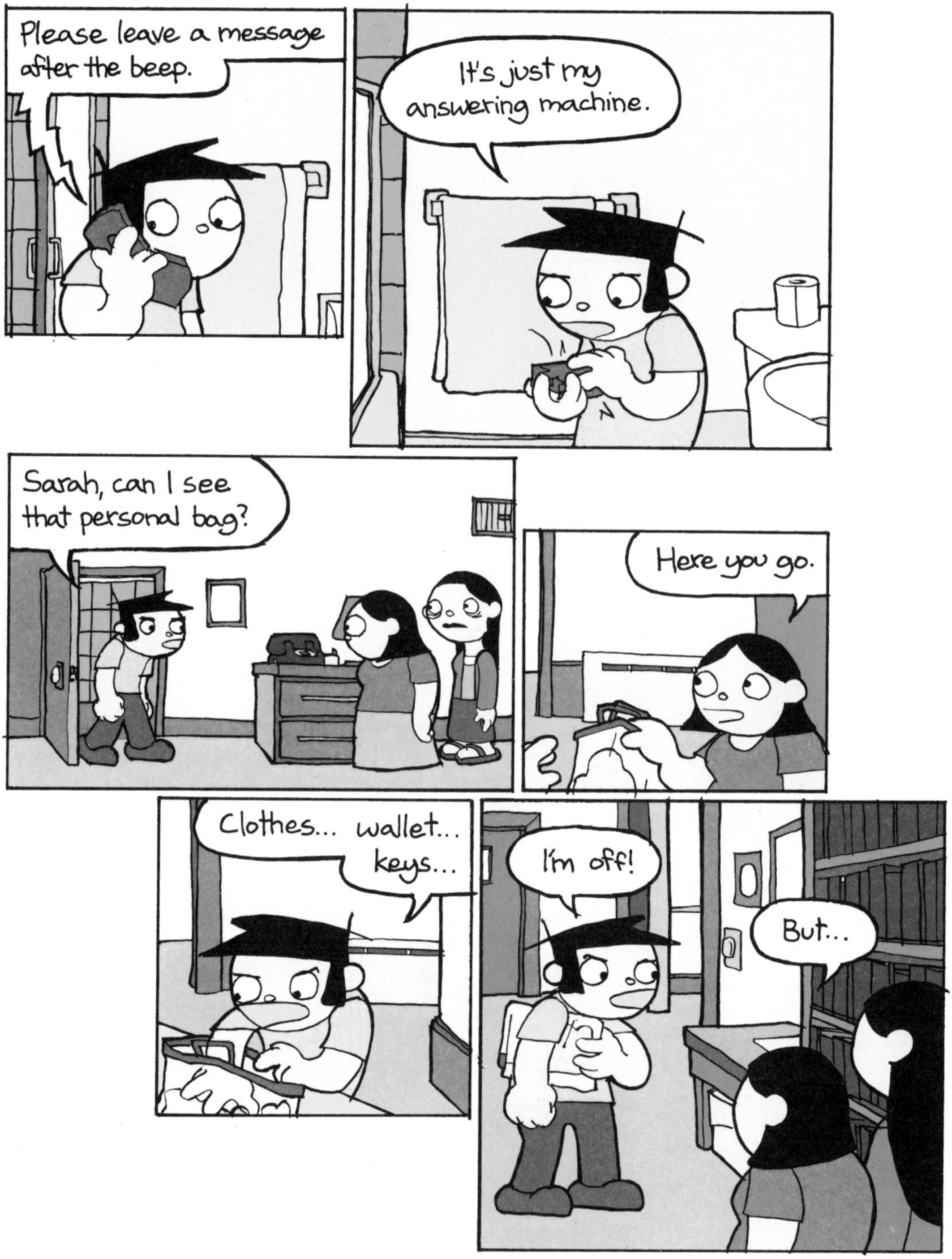
Please leave a message after the beep.
It's just my answering machine.
Sarah, can I see that personal bag?
Here you go.
Clothes... wallet... keys...
I'm off!
But...

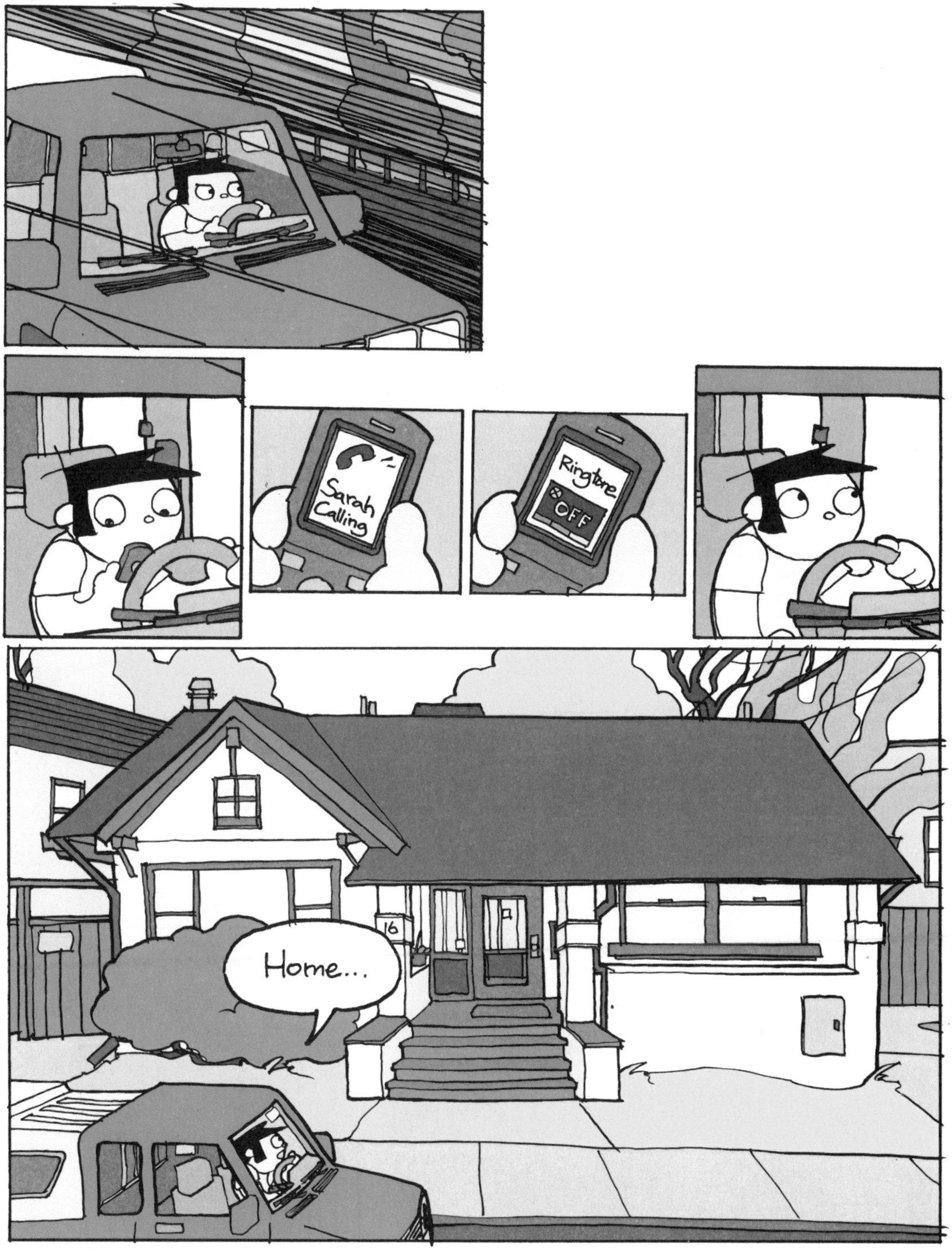
Sarah Calling
Ringtone
OFF
16
Home...

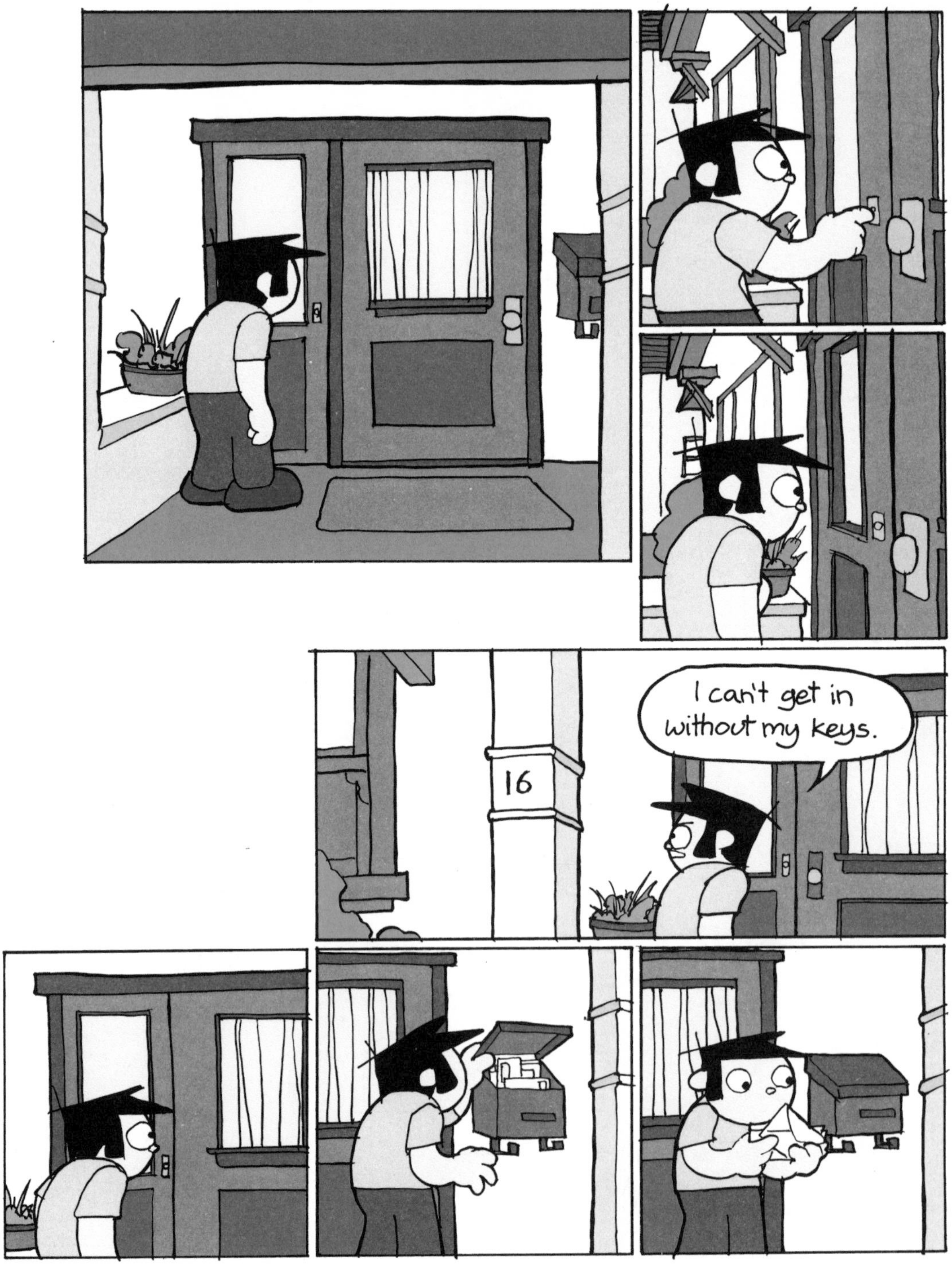
16
I can't get in without my keys.

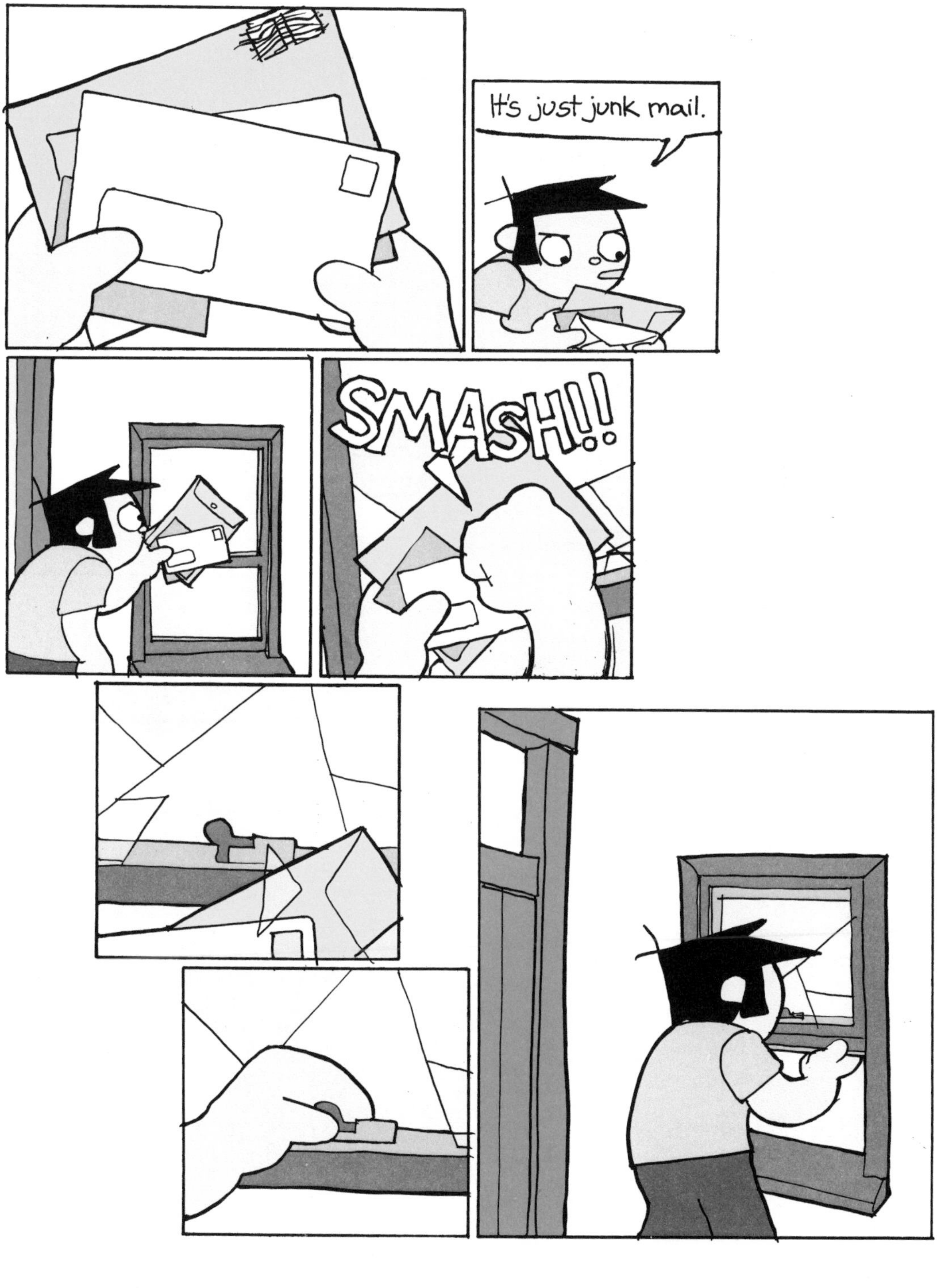
It's just junk mail.
SMASH!!

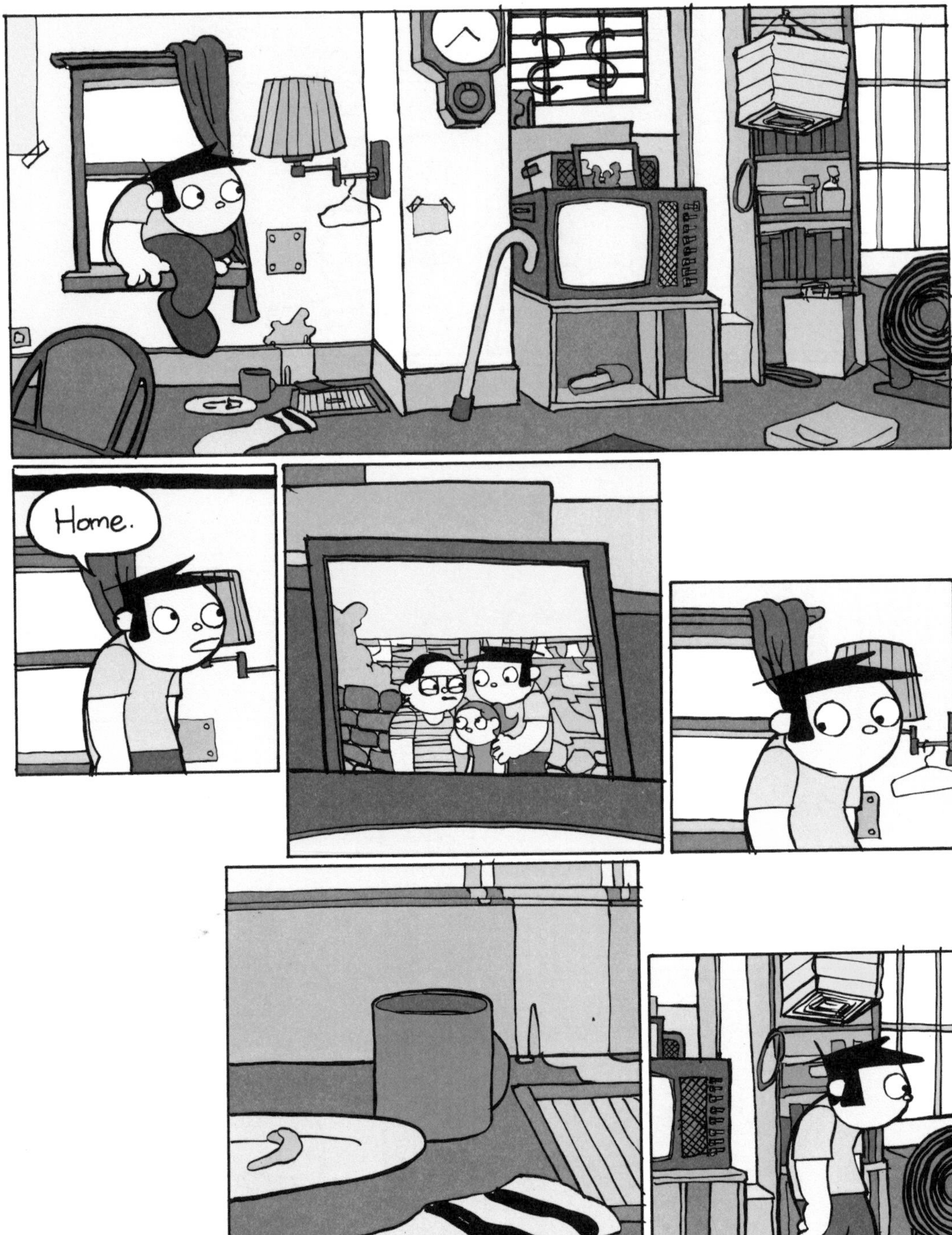
Home.

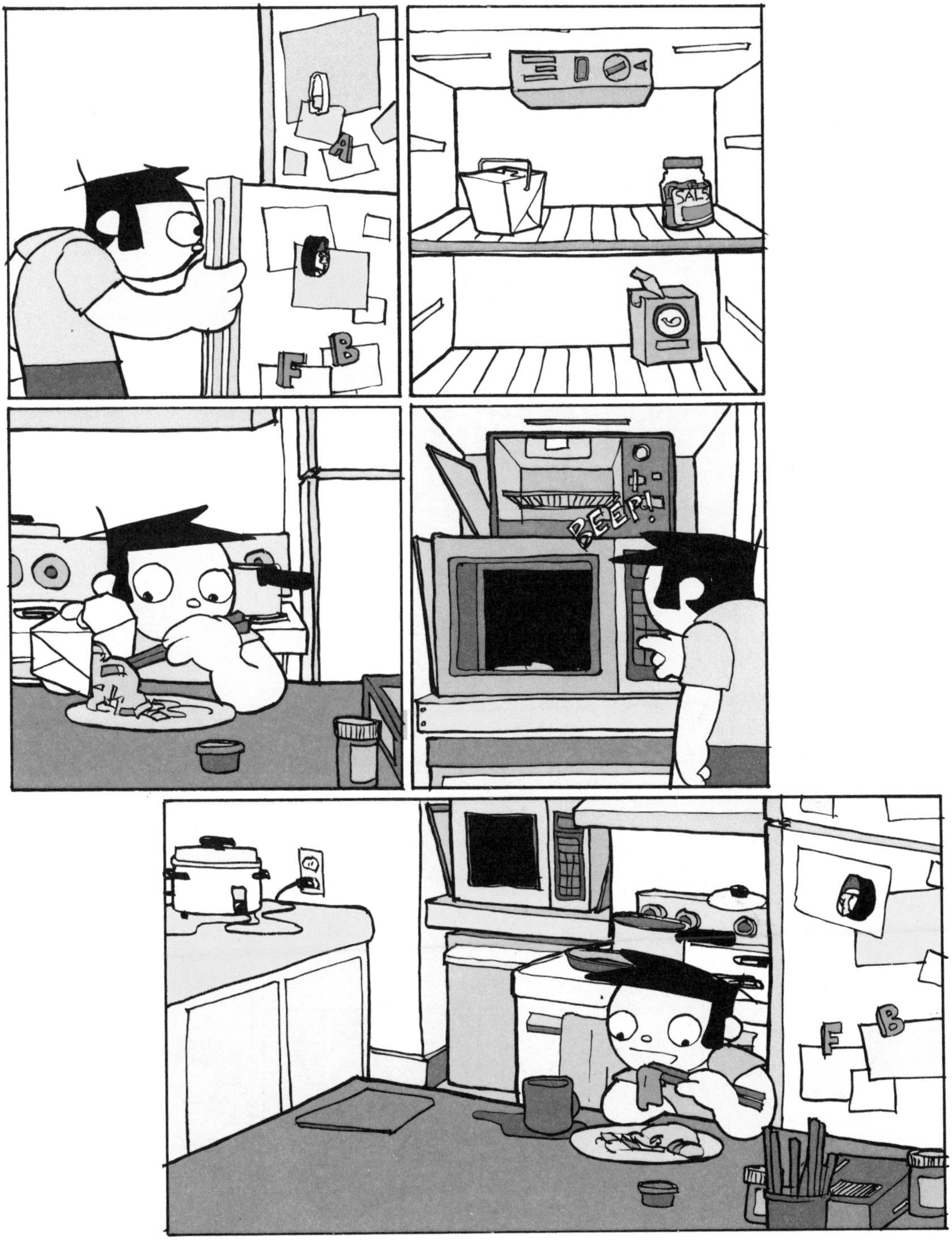
SALS
BEEP!

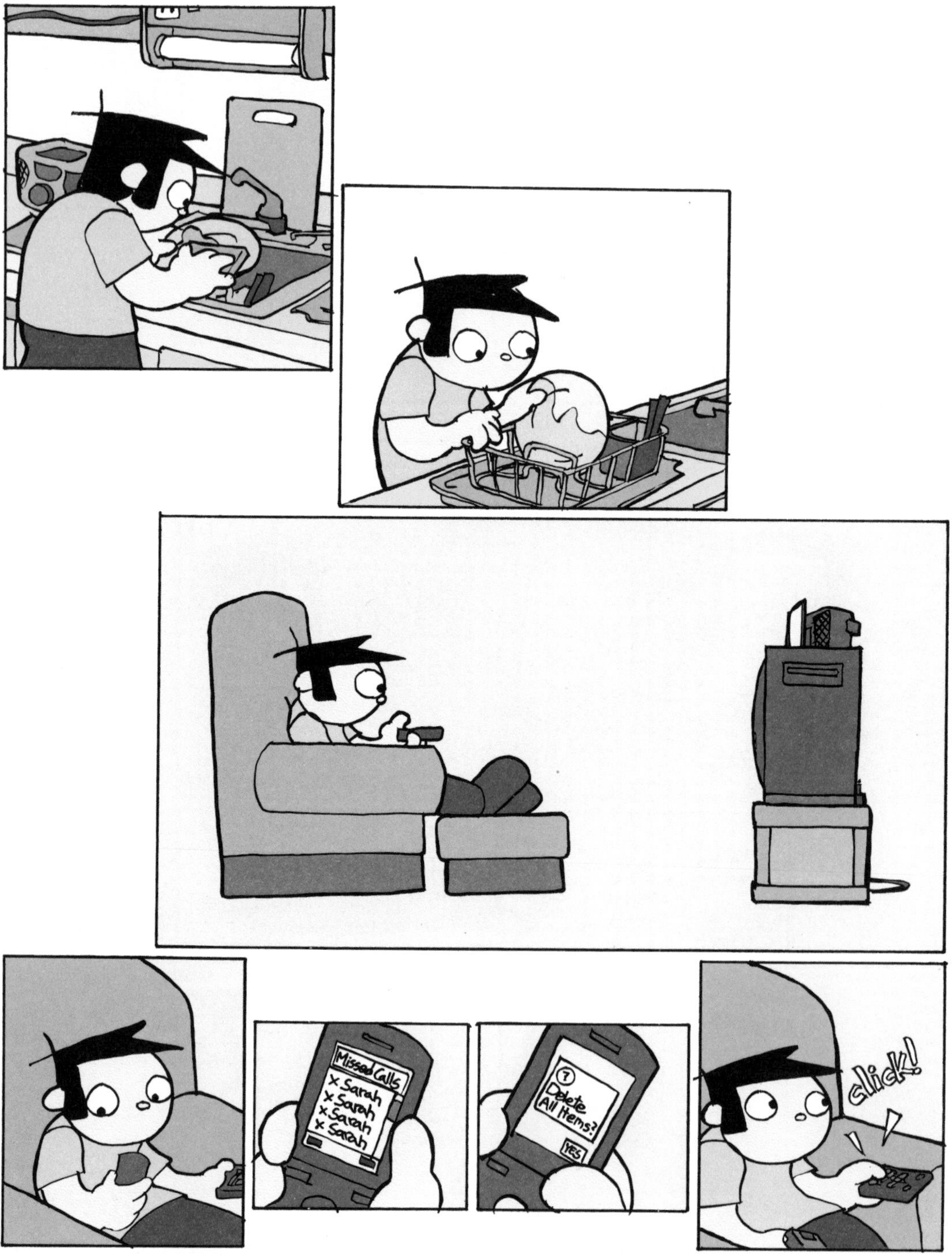
Missed Calls
x Sarah
x Sarah
x Sarah
x Sarah
?
Delete All Items?
YES
click!

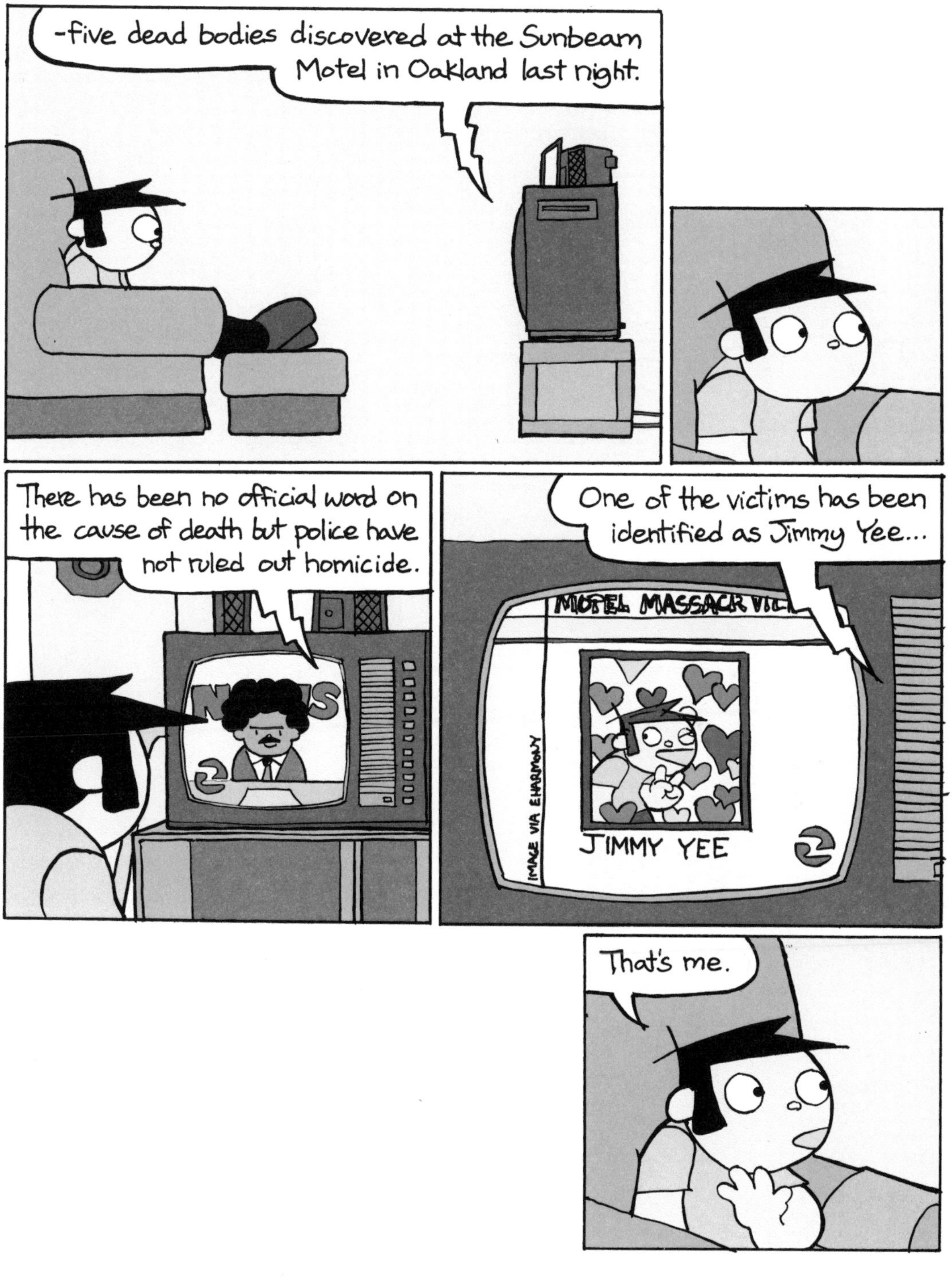
-five dead bodies discovered at the Sunbeam Motel in Oakland last night.
There has been no official word on the cause of death but police have not ruled out homicide.
One of the victims has been identified as Jimmy Yee...
IMAGE VIA EHARMONY
JIMMY YEE
That's me.

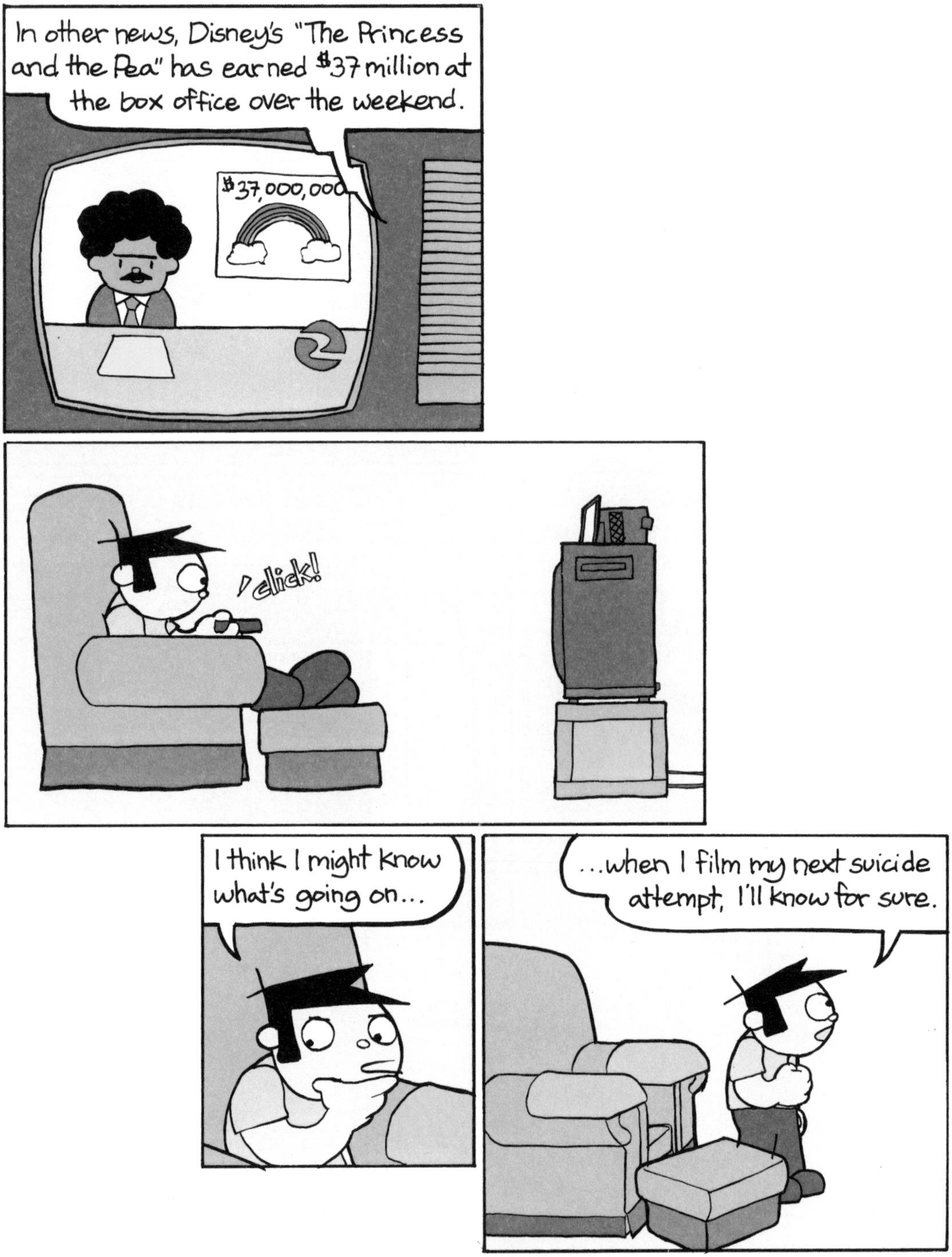
In other news, Disney's "The Princess and the Pea" has earned $37 million at the box office over the weekend.
$37,000,000
click!
I think I might know what's going on...
...when I film my next suicide attempt, I'll know for sure.

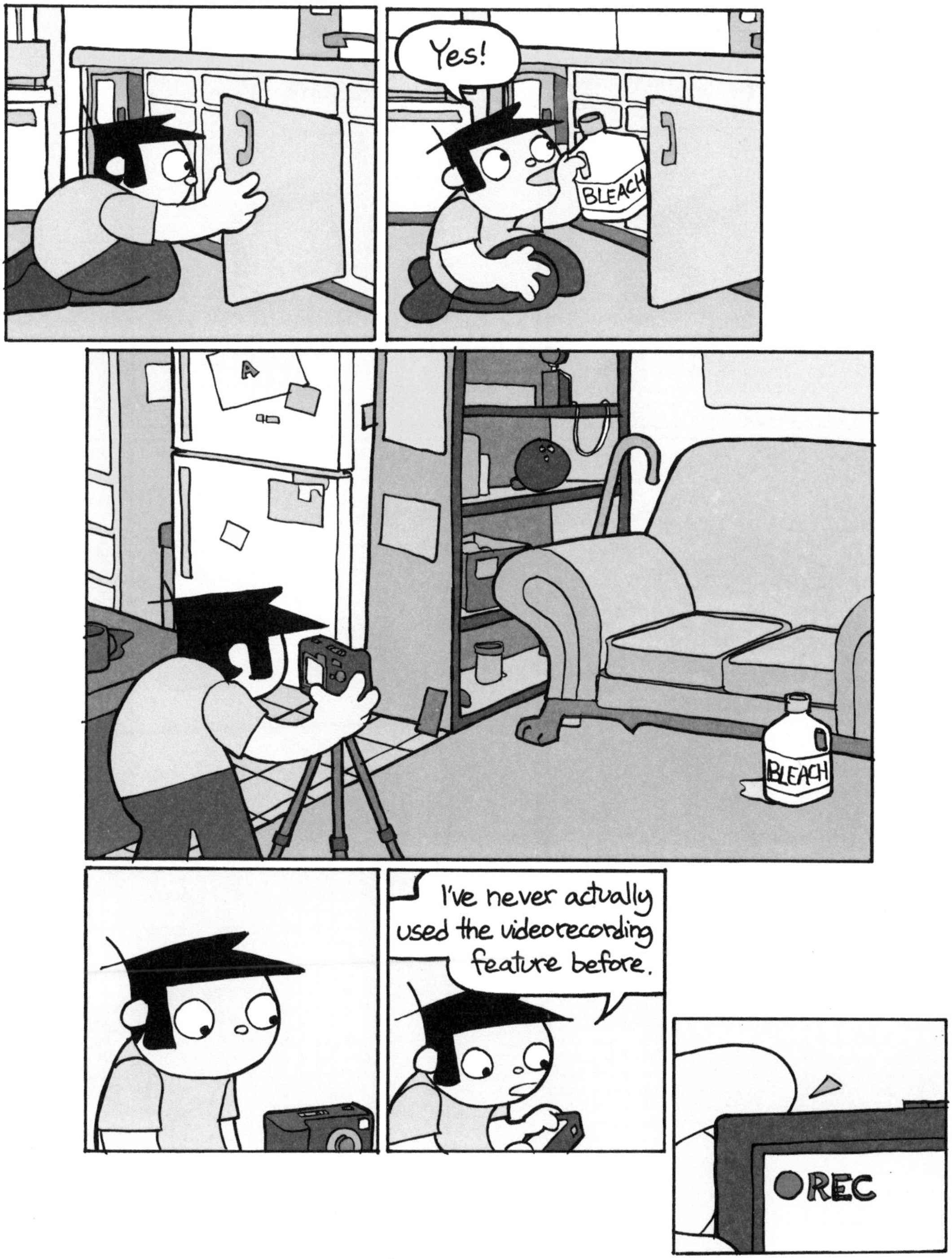
Yes!
BLEACH
BLEACH
I've never actually used the videorecording feature before.
REC

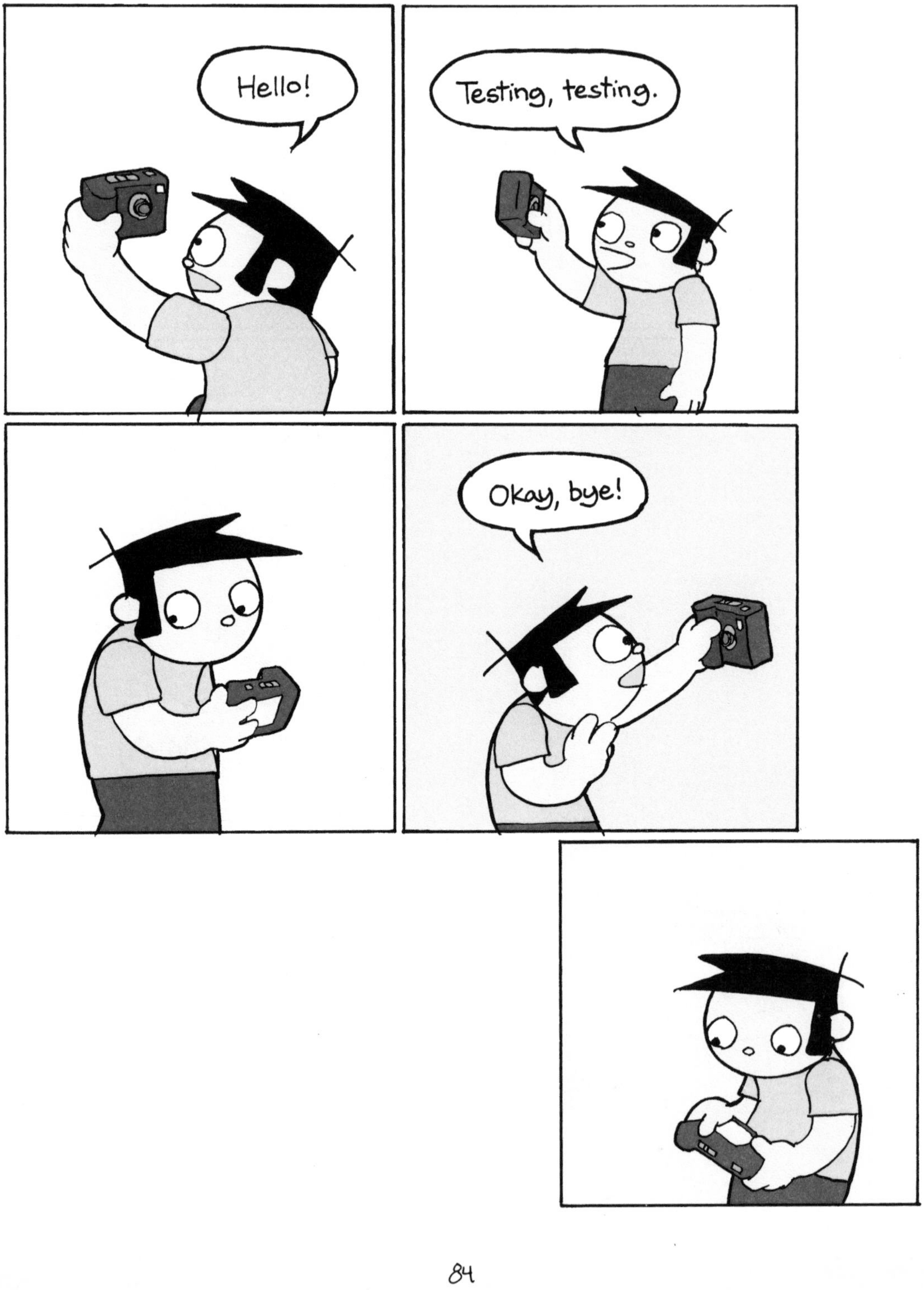
Hello!
Testing, testing.
Okay, bye!

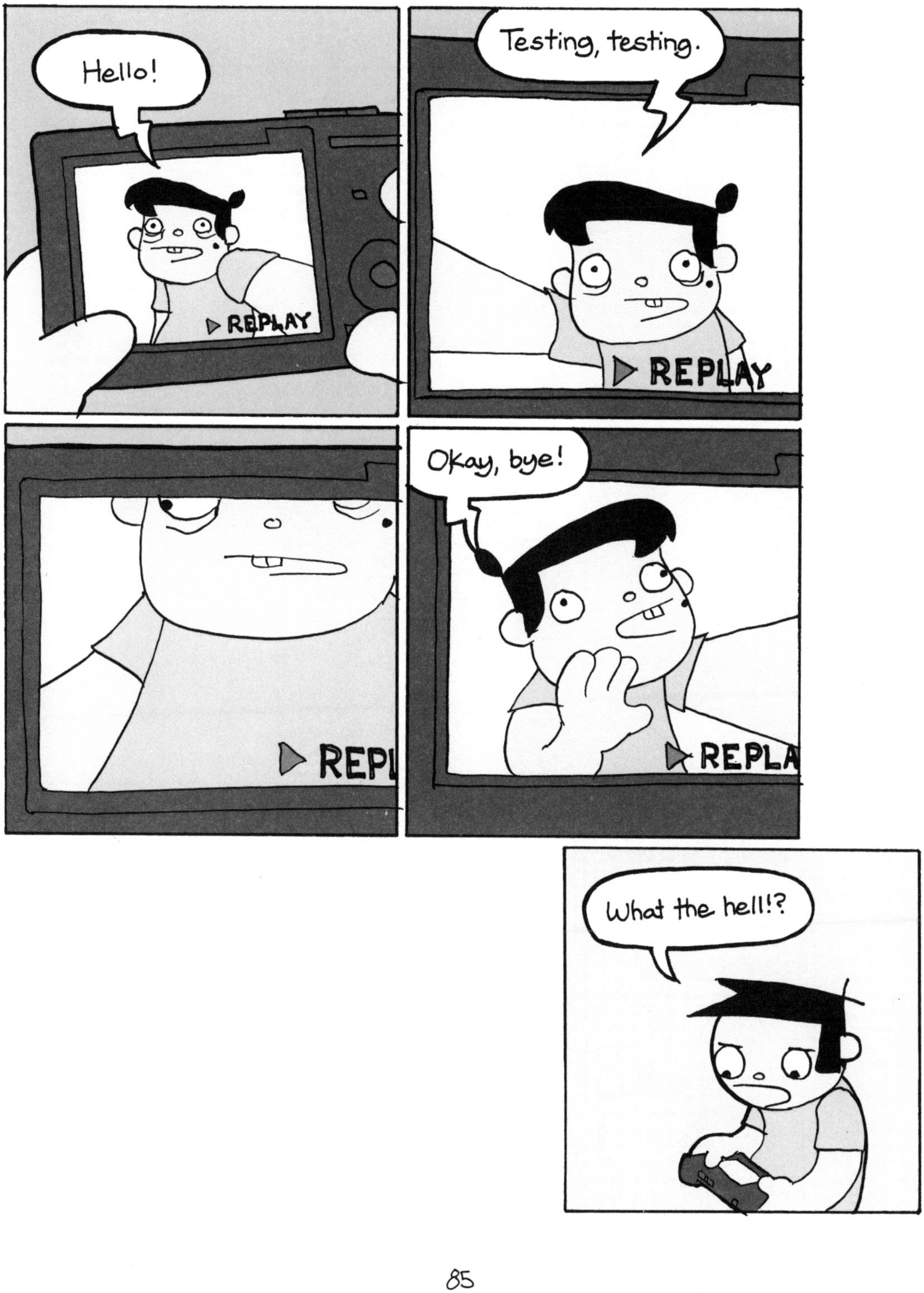
Hello!
REPLAY
Testing, testing.
REPLAY
REPL
Okay, bye!
REPLA
What the hell!?

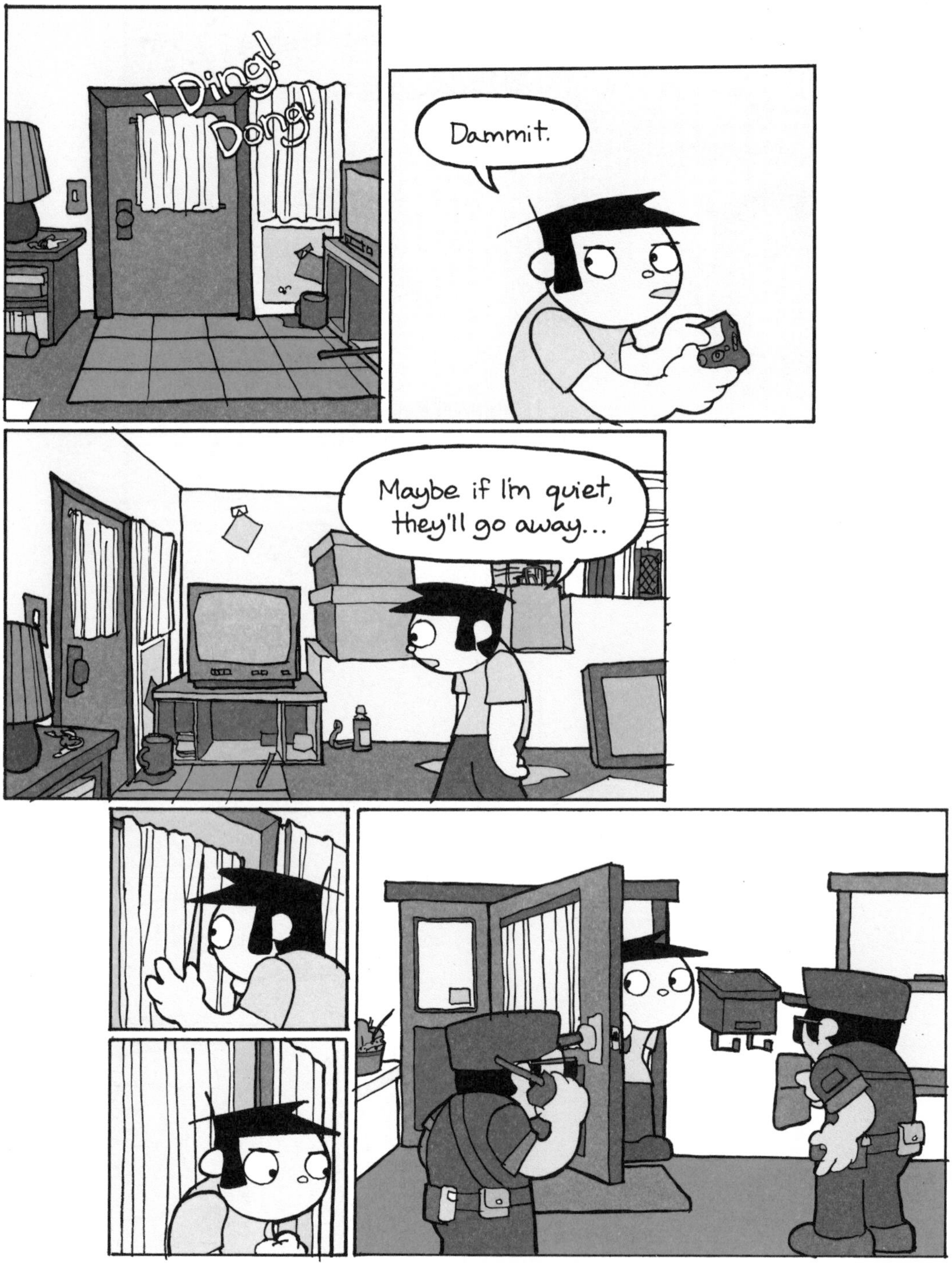
Ding! Dong!
Dammit.
Maybe if I'm quiet, they'll go away...

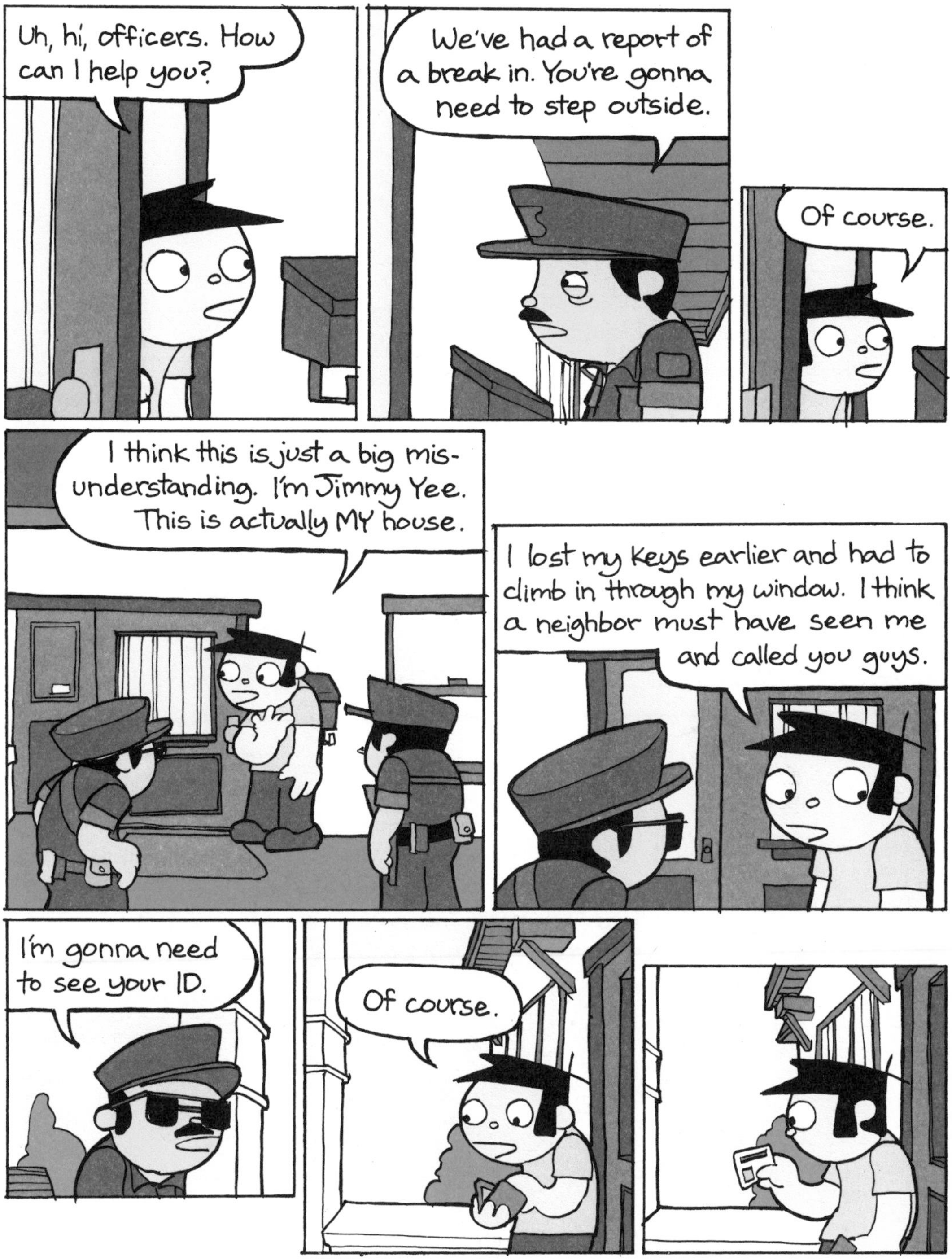
Uh, hi, officers. How can I help you?
We've had a report of a break in. You're gonna need to step outside.
Of course.
I think this is just a big mis-understanding. I'm Jimmy Yee. This is actually MY house.
I lost my keys earlier and had to climb in through my window. I think a neighbor must have seen me and called you guys.
I'm gonna need to see your ID.
Of course.

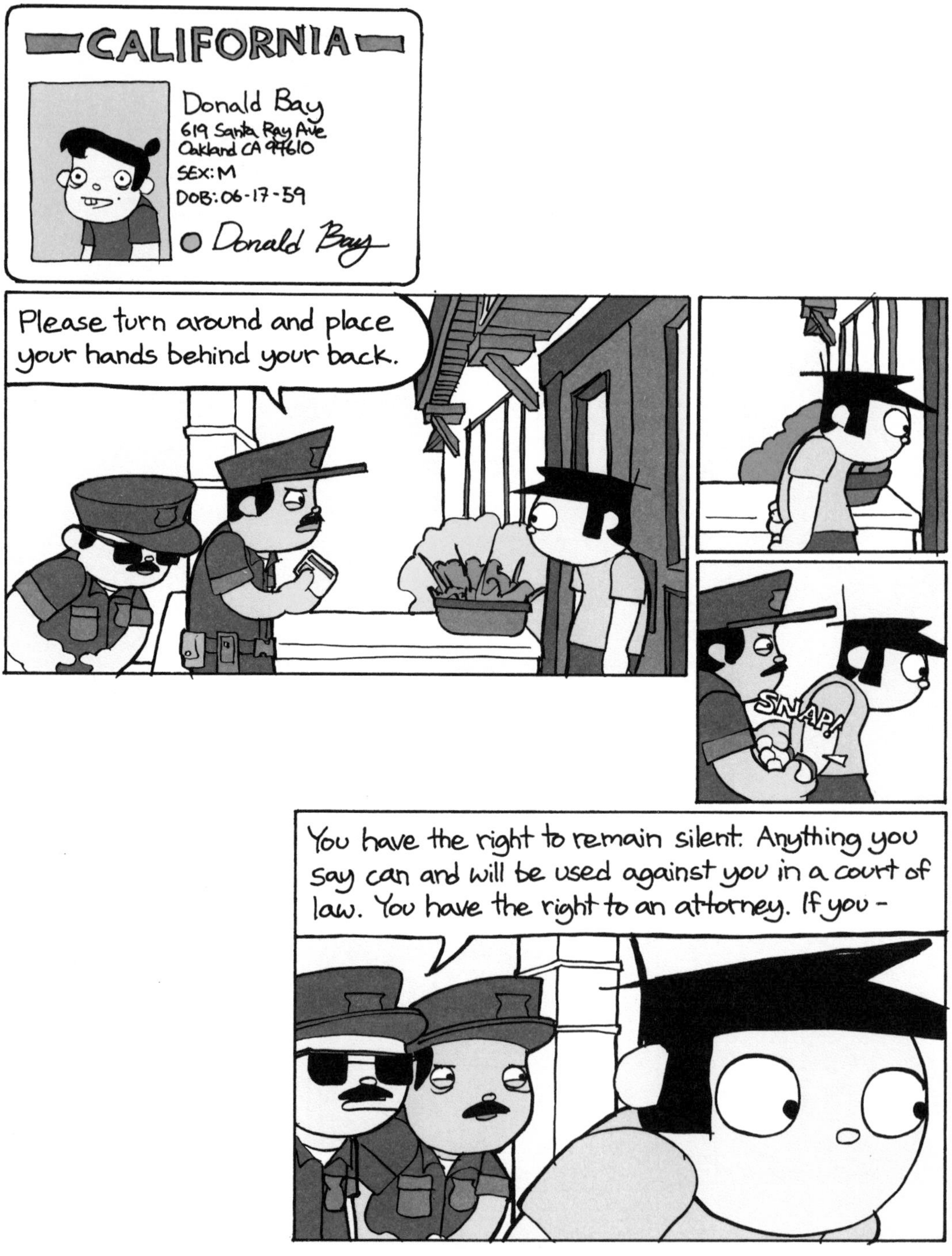
CALIFORNIA
Donald Bay
619 Santa Ray Ave
Oakland CA 94610
SEX: M
DOB: 06-17-59
Donald Bay
Please turn around and place your hands behind your back.
SNAP!
You have the right to remain silent. Anything you say can and will be used against you in a court of law. You have the right to an attorney. If you -

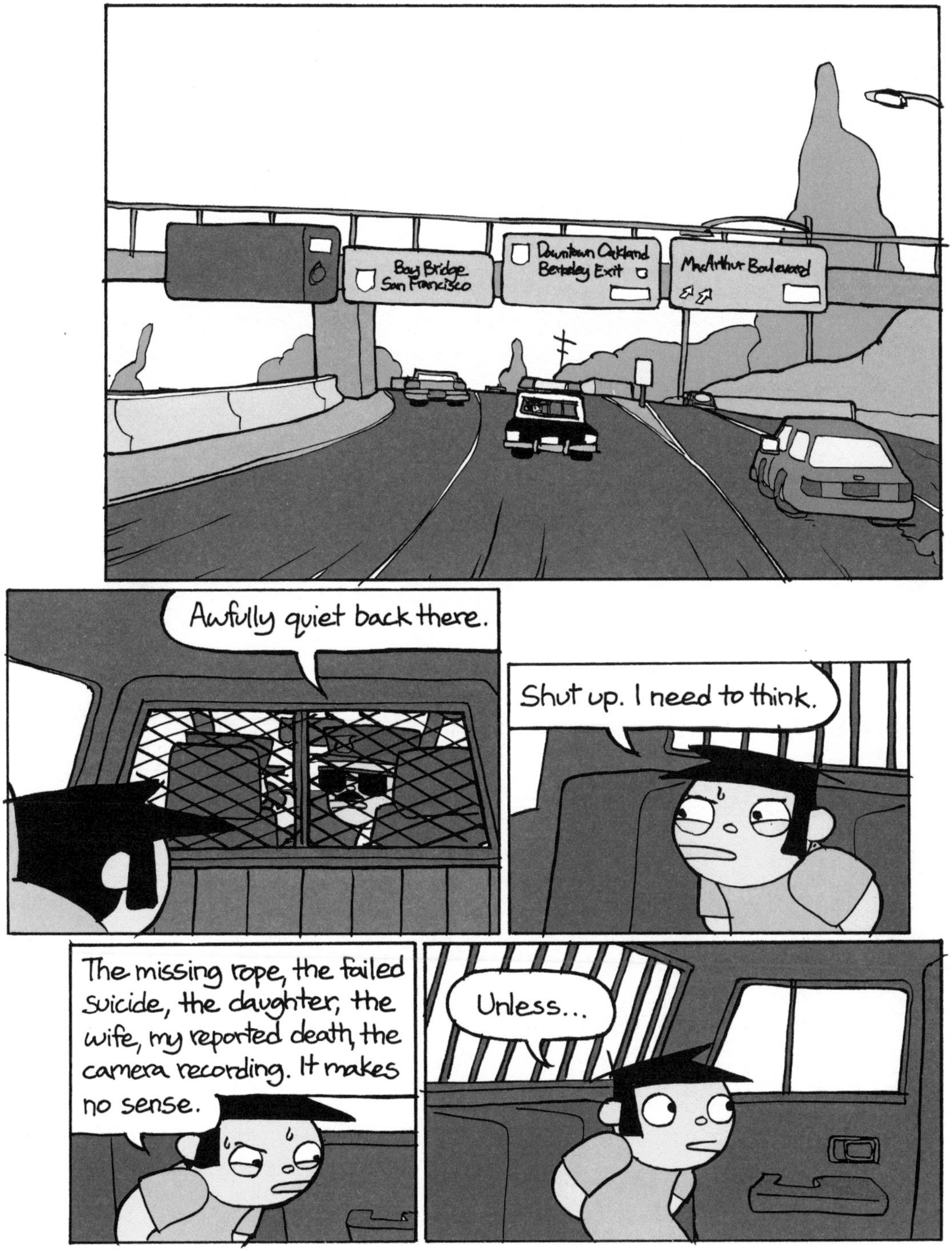
Bay Bridge
San Francisco
Downtown Oakland
Berkeley Exit
MacArthur Boulevard
Awfully quiet back there.
Shut up. I need to think.
The missing rope, the failed suicide, the daughter, the wife, my reported death, the camera recording. It makes no sense.
Unless...

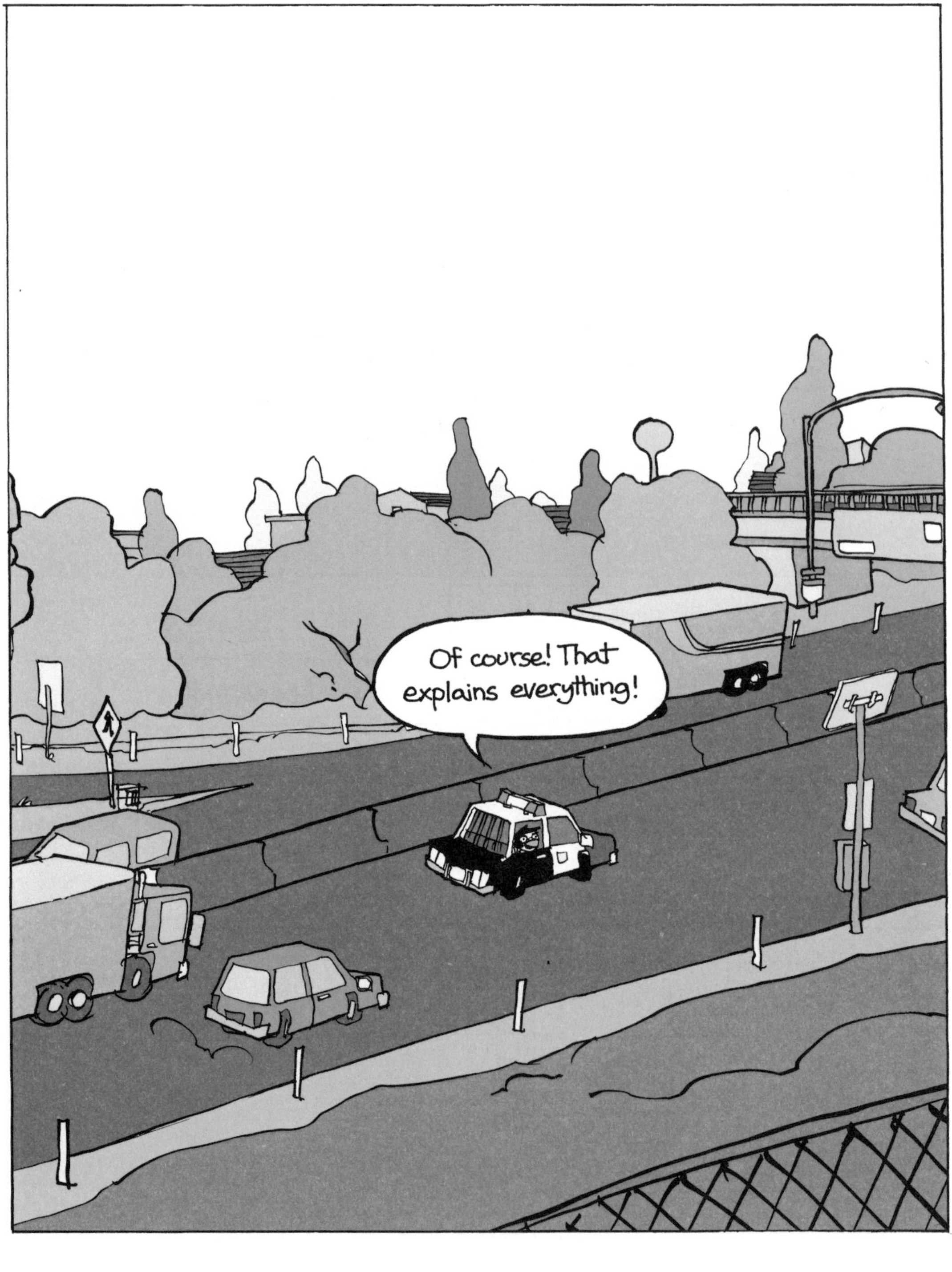
Of course! That explains everything!

CHAPTER 4

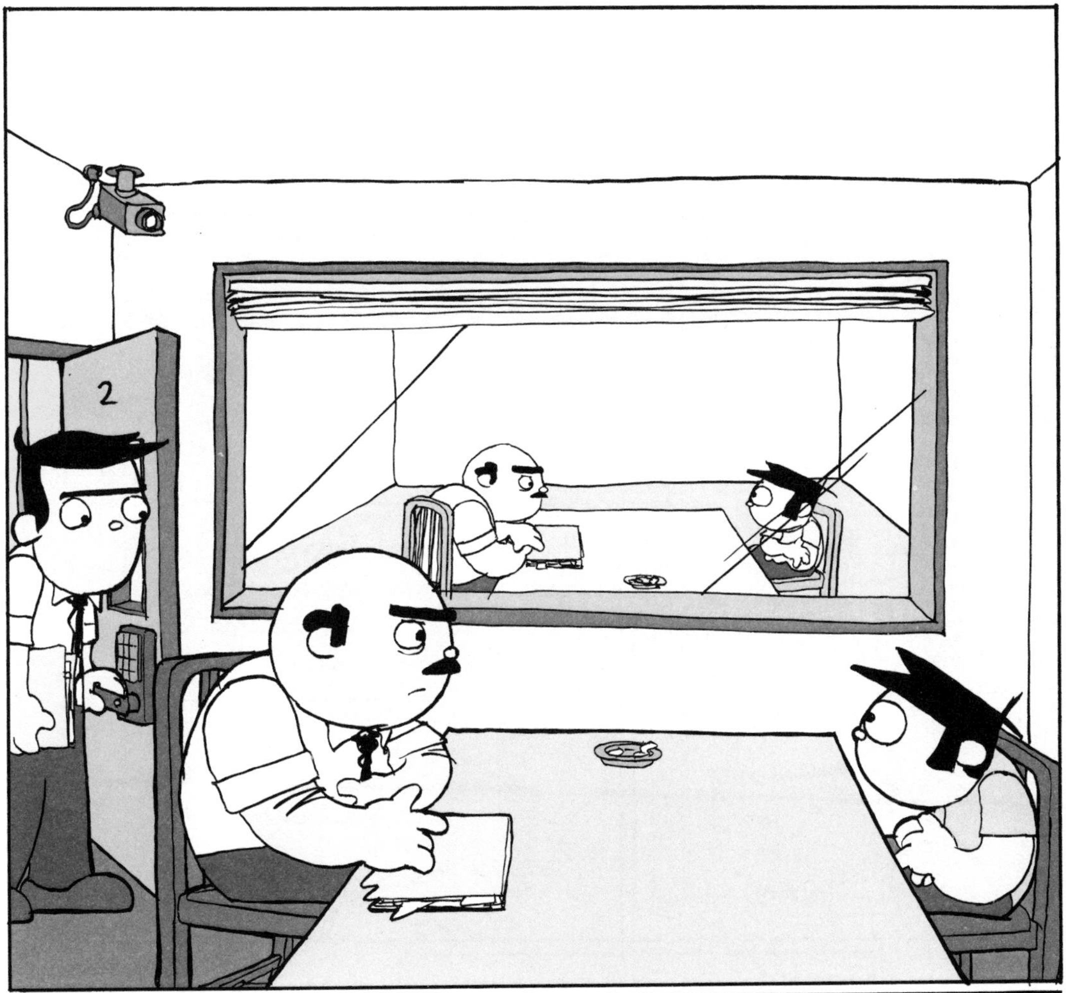

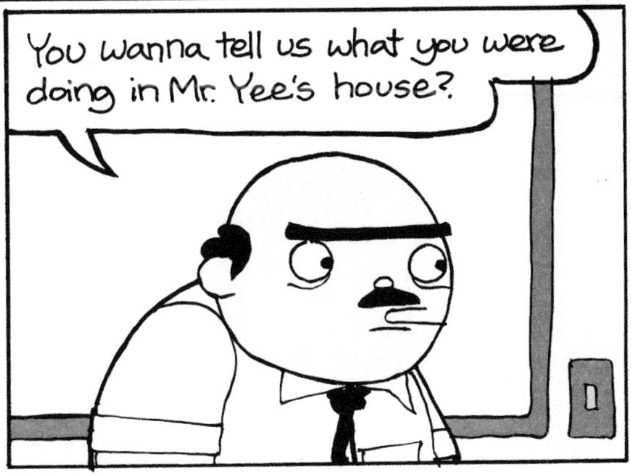
You wanna tell us what you were doing in Mr. Yee's house?

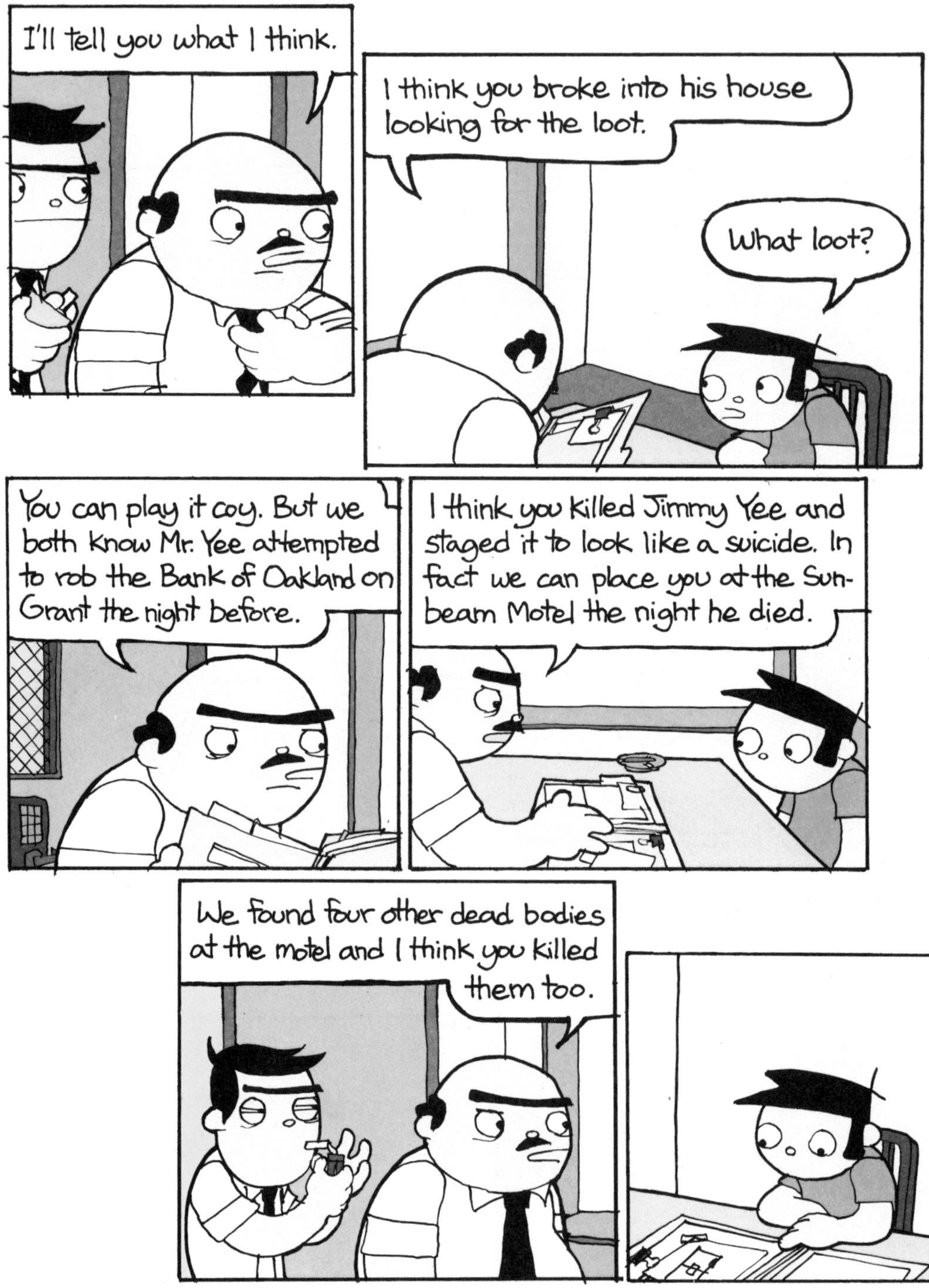
I'll tell you what I think.
I think you broke into his house looking for the loot.
What loot?
You can play it coy. But we both know Mr. Yee attempted to rob the Bank of Oakland on Grant the night before.
I think you killed Jimmy Yee and staged it to look like a suicide. In fact we can place you at the Sunbeam Motel the night he died.
We found four other dead bodies at the motel and I think you killed them too.

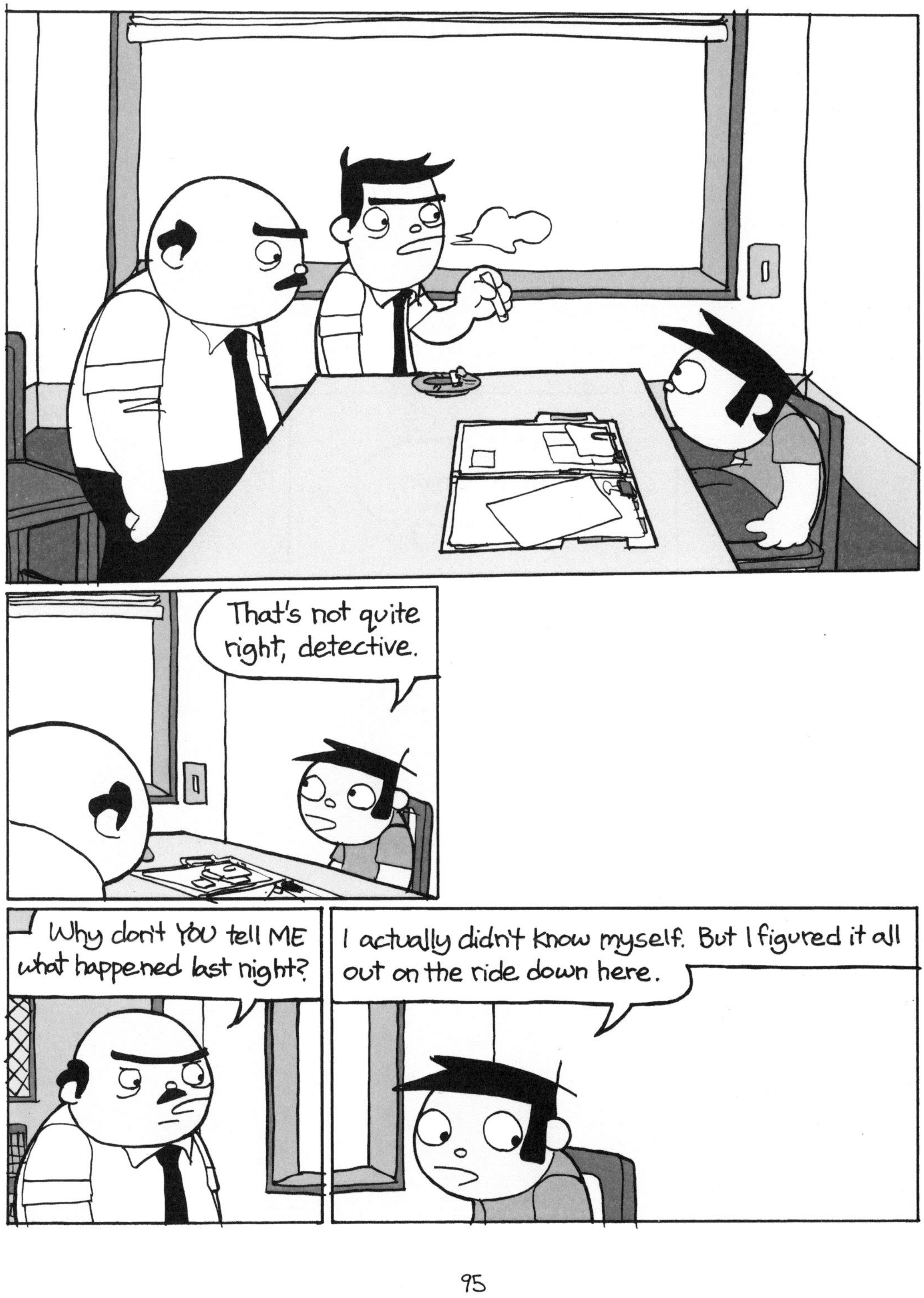
That's not quite right, detective.
Why don't YOU tell ME what happened last night?
I actually didn't know myself. But I figured it all out on the ride down here.

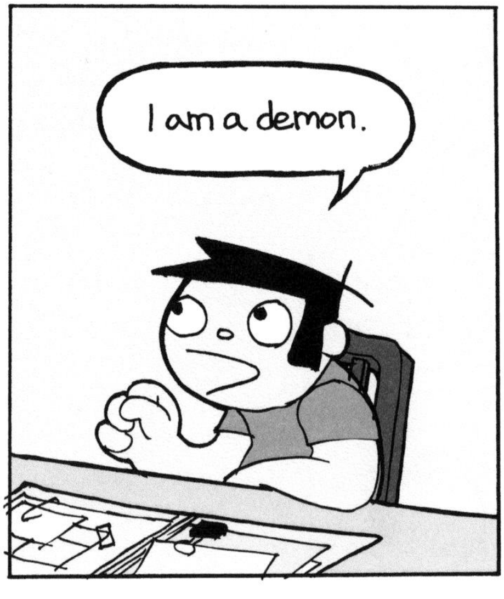
I am a demon.

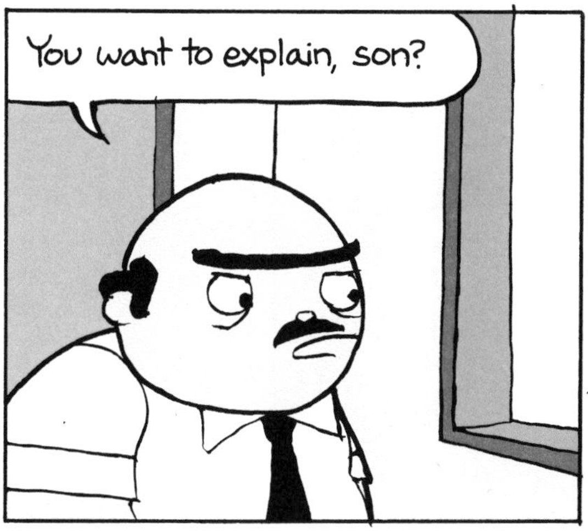
You want to explain, son?

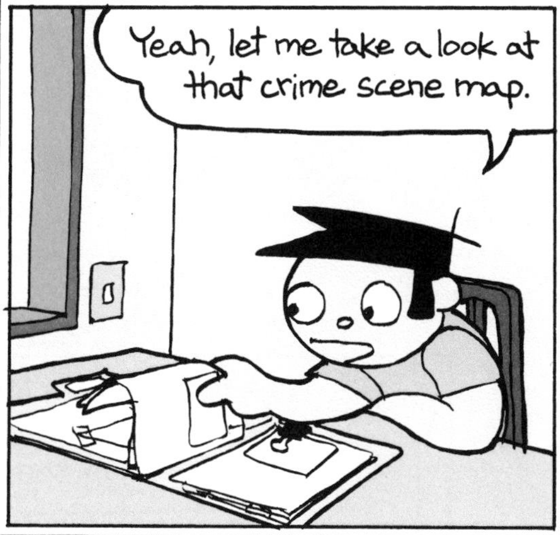
Yeah, let me take a look at that crime scene map.

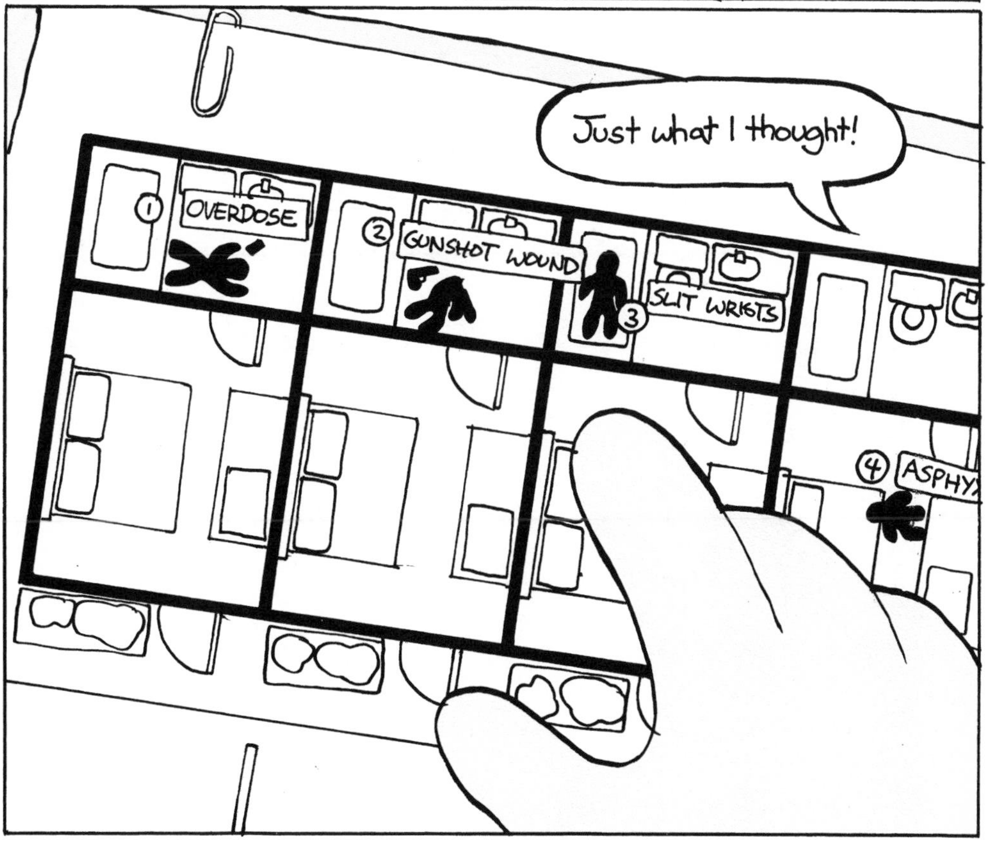
Just what I thought!
1 OVERDOSE
2 GUNSHOT WOUND
3 SLIT WRISTS
4 ASPHYX

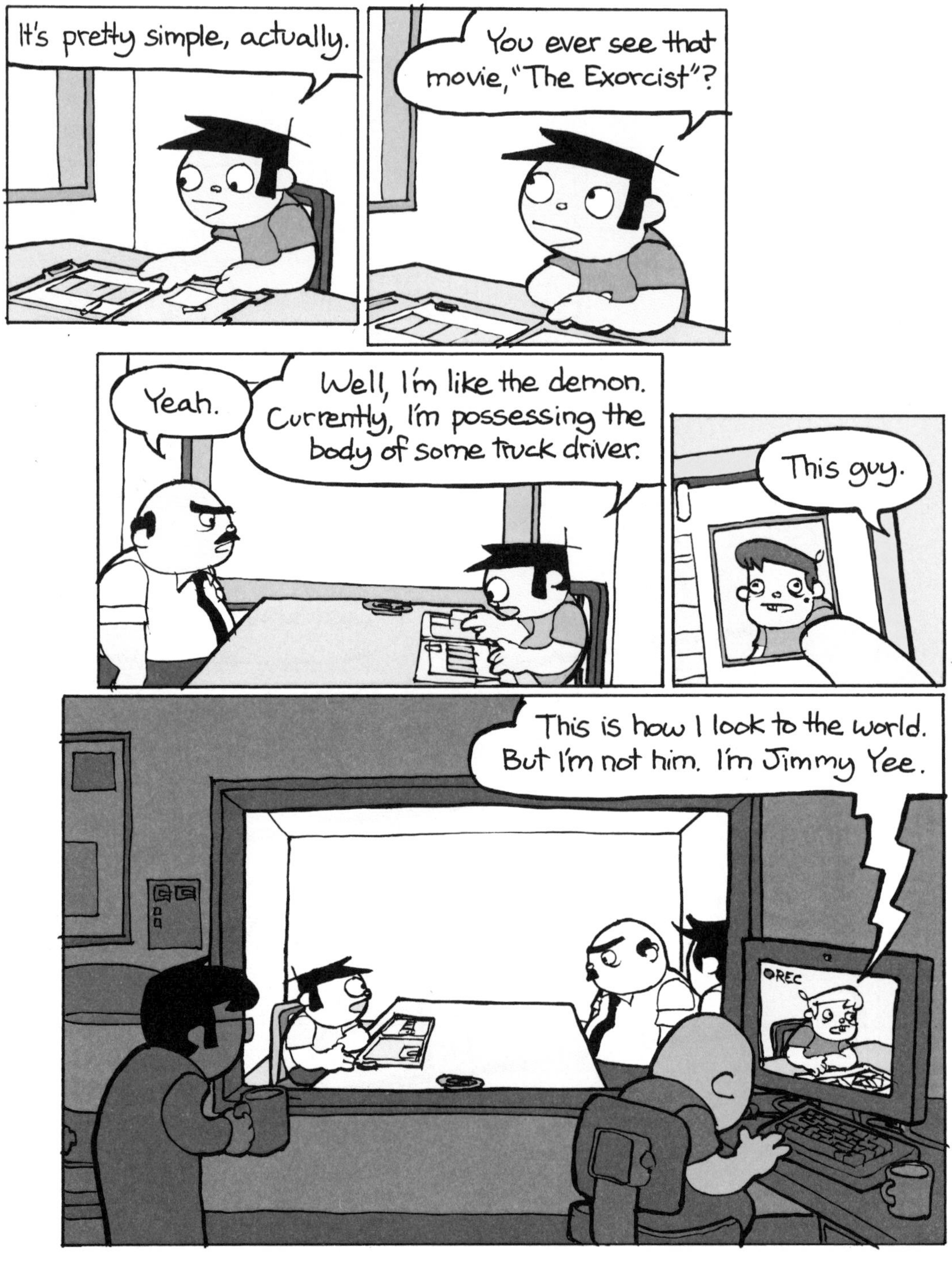
It's pretty simple, actually.
You ever see that movie, "The Exorcist"?
Yeah.
Well, I'm like the demon. Currently, I'm possessing the body of some truck driver.
This guy.
This is how I look to the world. But I'm not him. I'm Jimmy Yee.
REC

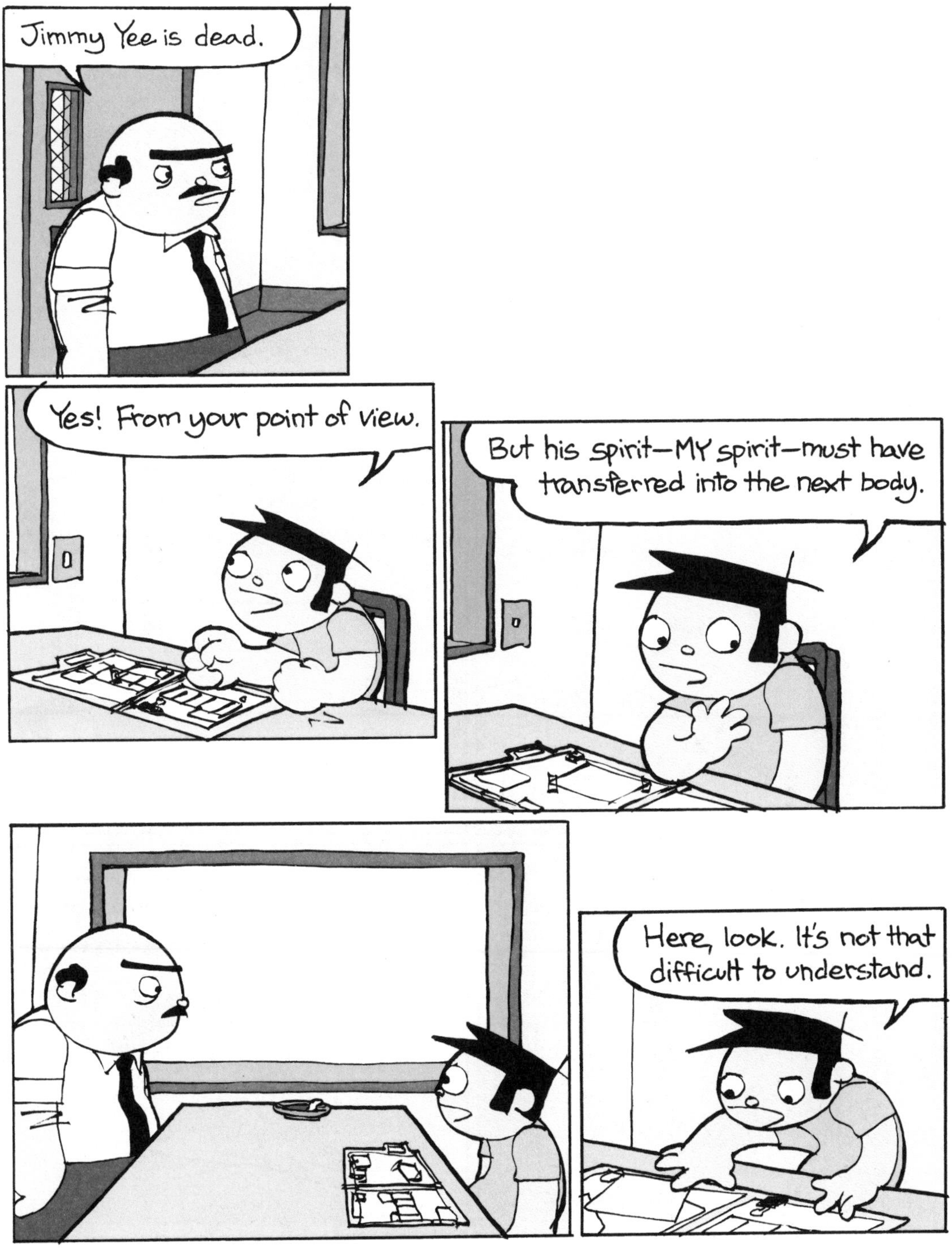
Jimmy Yee is dead.
Yes! From your point of view.
But his spirit—MY spirit—must have transferred into the next body.
Here, look. It's not that difficult to understand.

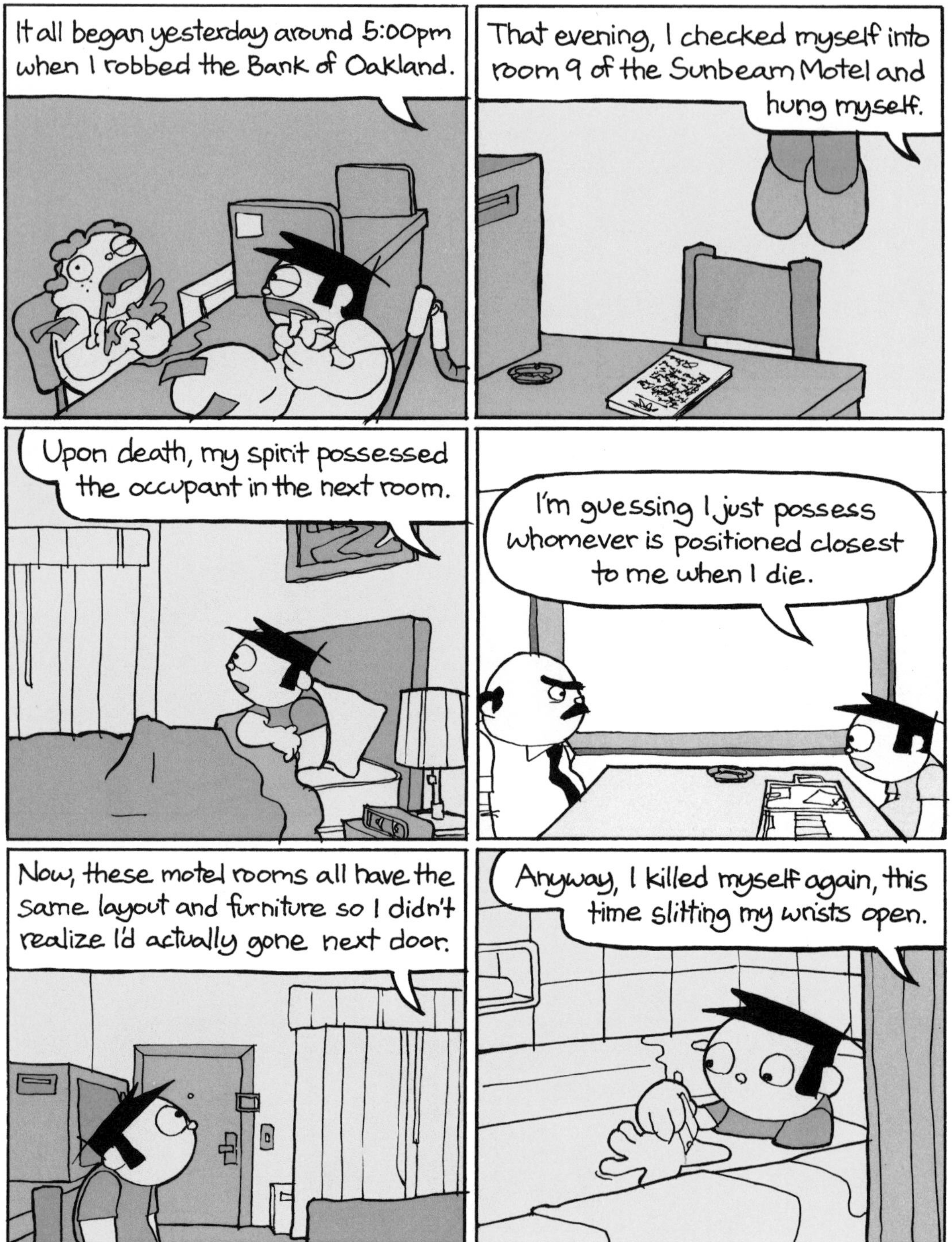
It all began yesterday around 5:00pm when I robbed the Bank of Oakland.
That evening, I checked myself into room 9 of the Sunbeam Motel and hung myself.
Upon death, my spirit possessed the occupant in the next room.
I'm guessing I just possess whomever is positioned closest to me when I die.
Now, these motel rooms all have the same layout and furniture so I didn't realize I'd actually gone next door.
Anyway, I killed myself again, this time slitting my wrists open.

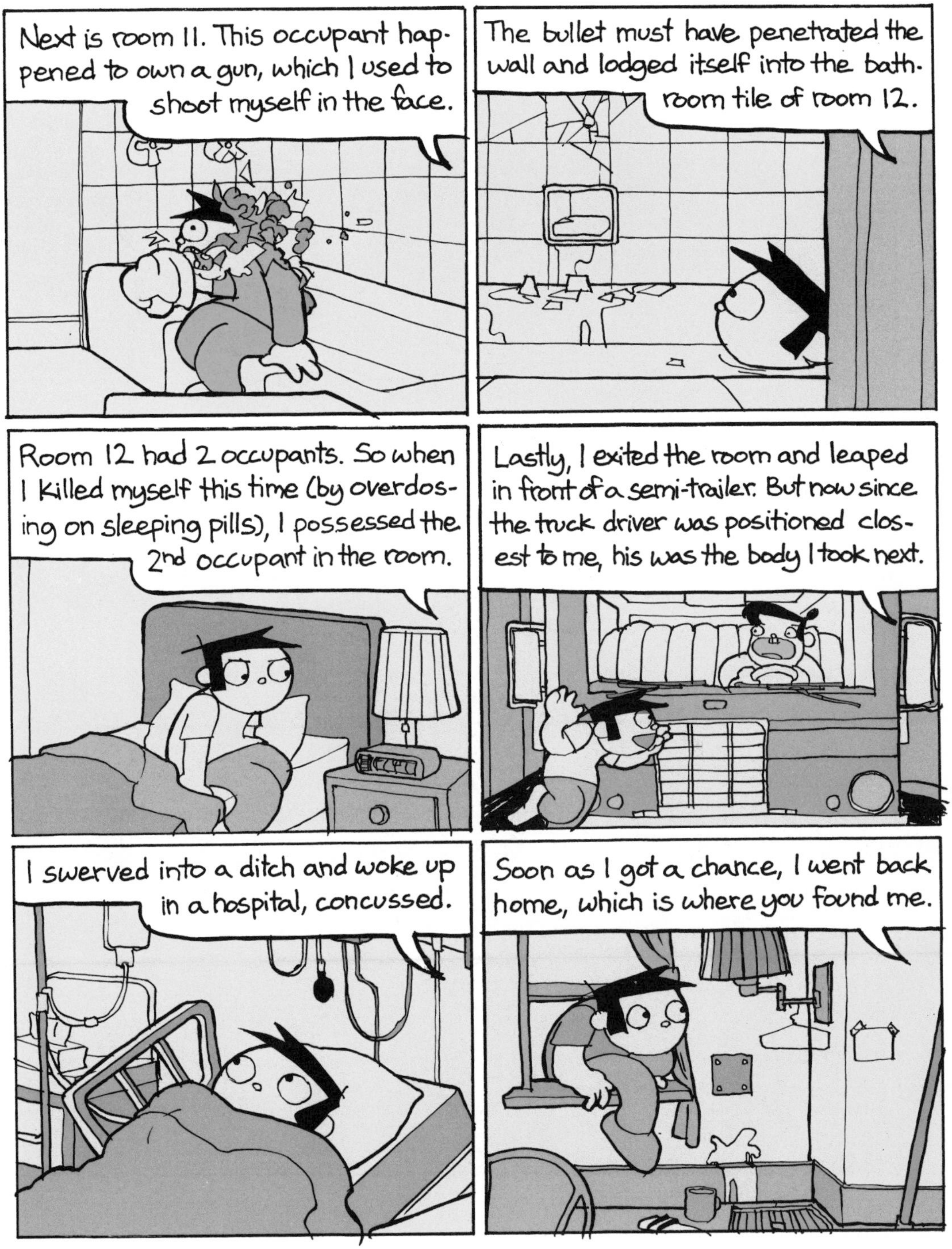
Next is room 11. This occupant happened to own a gun, which I used to shoot myself in the face.
The bullet must have penetrated the wall and lodged itself into the bathroom tile of room 12.
Room 12 had 2 occupants. So when I killed myself this time (by overdosing on sleeping pills), I possessed the 2nd occupant in the room.
Lastly, I exited the room and leaped in front of a semi-trailer. But now since the truck driver was positioned closest to me, his was the body I took next.
I swerved into a ditch and woke up in a hospital, concussed.
Soon as I got a chance, I went back home, which is where you found me.

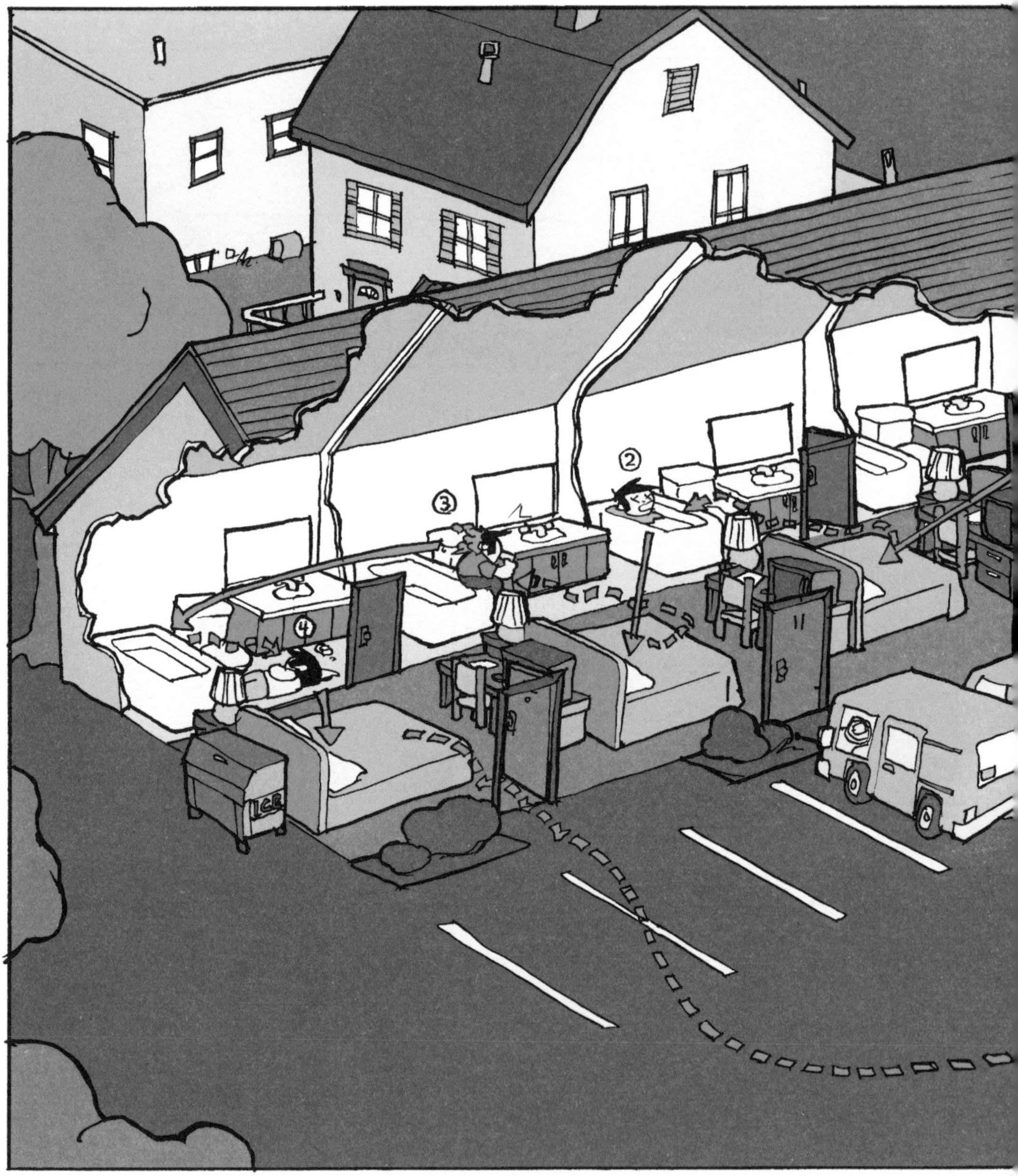
2
3
4
ICE

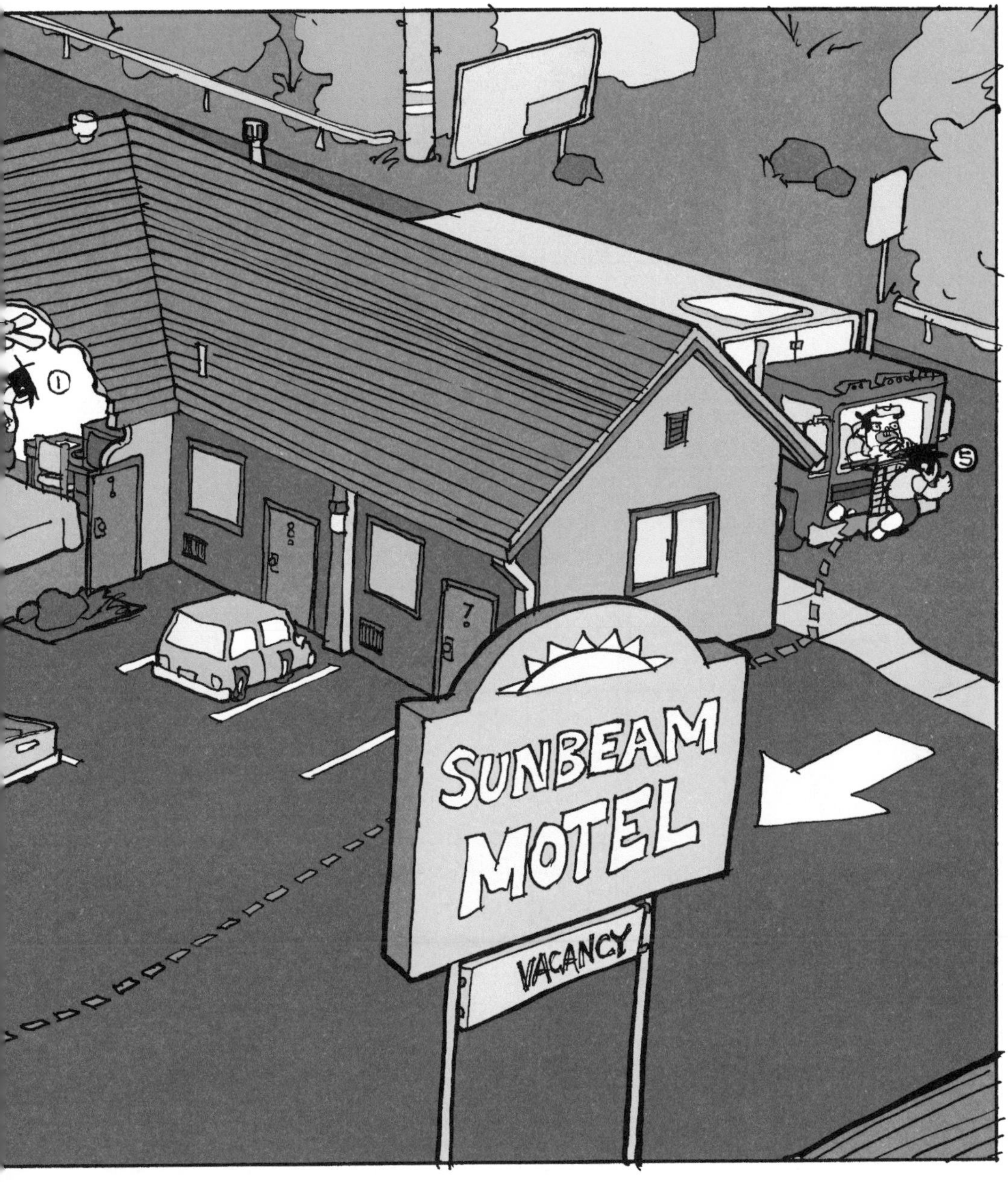
SUNBEAM MOTEL
VACANCY

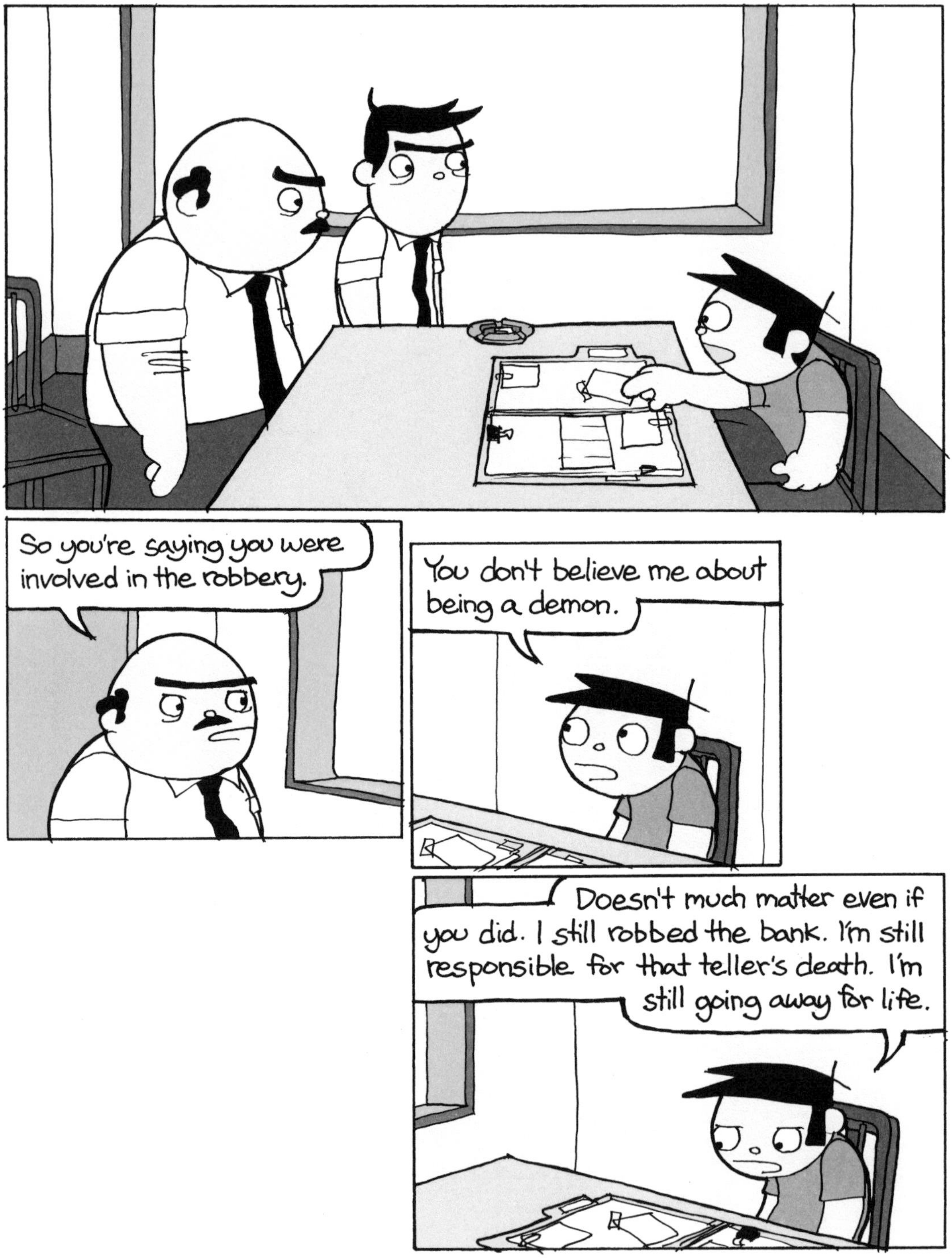
So you're saying you were involved in the robbery.
You don't believe me about being a demon.
Doesn't much matter even if you did. I still robbed the bank. I'm still responsible for that teller's death. I'm still going away for life.

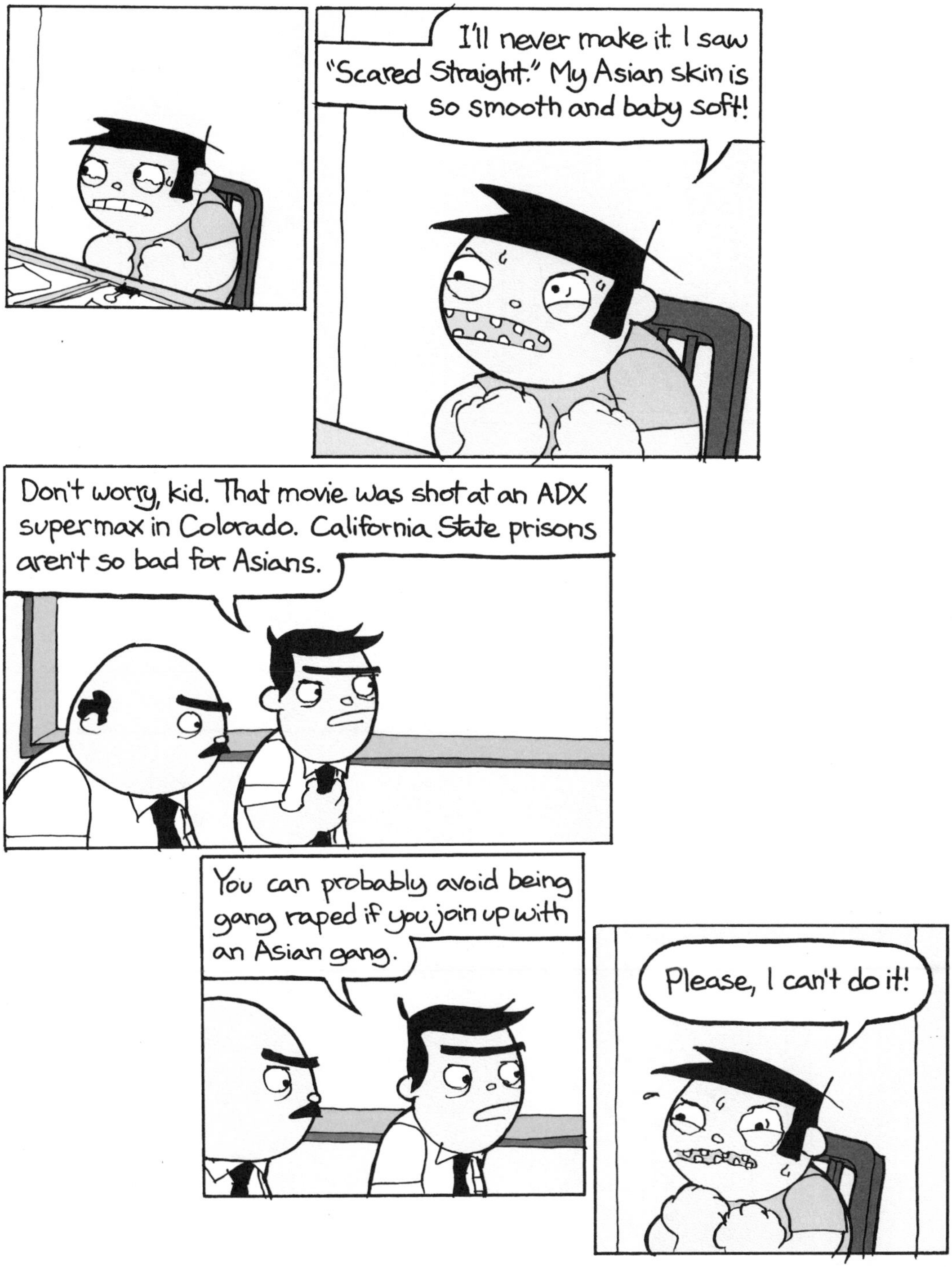
I'll never make it. I saw "Scared Straight." My Asian skin is so smooth and baby soft!
Don't worry, kid. That movie was shot at an ADX supermax in Colorado. California State prisons aren't so bad for Asians.
You can probably avoid being gang raped if you join up with an Asian gang.
Please, I can't do it!

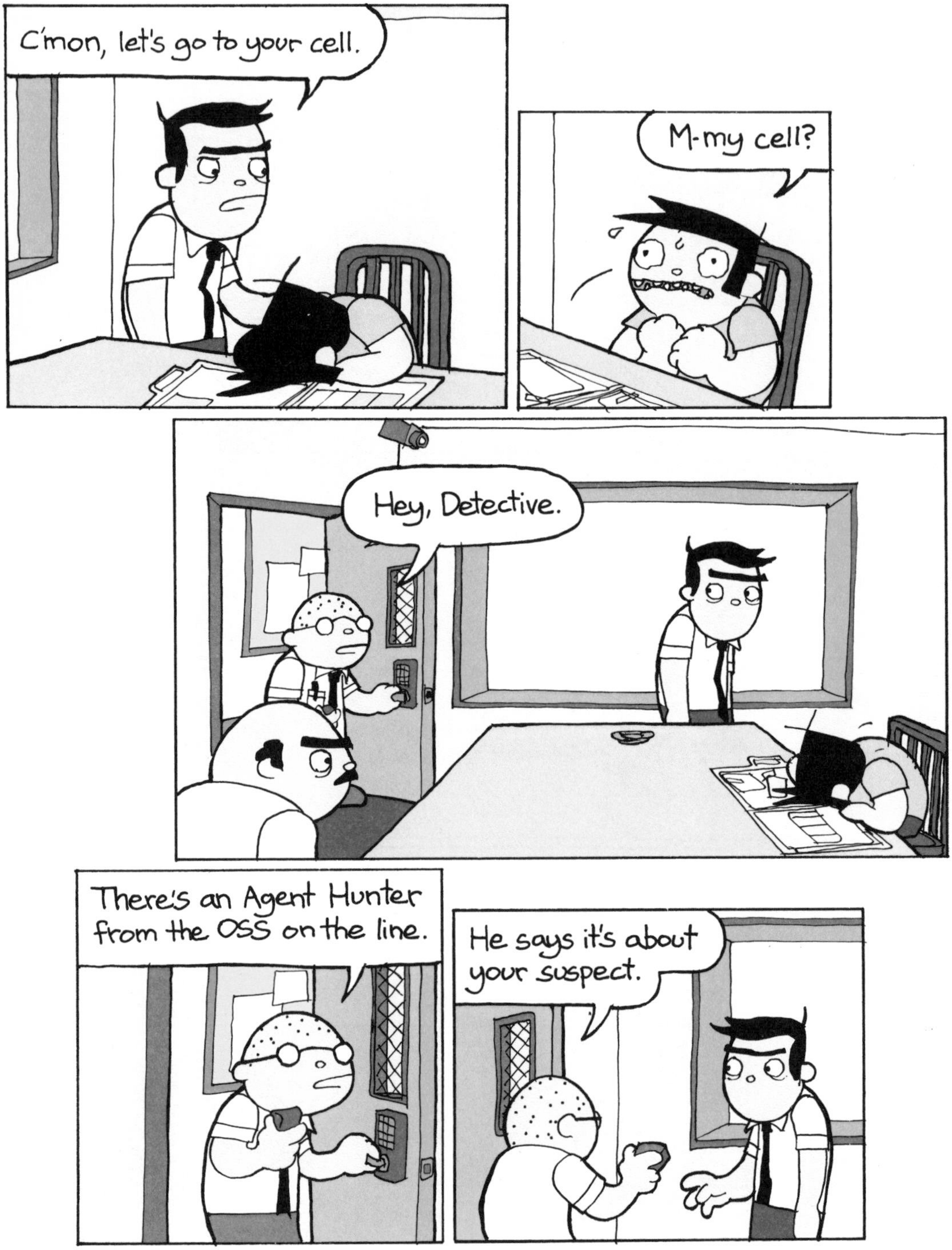
C'mon, let's go to your cell.
M-my cell?
Hey, Detective.
There's an Agent Hunter from the OSS on the line.
He says it's about your suspect.

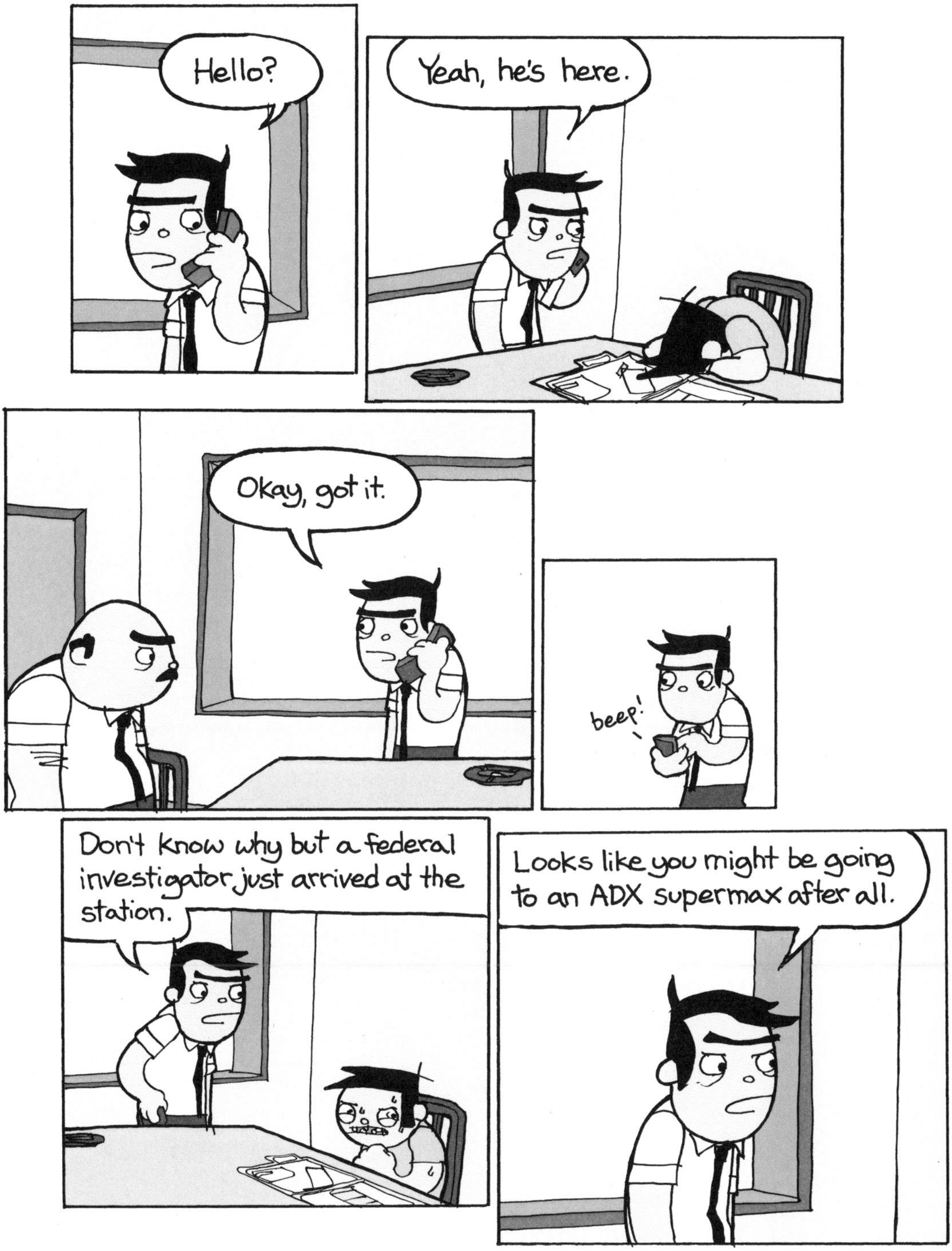
Hello?
Yeah, he's here.
Okay, got it.
beep!
Don't know why but a federal investigator just arrived at the station.
Looks like you might be going to an ADX supermax after all.

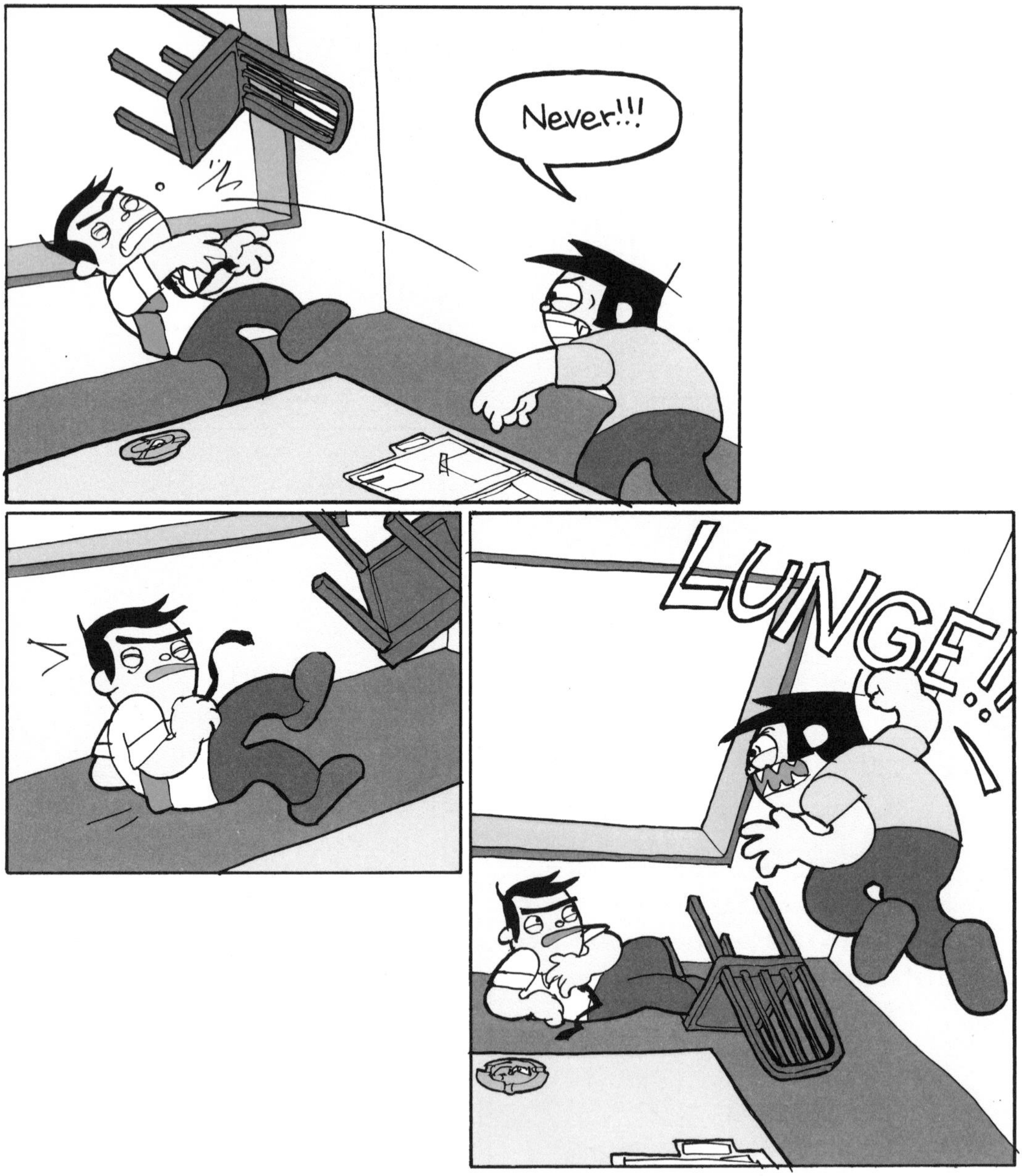
Never!!!
LUNGE!!

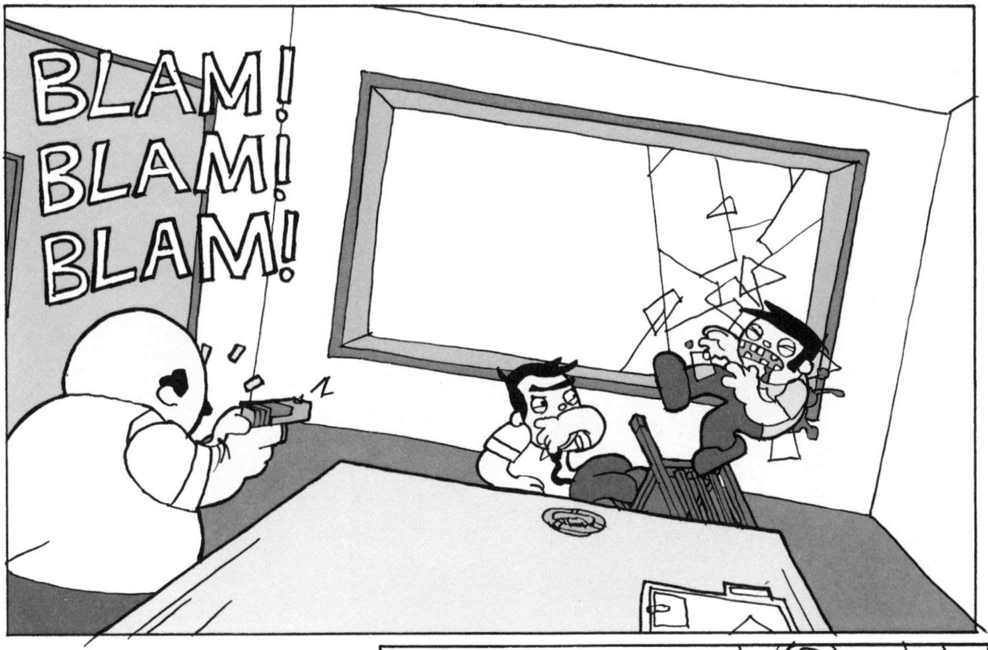
BLAM! BLAM! BLAM!

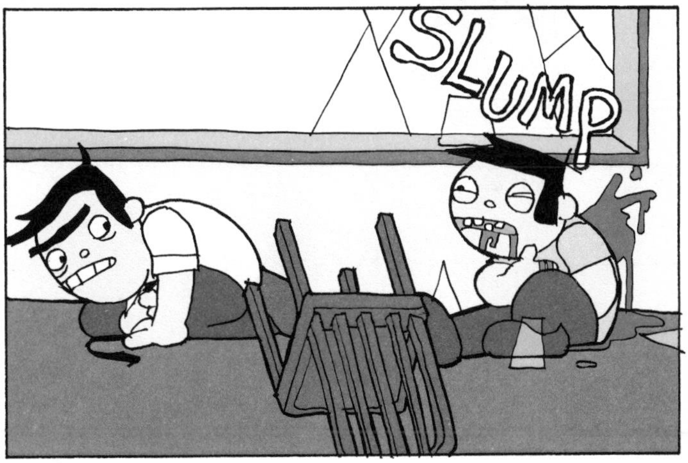
SLUMP

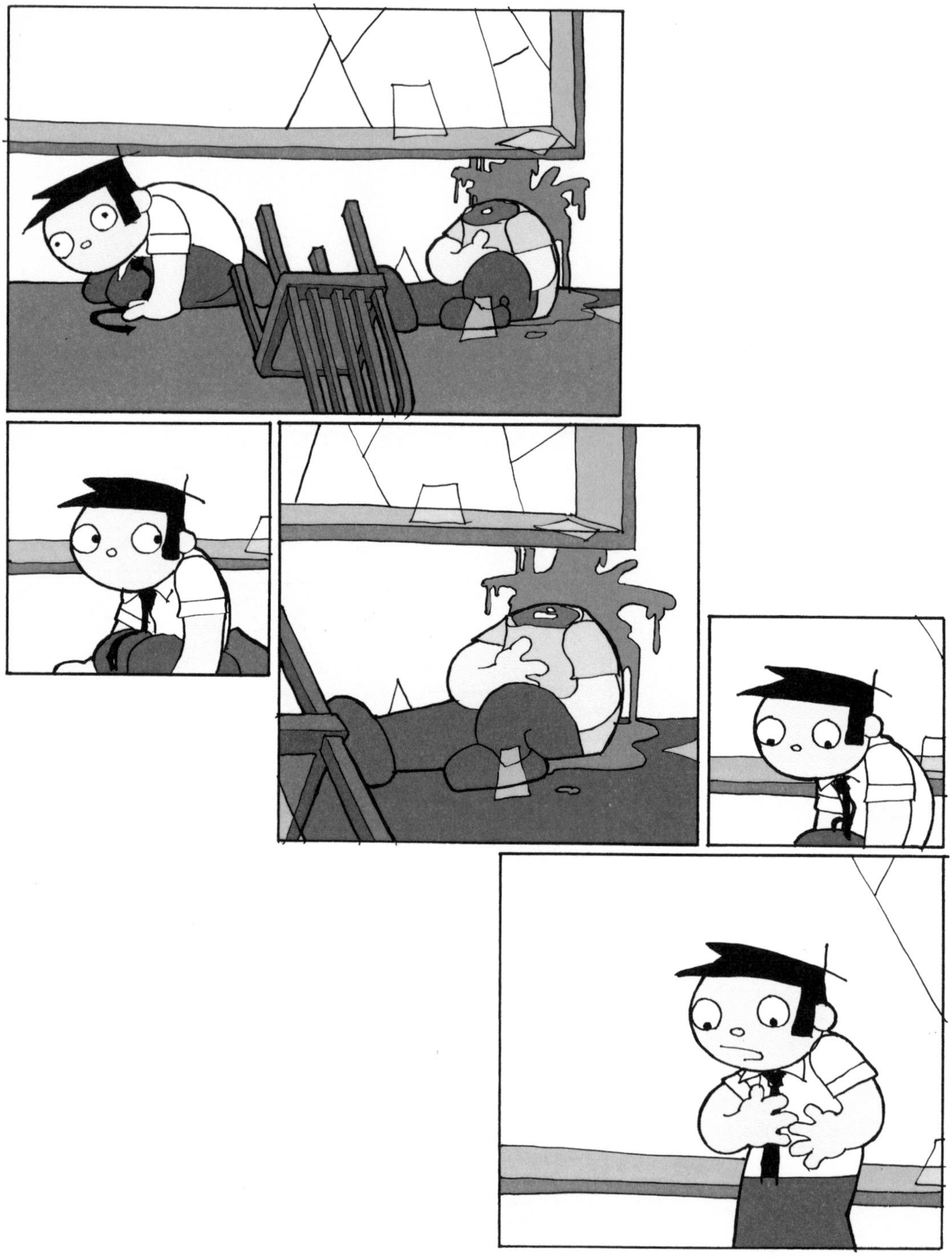

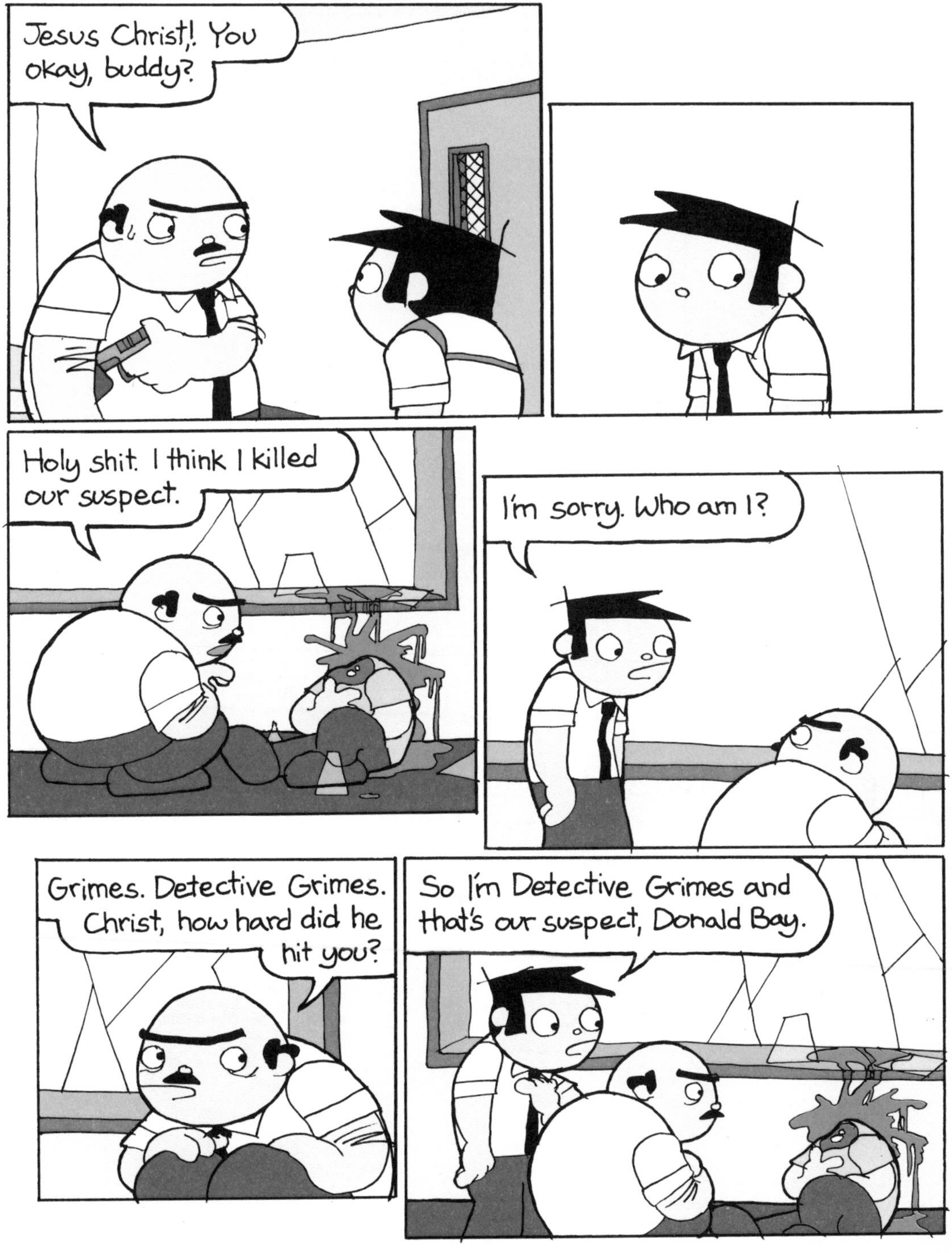
Jesus Christ!. You okay, buddy?
Holy shit. I think I killed our suspect.
I'm sorry. Who am I?
Grimes. Detective Grimes. Christ, how hard did he hit you?
So I'm Detective Grimes and that's our suspect, Donald Bay.

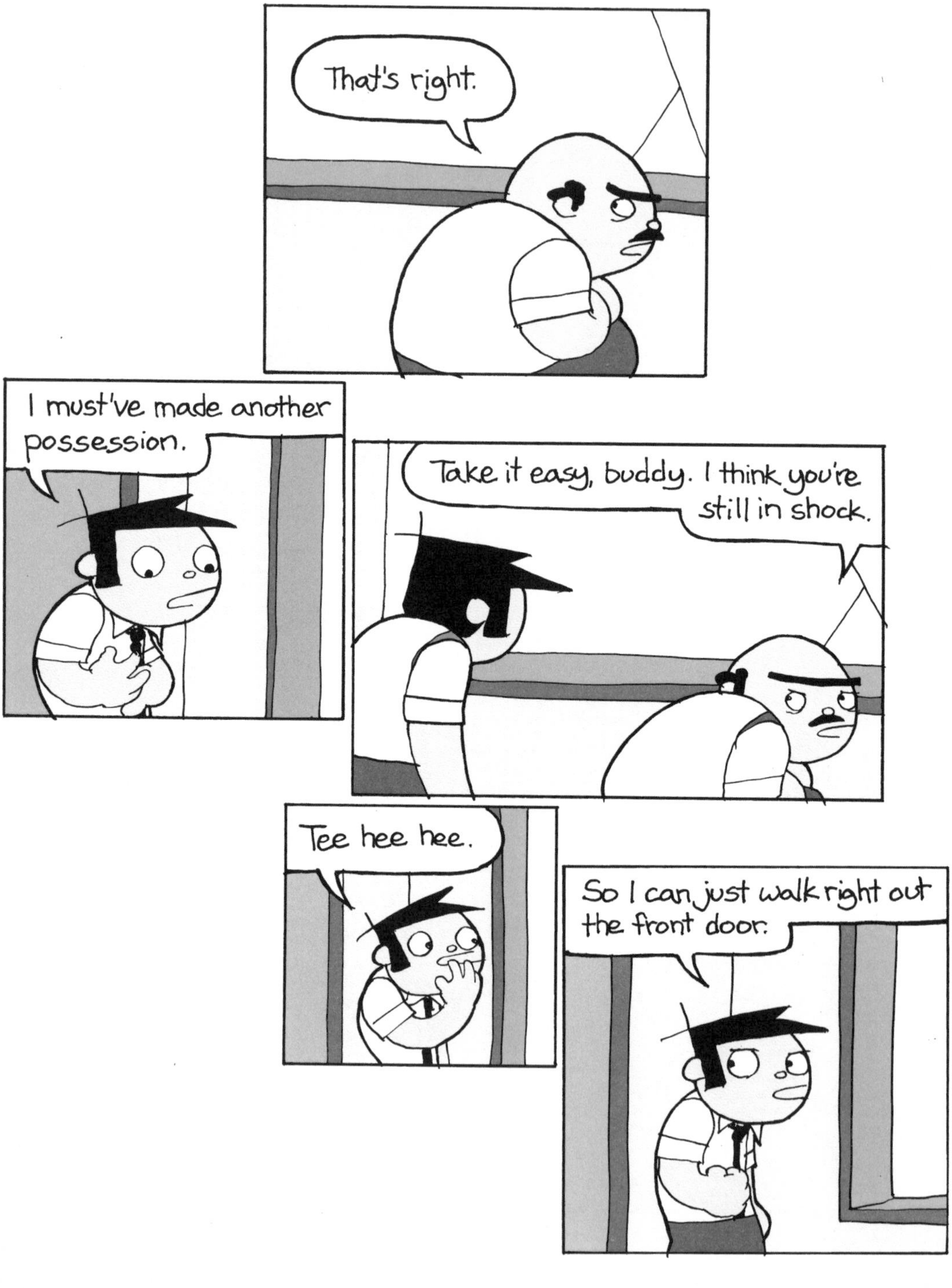
That's right.
I must've made another possession.
Take it easy, buddy. I think you're still in shock.
Tee hee hee.
So I can just walk right out the front door.

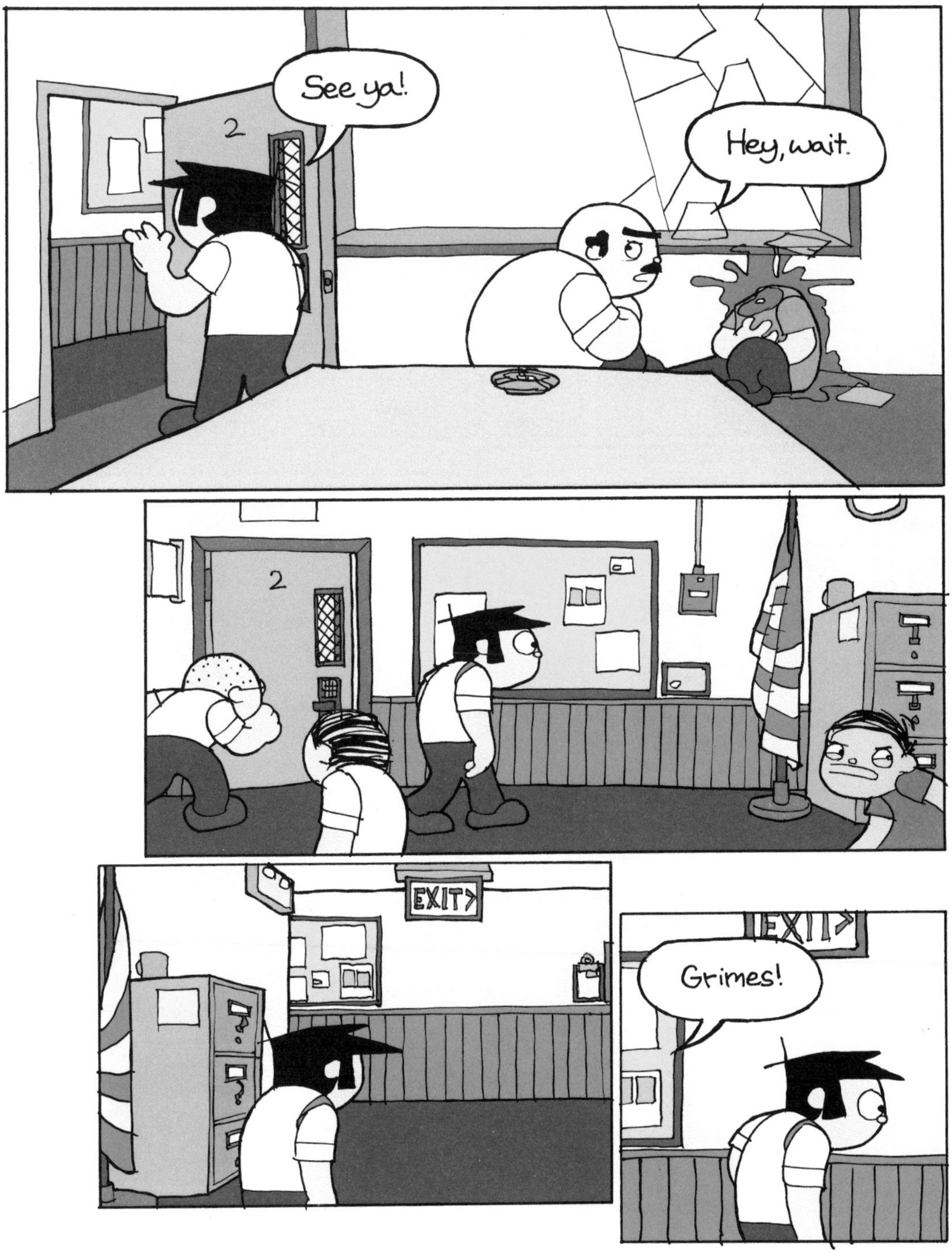
2
See ya!
Hey, wait.
2
EXIT>
EXIT>
Grimes!

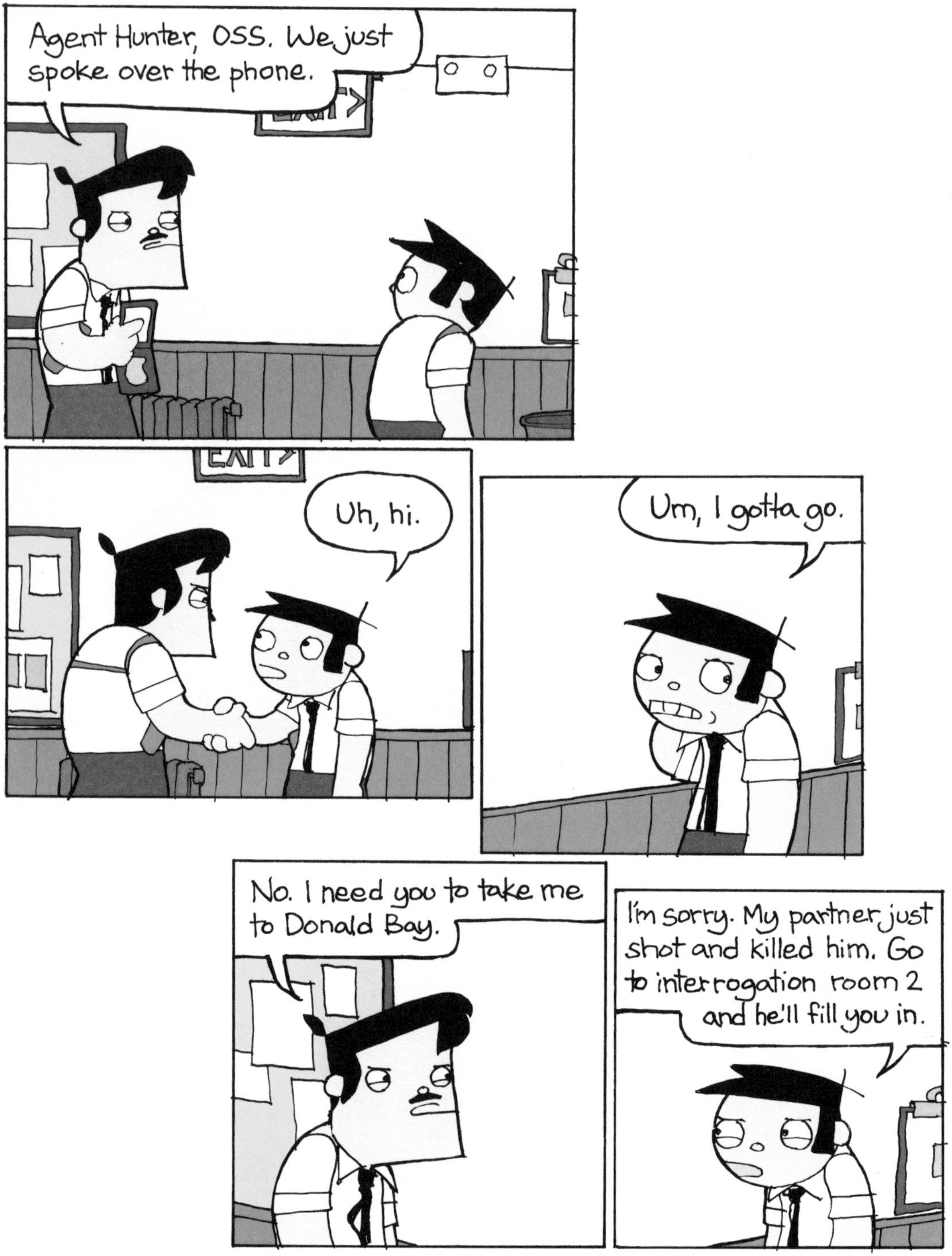
Agent Hunter, OSS. We just spoke over the phone.
EXIT
Uh, hi.
Um, I gotta go.
No. I need you to take me to Donald Bay.
I'm sorry. My partner just shot and killed him. Go to interrogation room 2 and he'll fill you in.

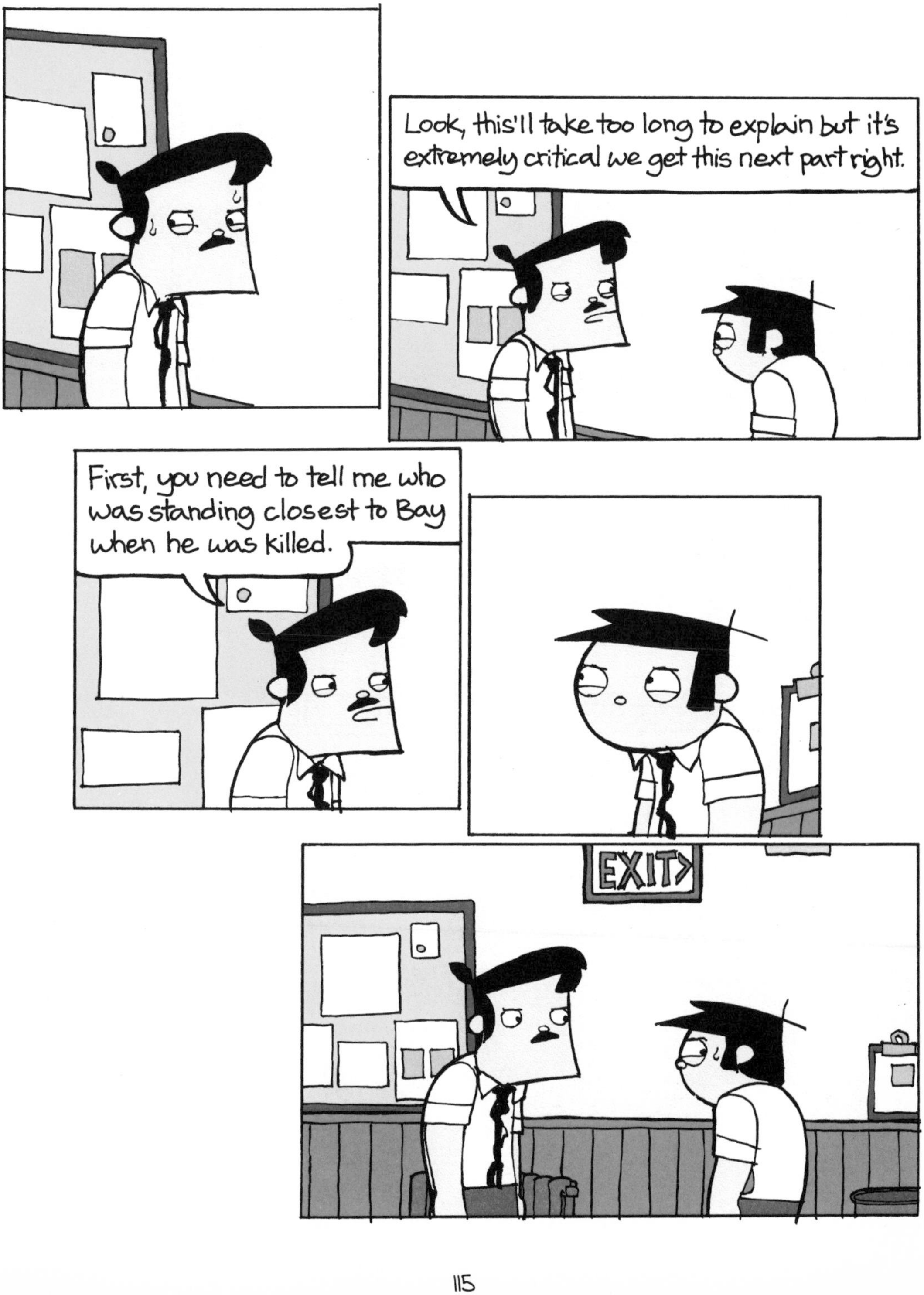
Look, this'll take too long to explain but it's extremely critical we get this next part right.
First, you need to tell me who was standing closest to Bay when he was killed.
EXIT

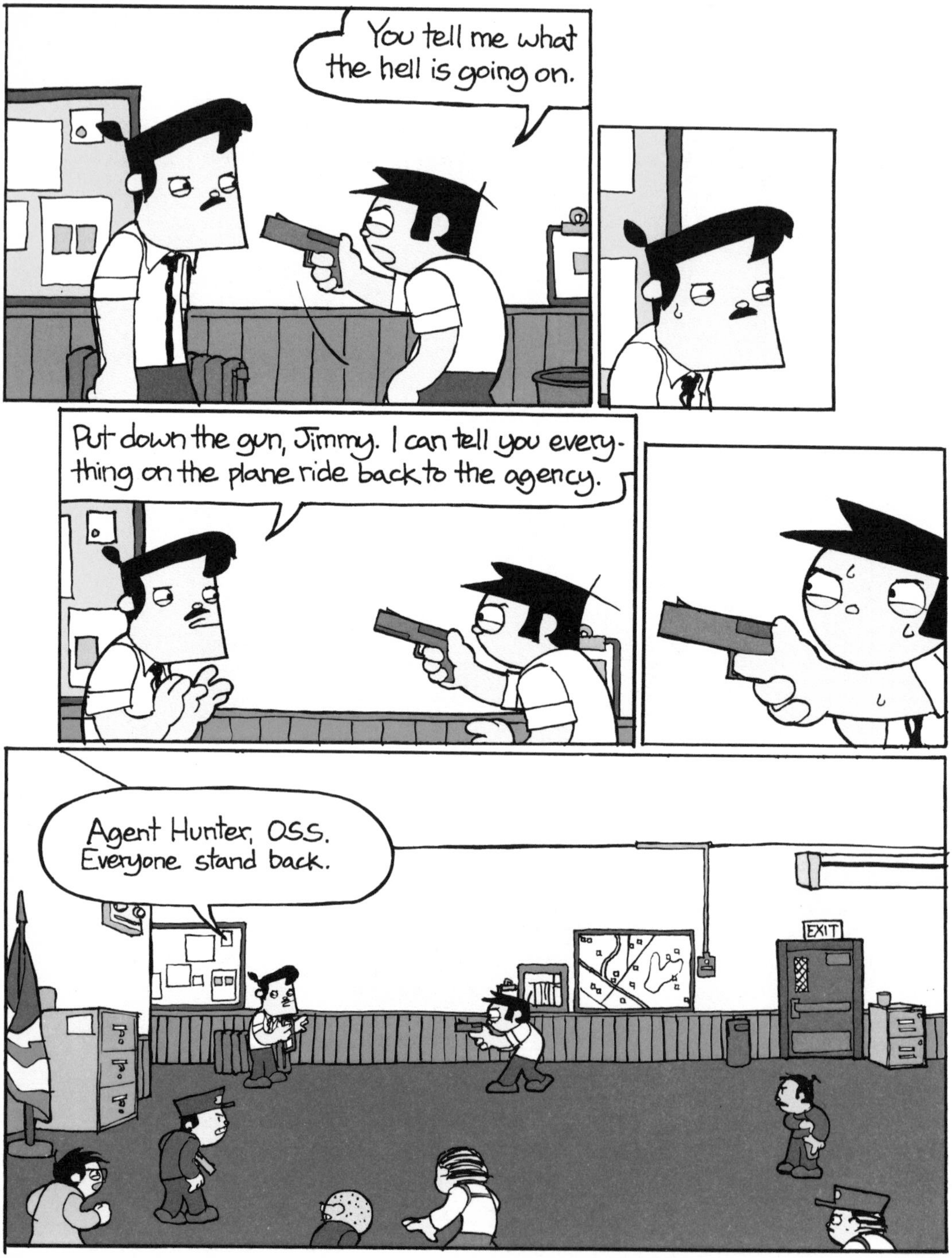
You tell me what the hell is going on.
Put down the gun, Jimmy. I can tell you everything on the plane ride back to the agency.
Agent Hunter, OSS. Everyone stand back.
EXIT

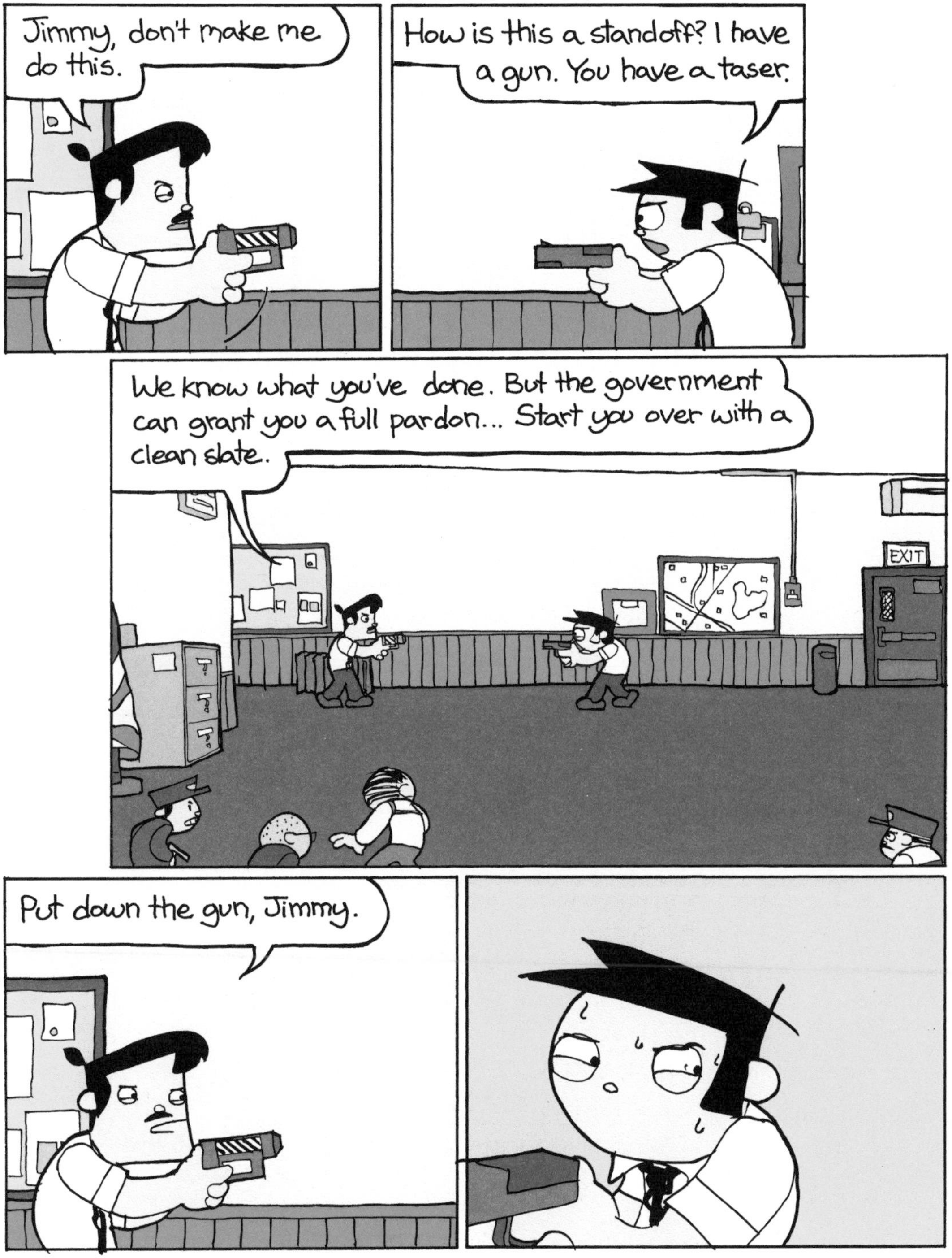
Jimmy, don't make me do this.
How is this a standoff? I have a gun. You have a taser.
We know what you've done. But the government can grant you a full pardon... Start you over with a clean slate.
EXIT
Put down the gun, Jimmy.

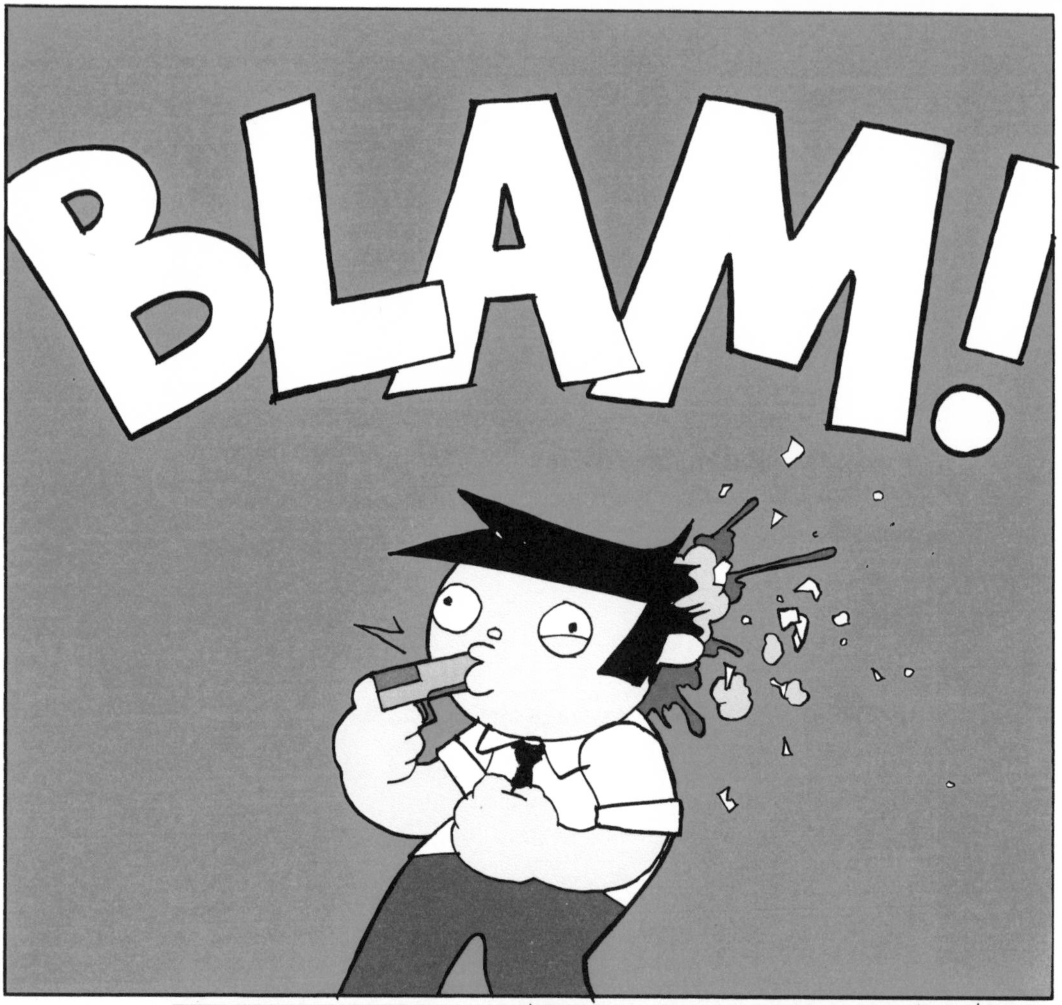
BLAM!

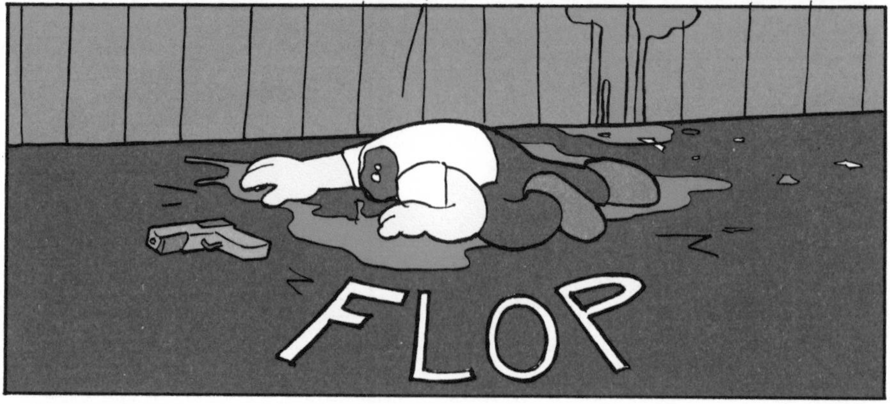
FLOP

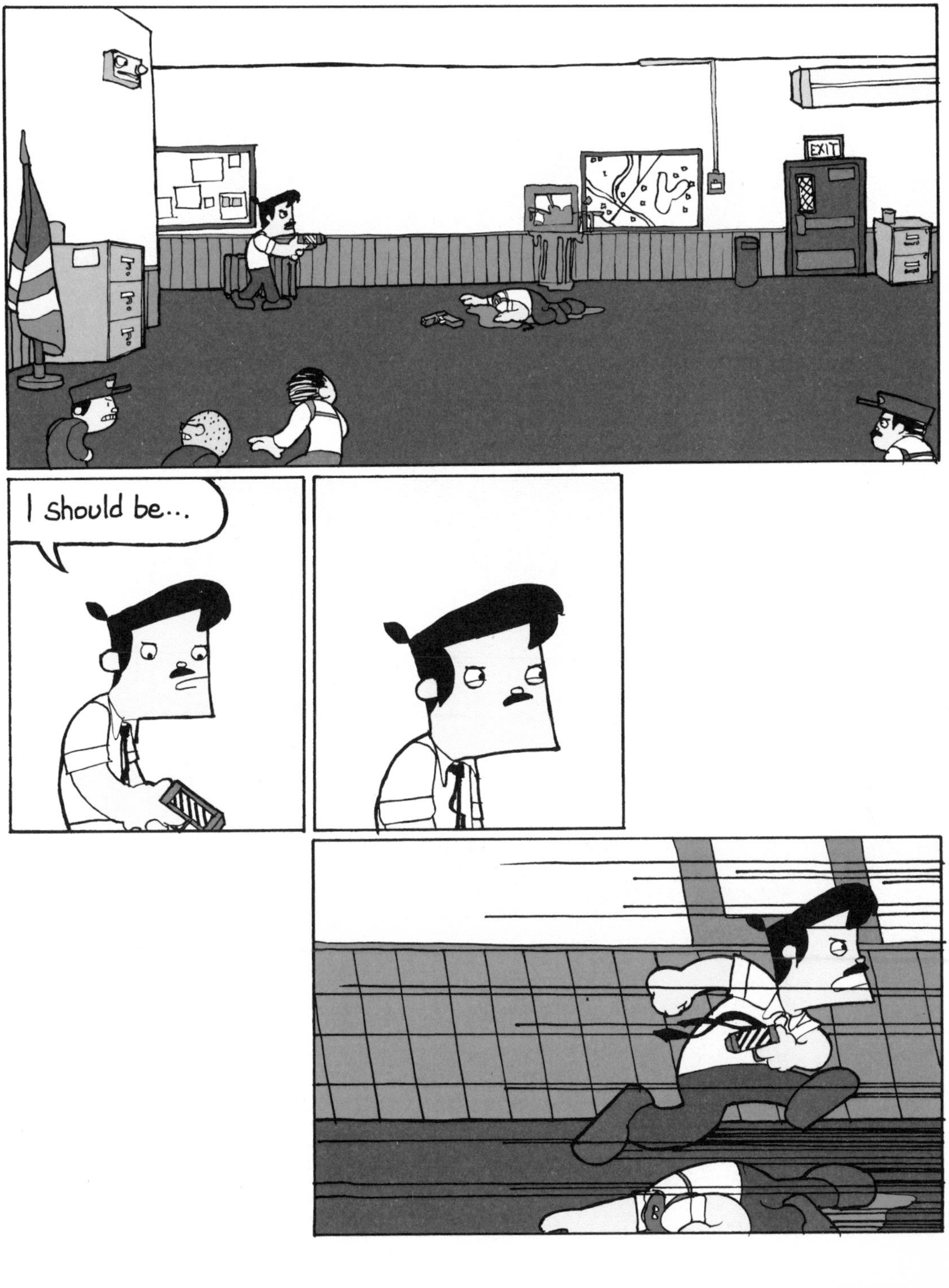
EXIT
I should be...

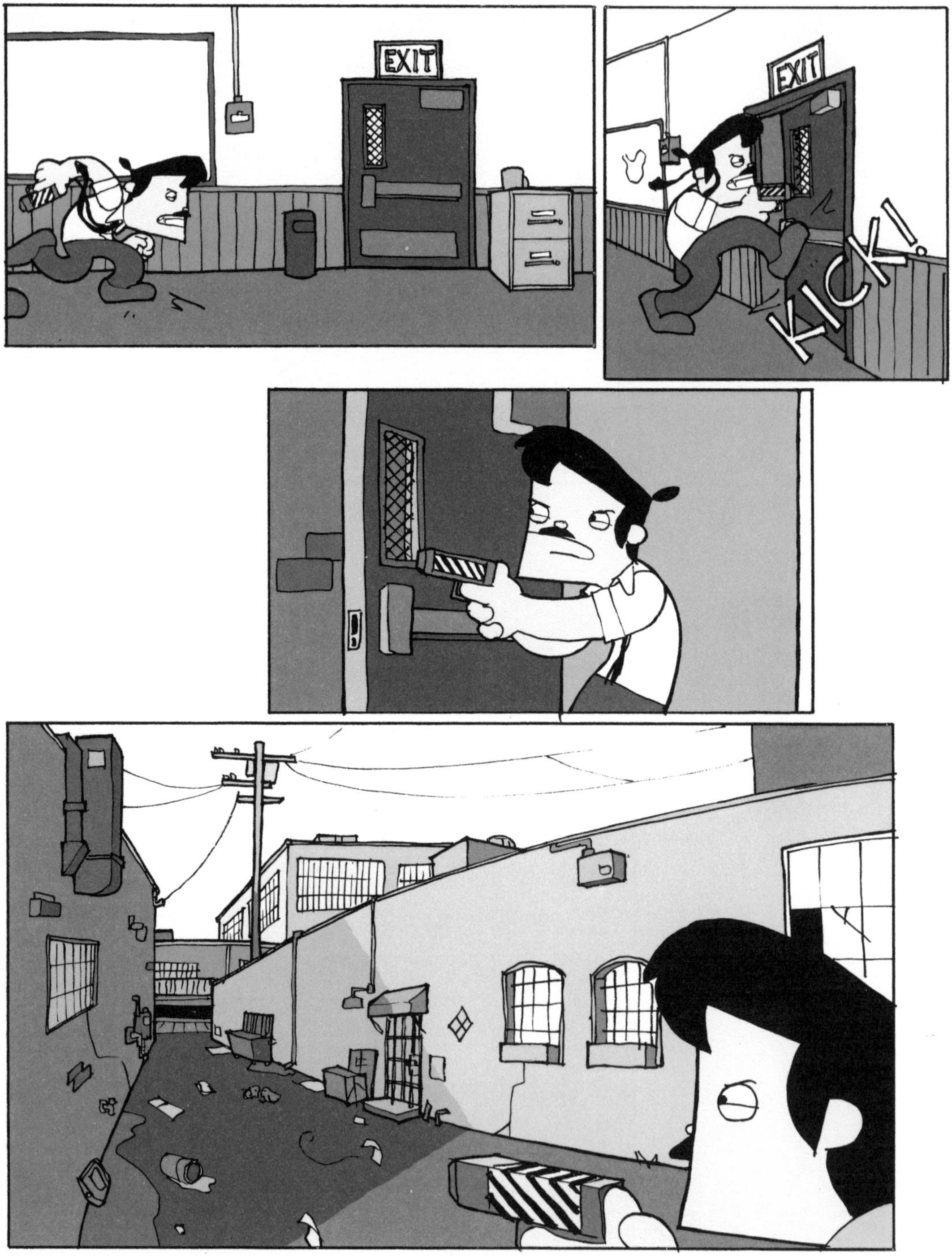
EXIT
EXIT
KICK!

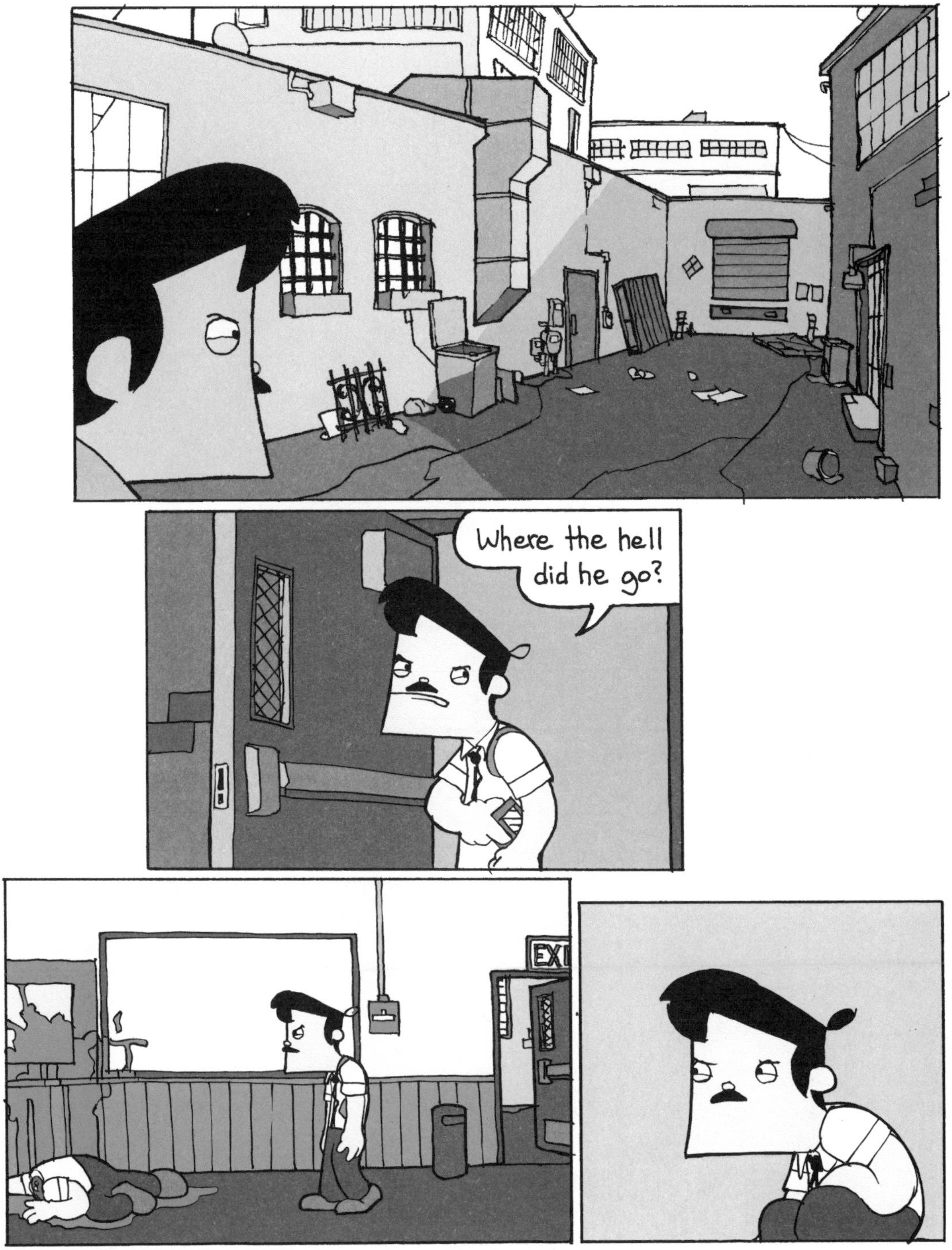
Where the hell did he go?

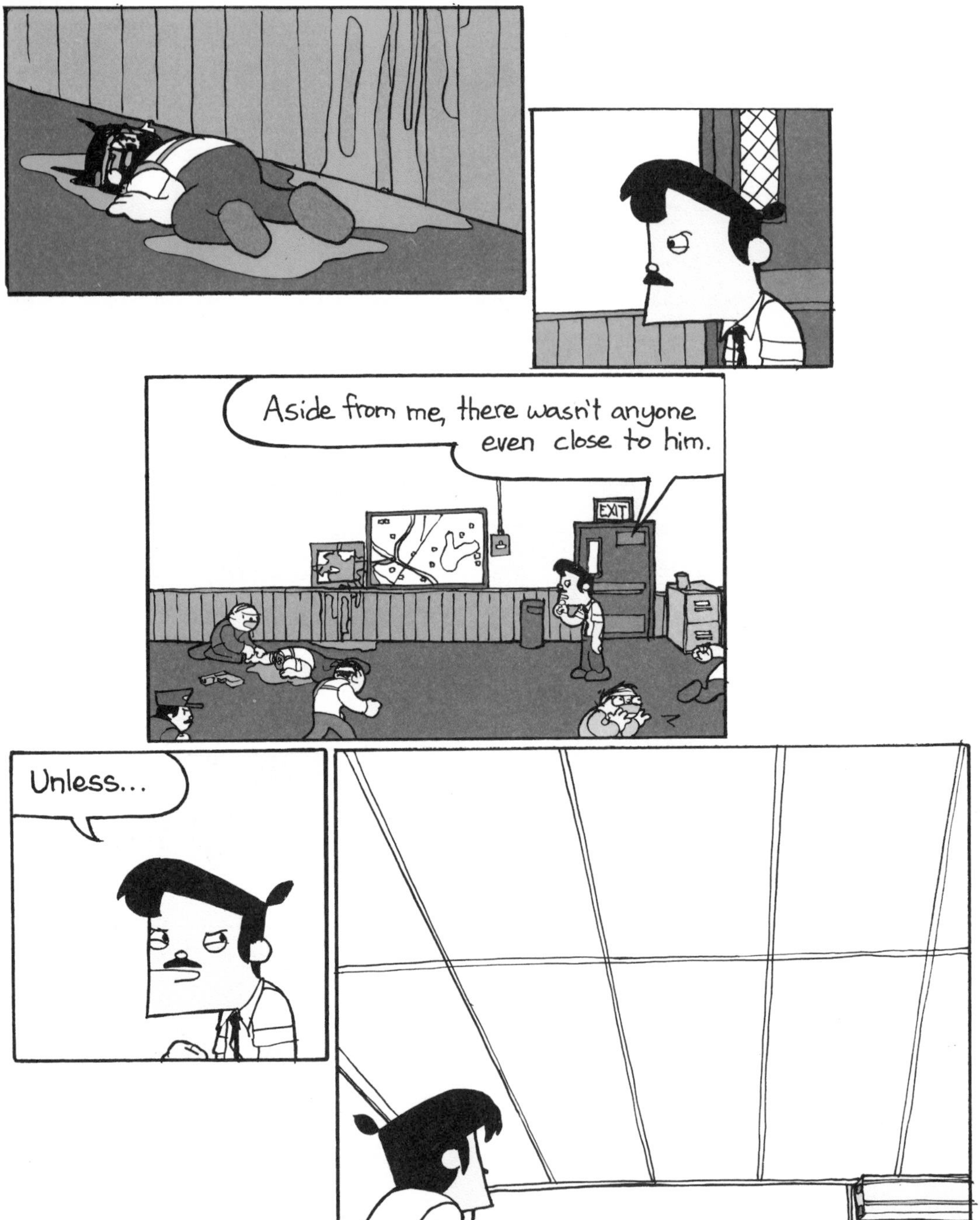
Aside from me, there wasn't anyone even close to him.
EXIT
Unless...

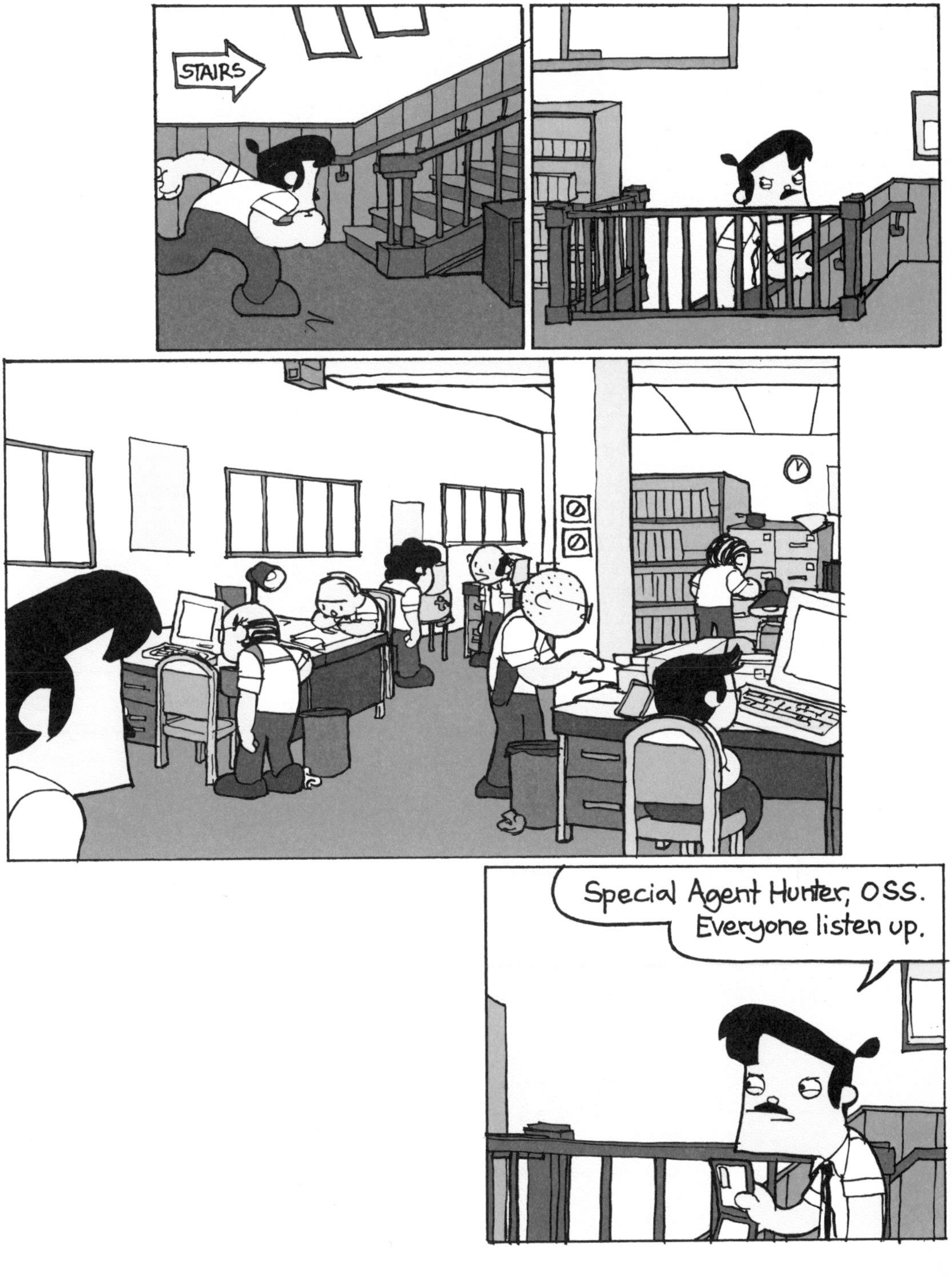
STAIRS
Special Agent Hunter, OSS. Everyone listen up.

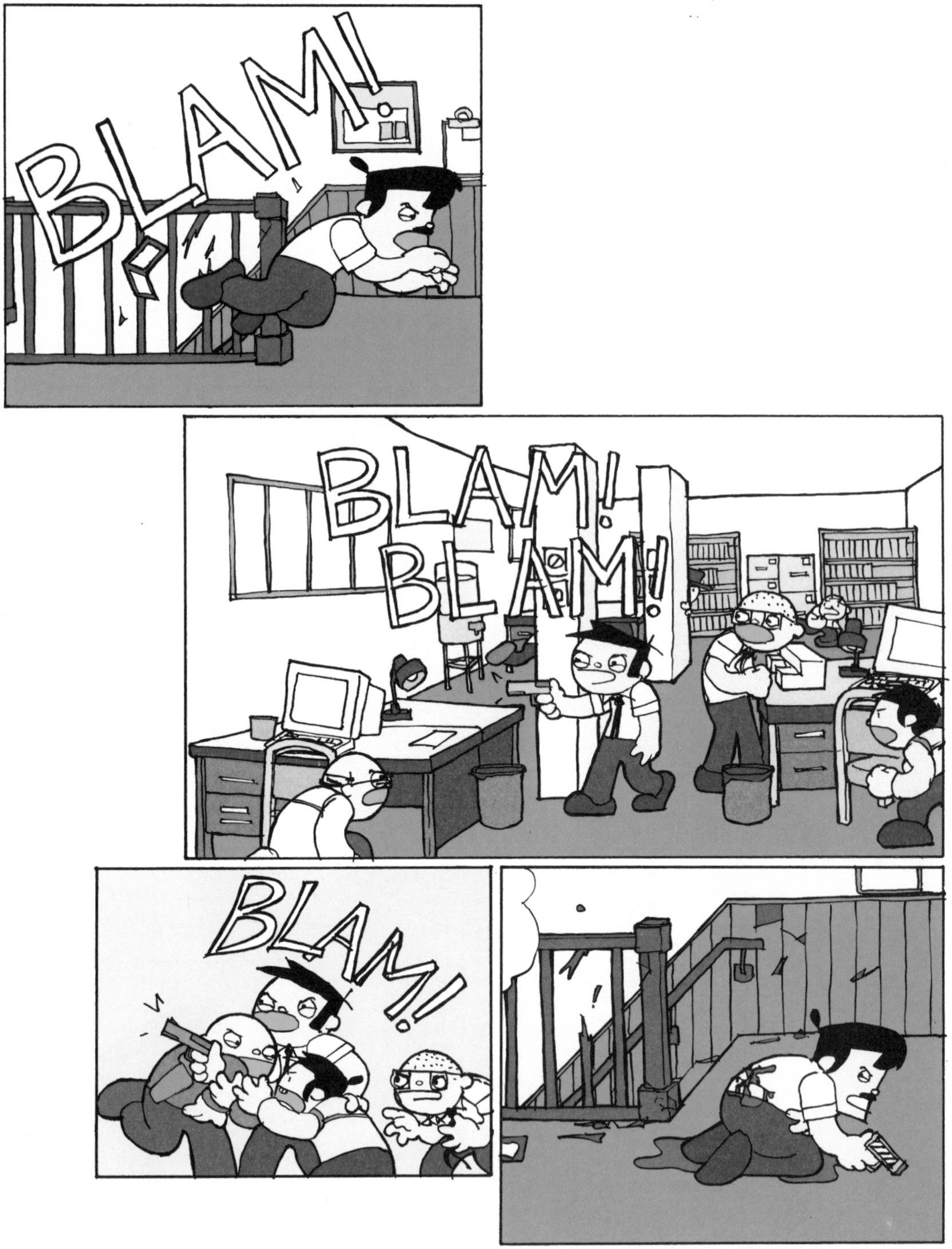
BLAM!
BLAM!
BLAM!
BLAM!

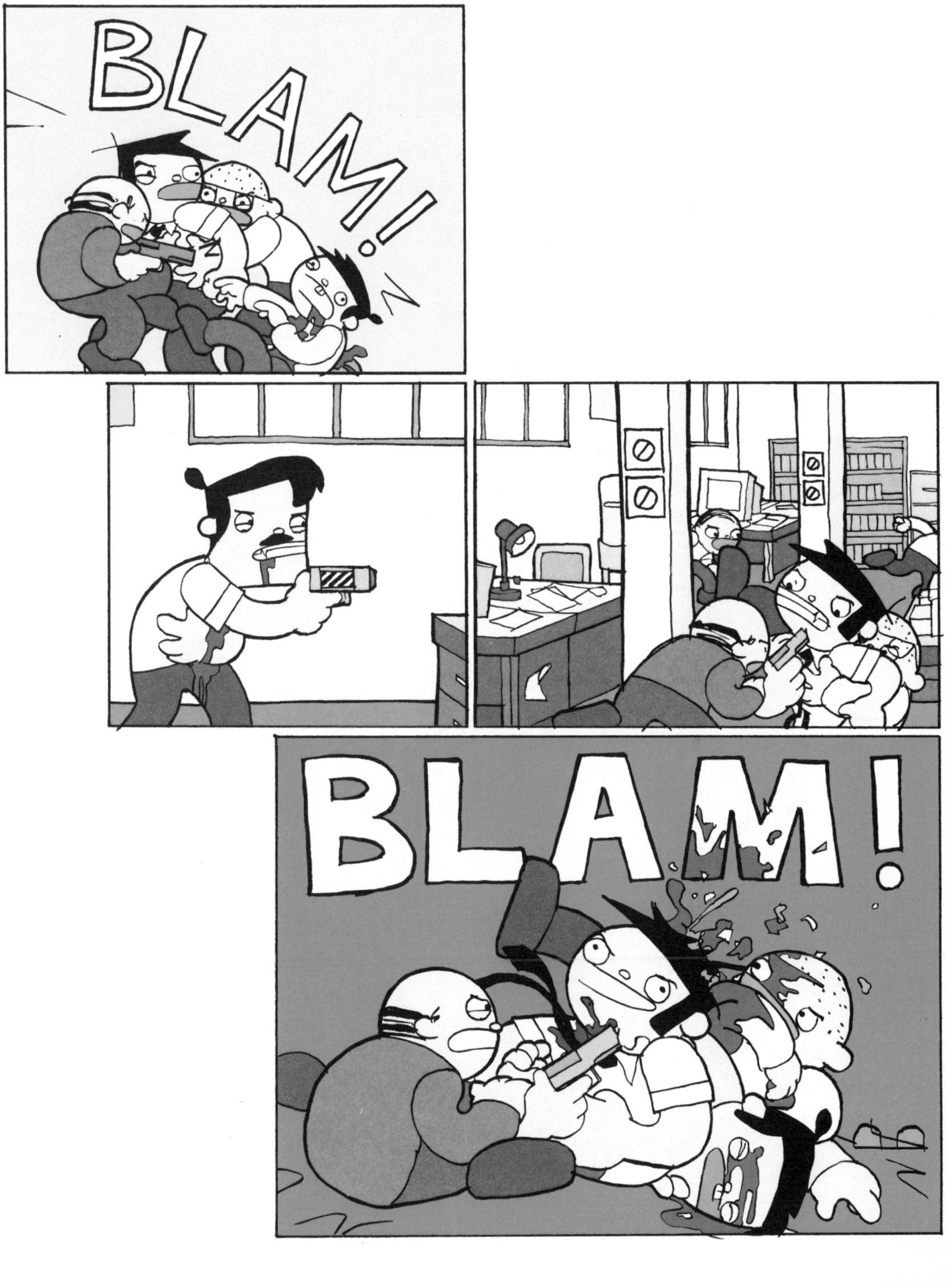
BLAM!
BLAM!

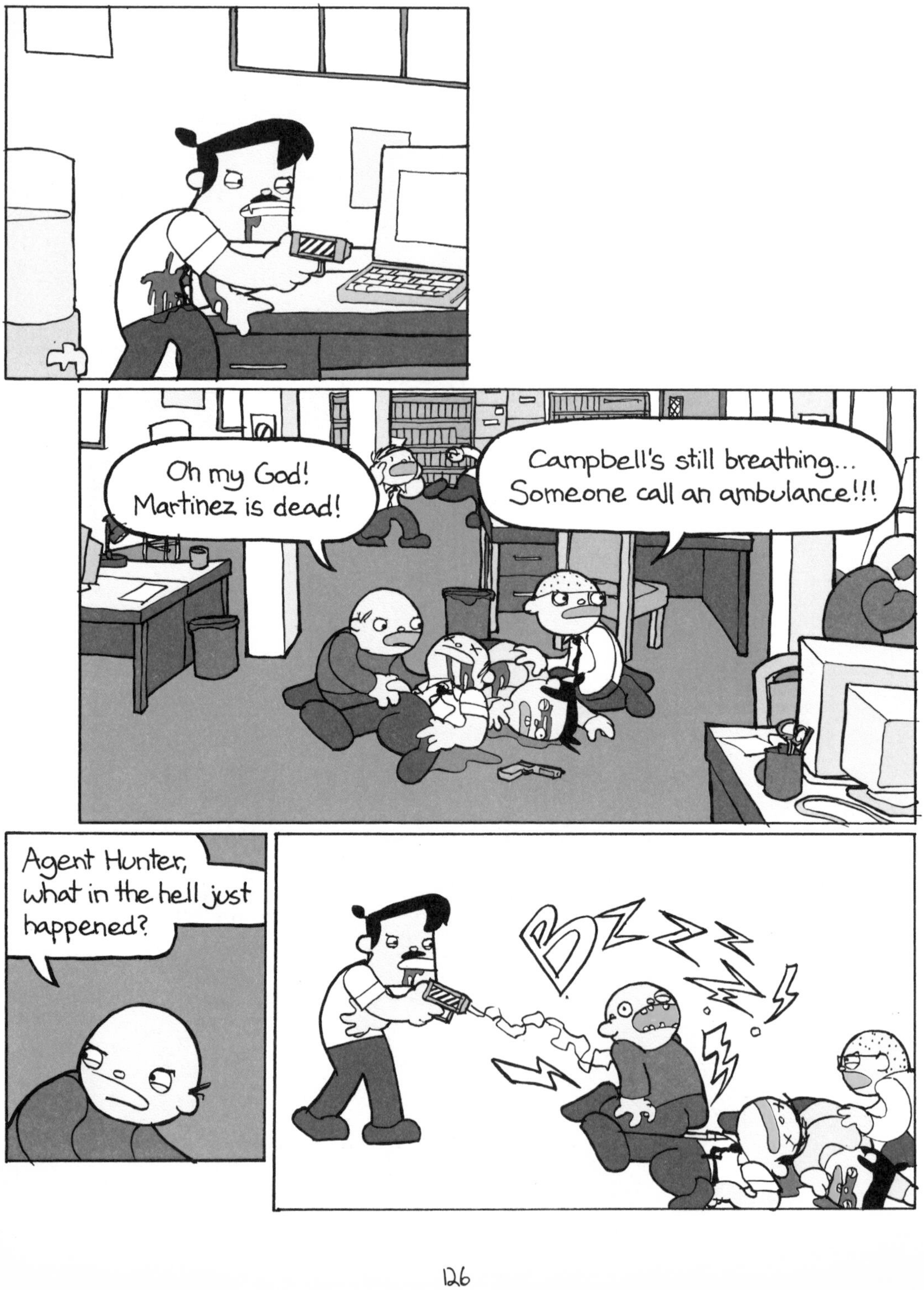
Oh my God! Martinez is dead!
Campbell's still breathing... Someone call an ambulance!!!
Agent Hunter, what in the hell just happened?

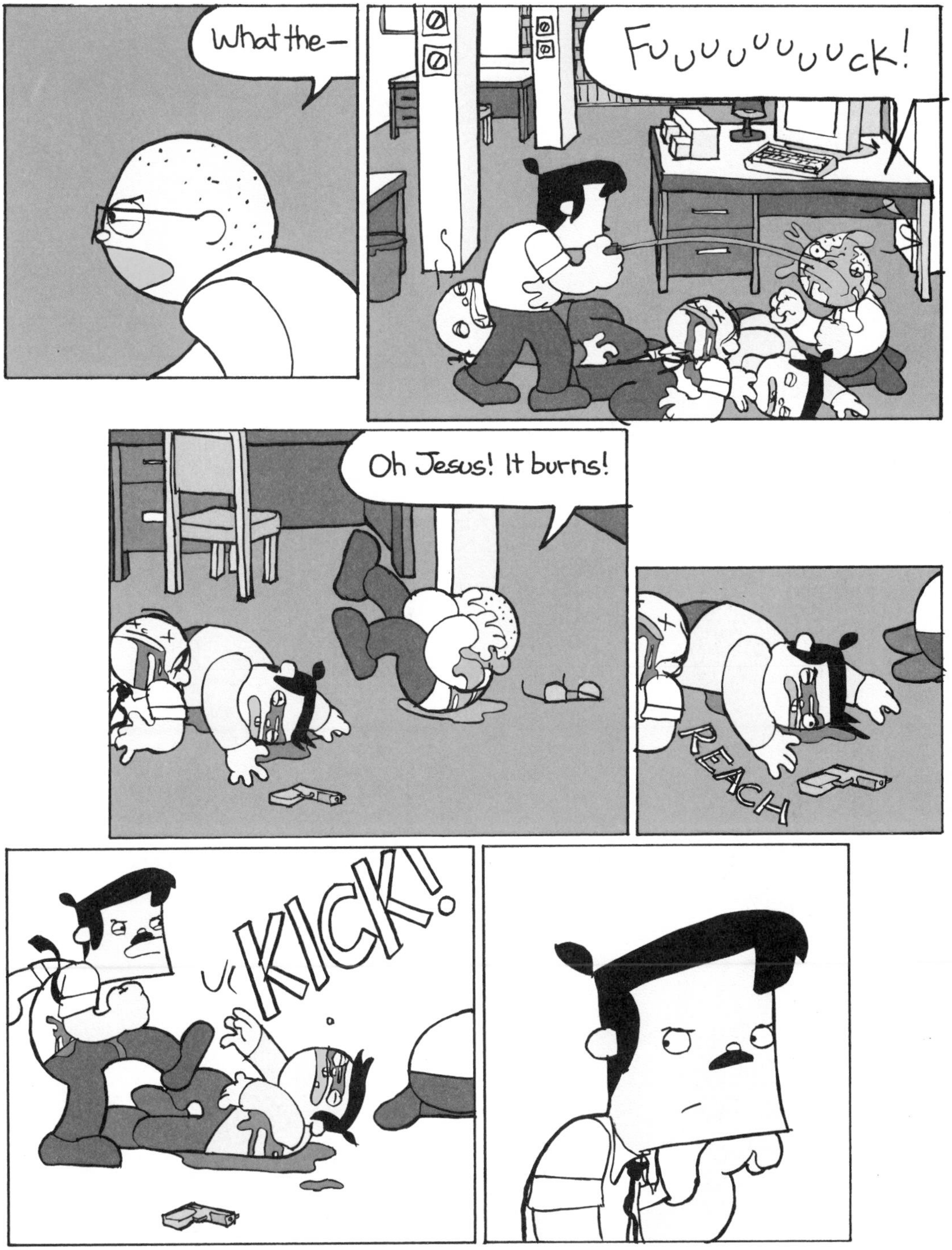
What the-
Fuuuuuuuuuck!
Oh Jesus! It burns!
REACH
KICK!

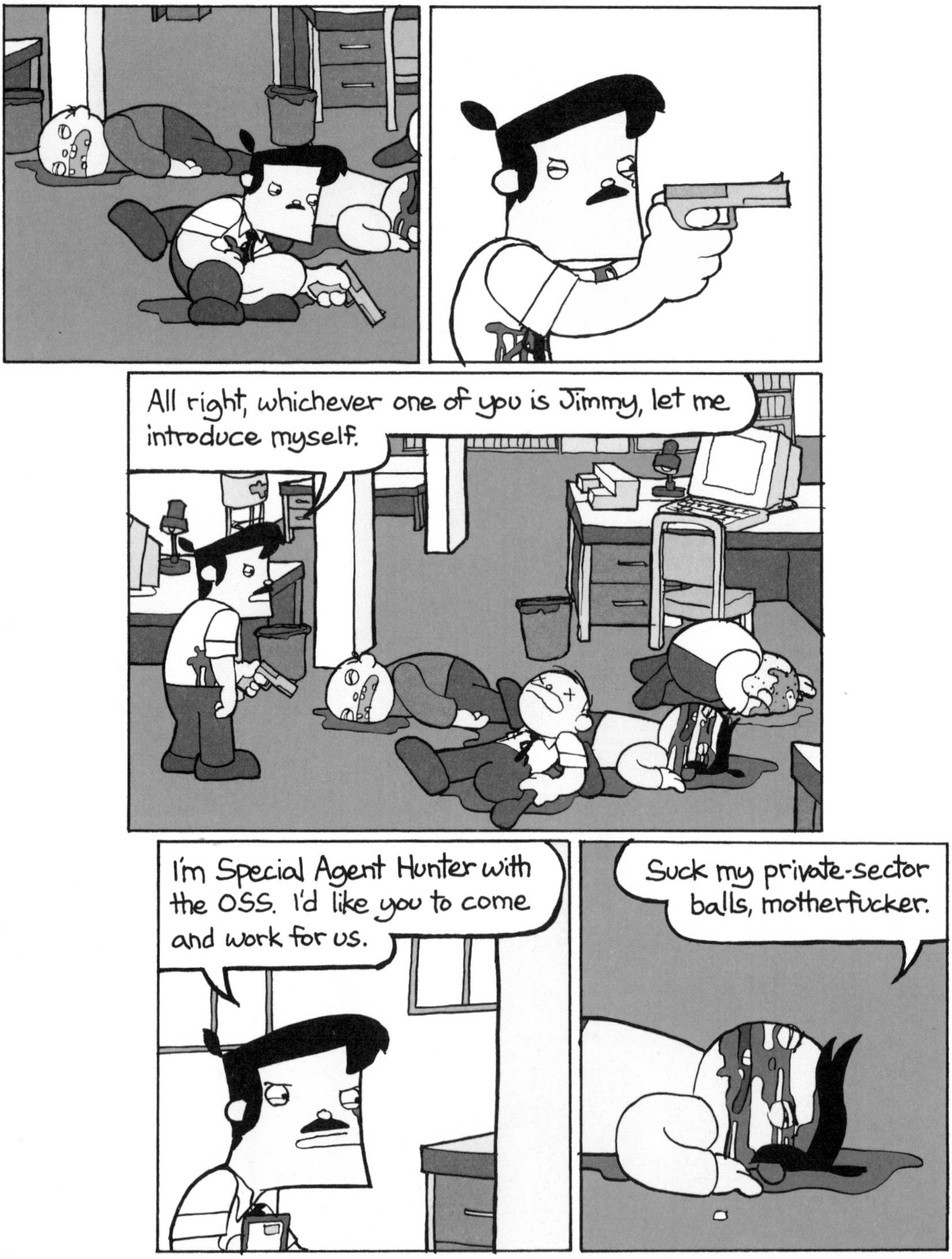
All right, whichever one of you is Jimmy, let me introduce myself.
I'm Special Agent Hunter with the OSS. I'd like you to come and work for us.
Suck my private-sector balls, motherfucker.

CHAPTER 5

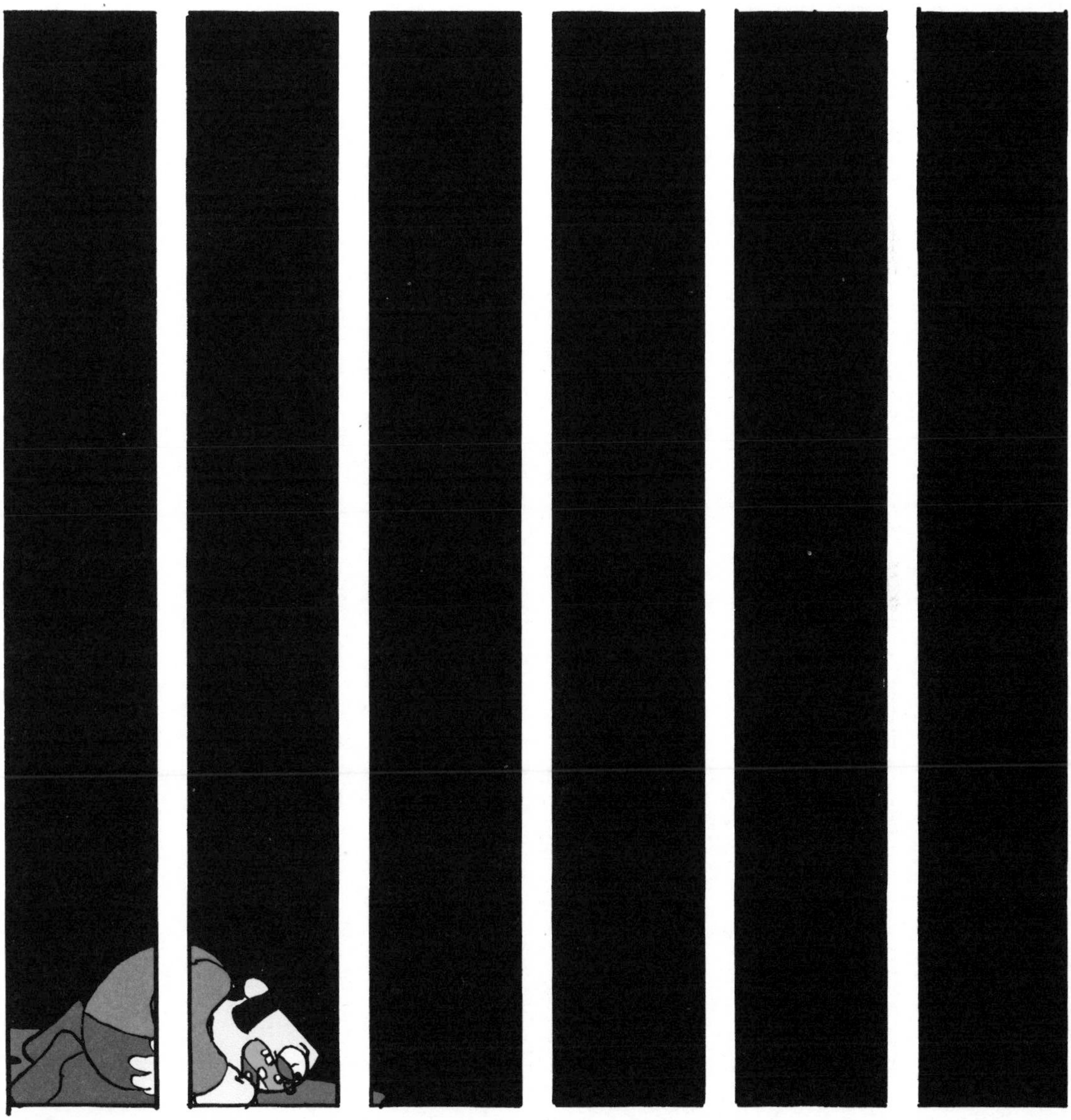

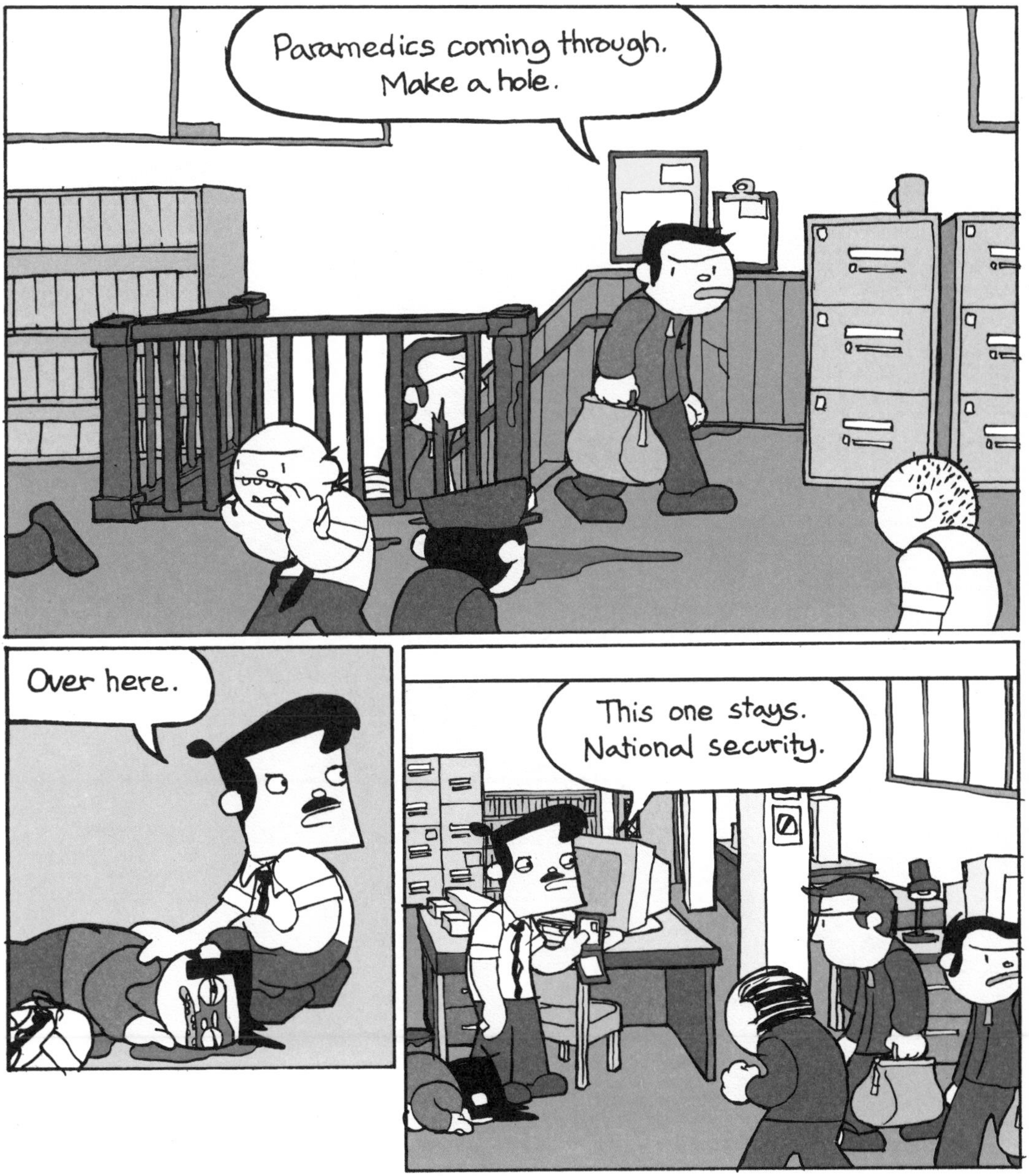
Paramedics coming through. Make a hole.
Over here.
This one stays. National security.

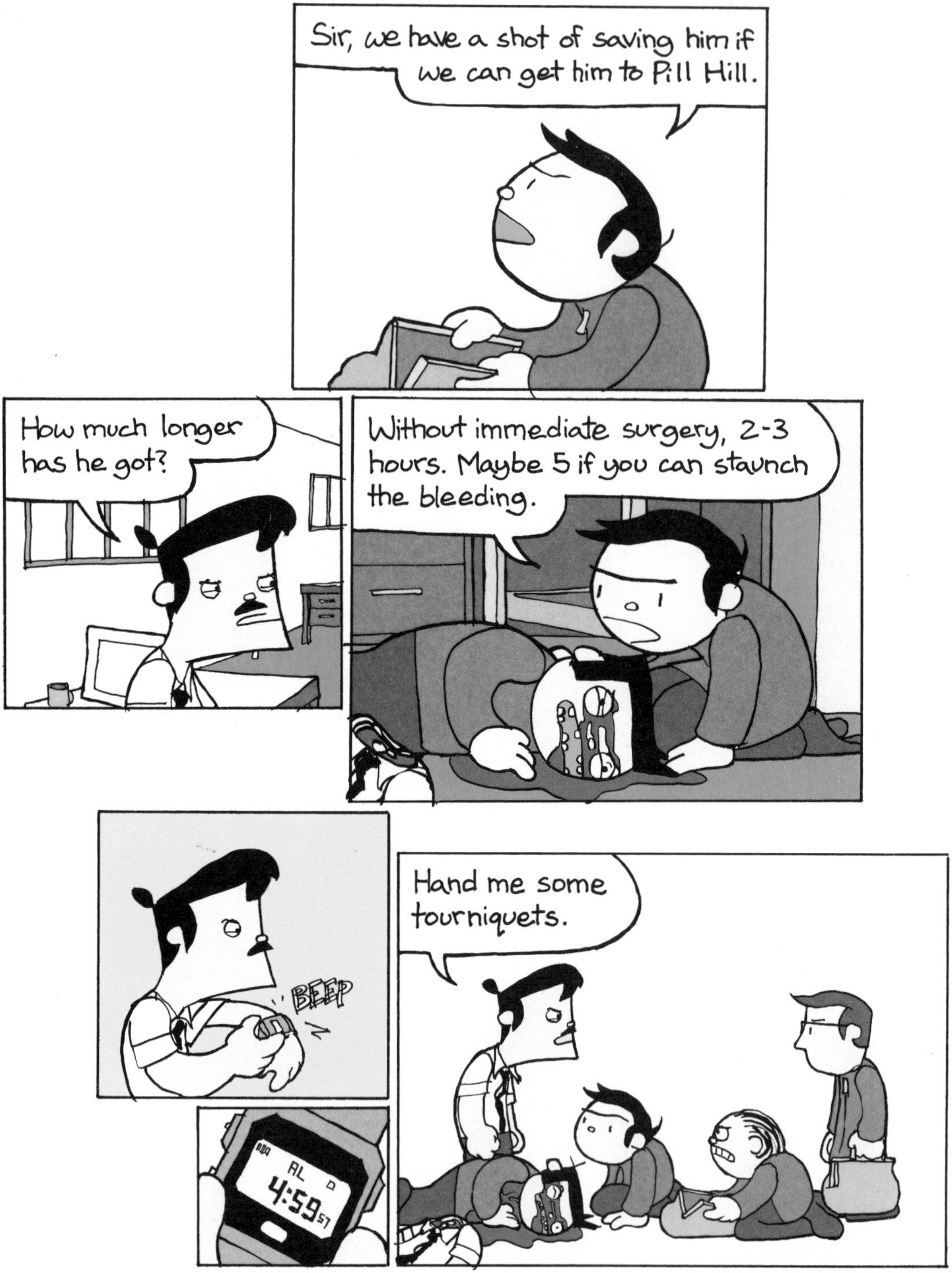
Sir, we have a shot of saving him if we can get him to Pill Hill.
How much longer has he got?
Without immediate surgery, 2-3 hours. Maybe 5 if you can staunch the bleeding.
BEEP
AL
4:59 57
Hand me some tourniquets.

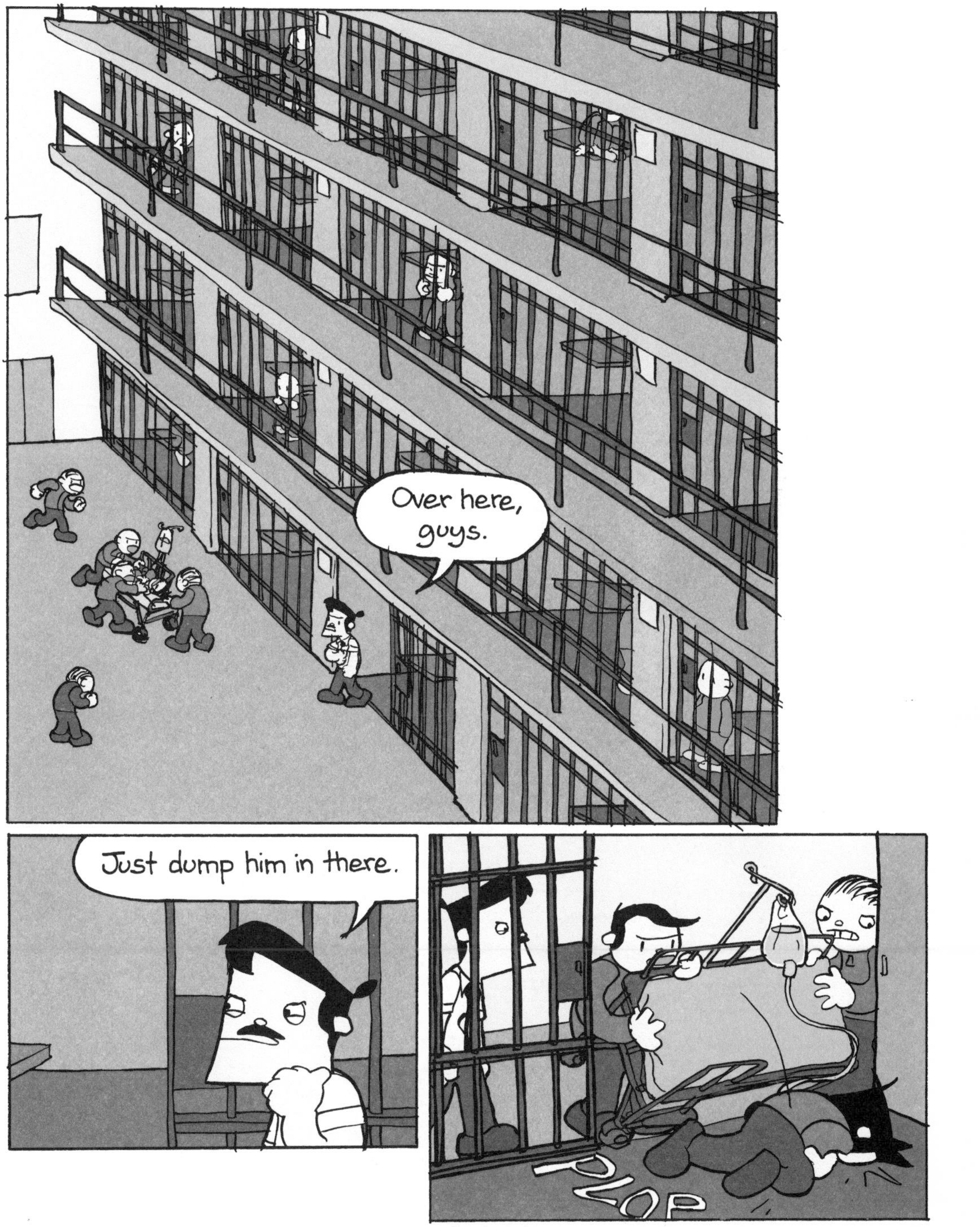
Over here, guys.
Just dump him in there.
PLOP

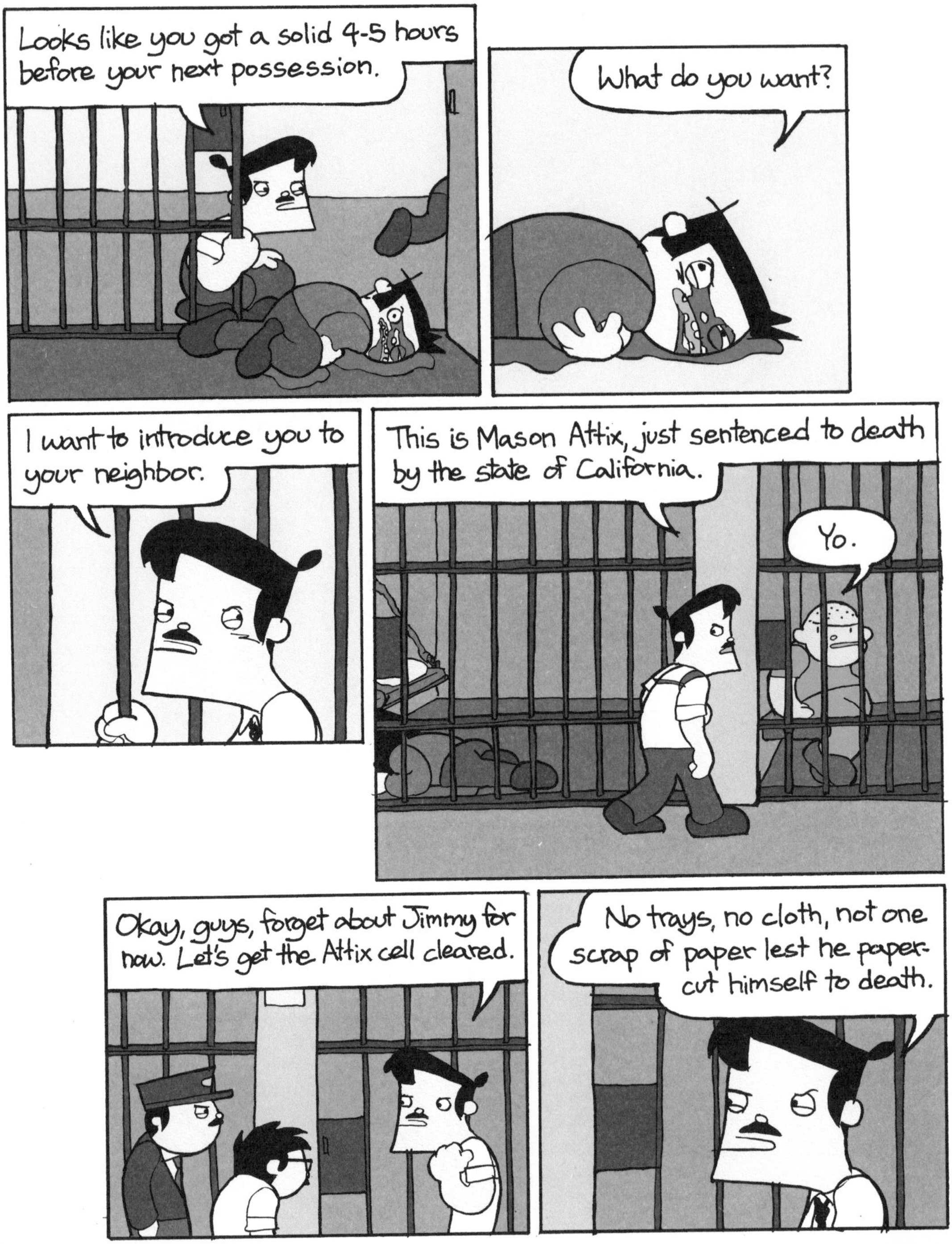
Looks like you got a solid 4-5 hours before your next possession.
What do you want?
I want to introduce you to your neighbor.
This is Mason Attix, just sentenced to death by the state of California.
Yo.
Okay, guys, forget about Jimmy for now. Let's get the Attix cell cleared.
No trays, no cloth, not one scrap of paper lest he paper-cut himself to death.

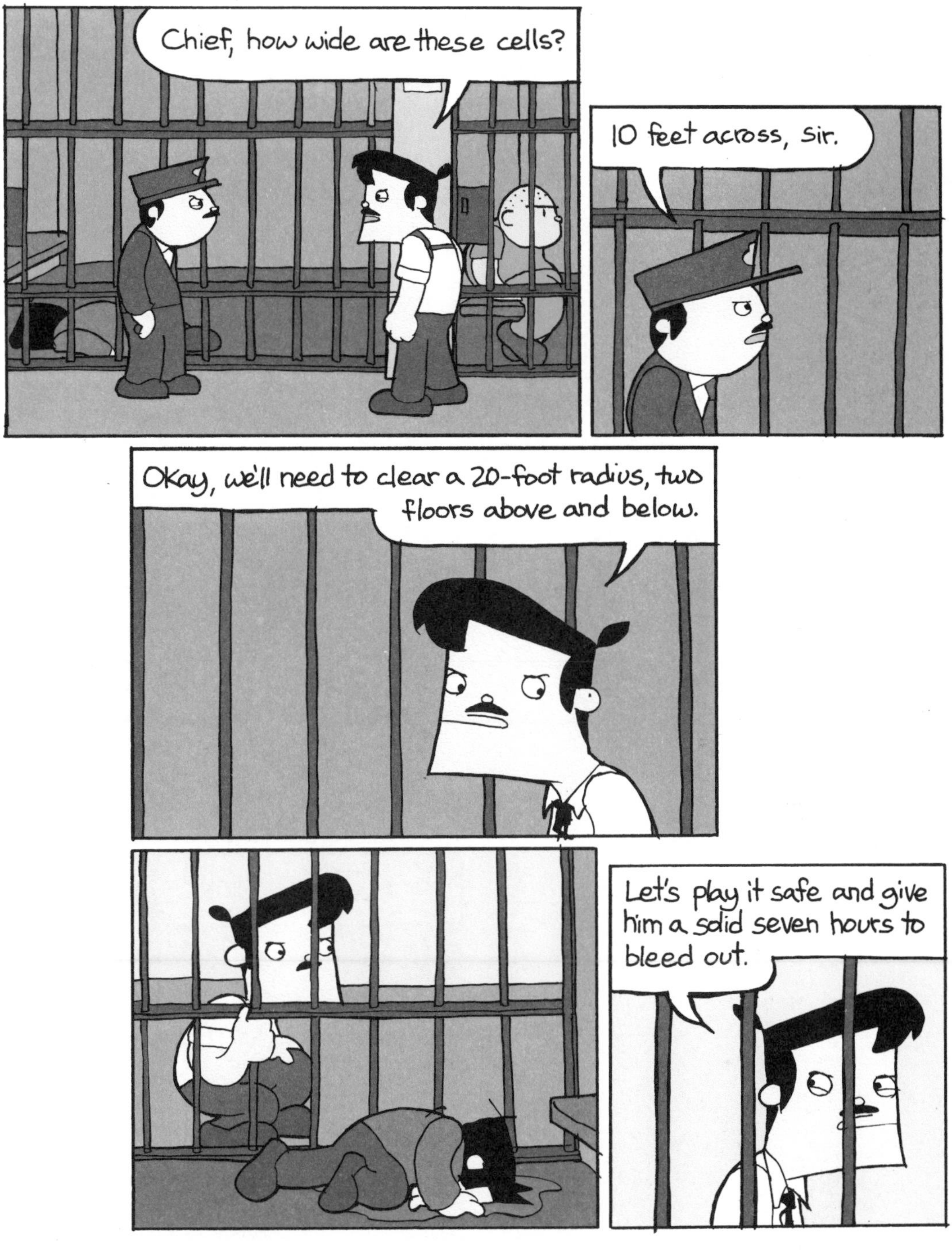
Chief, how wide are these cells?
10 feet across, sir.
Okay, we'll need to clear a 20-foot radius, two floors above and below.
Let's play it safe and give him a solid seven hours to bleed out.

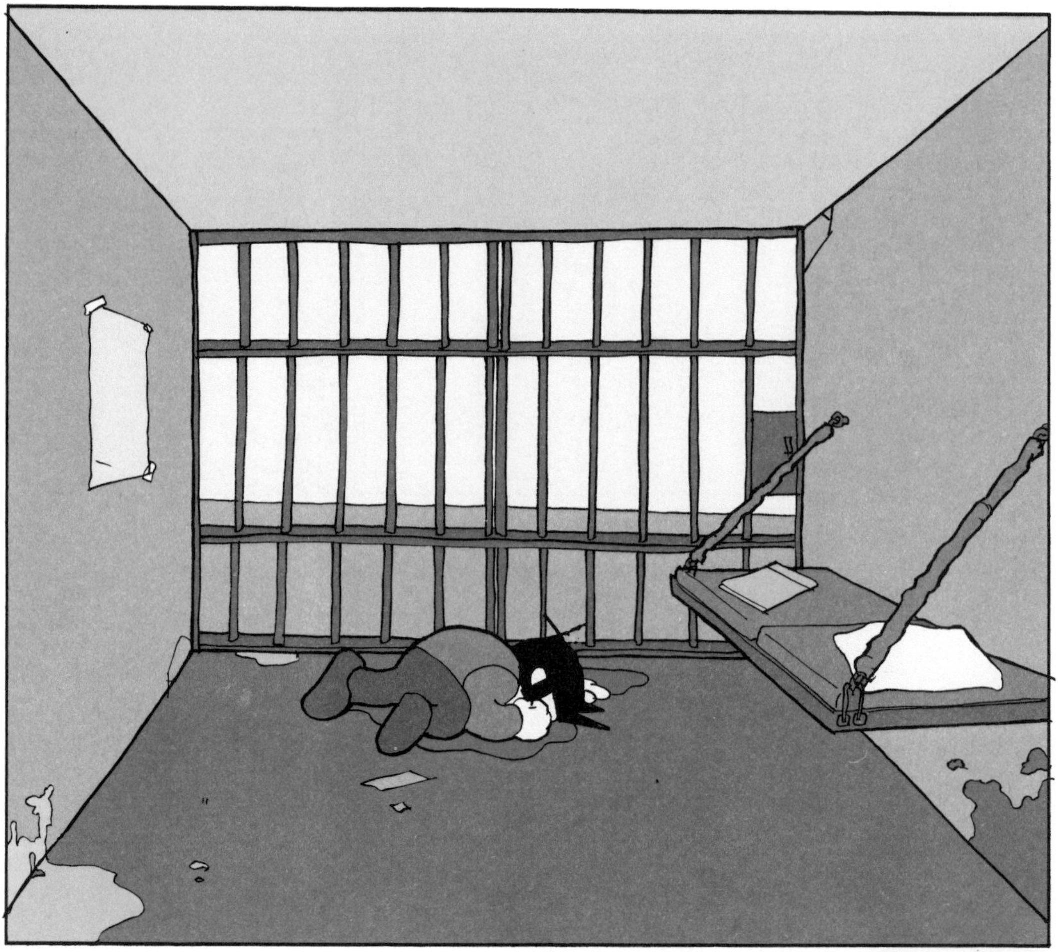

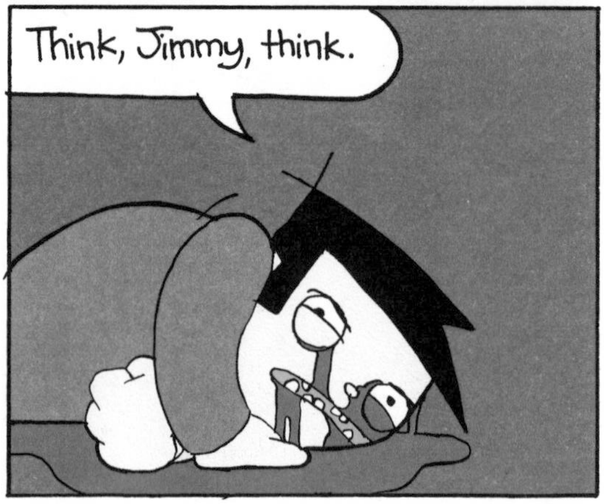
Think, Jimmy, think.

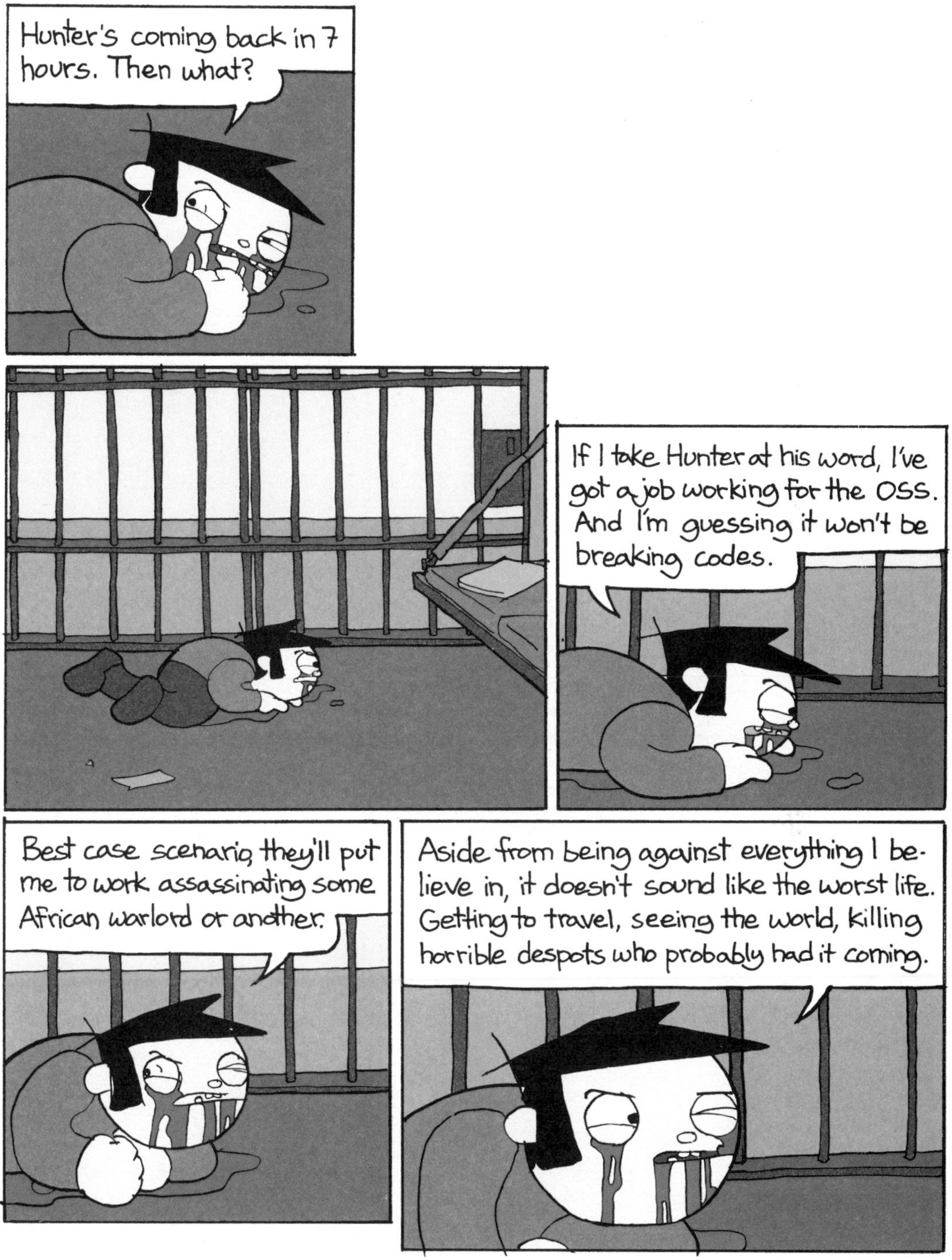
Hunter's coming back in 7 hours. Then what?
If I take Hunter at his word, I've got a job working for the OSS. And I'm guessing it won't be breaking codes.
Best case scenario, they'll put me to work assassinating some African warlord or another.
Aside from being against everything I believe in, it doesn't sound like the worst life. Getting to travel, seeing the world, killing horrible despots who probably had it coming.

Worst case, they dissect me up live, figure out how it all works, figure out how to demonize one of their own agents instead.

...But they don't figure out a way to kill me. Then I spend eternity in 4-point restraints, dying of bedsores every decade or so.

It's funny. 24 hours ago I just wanted to die. Still do I suppose.

There is one thing I want to take care of before I go. I'd given up hope of it ever happening. But anything can happen now that I'm a demon.

I just need to get out of here.

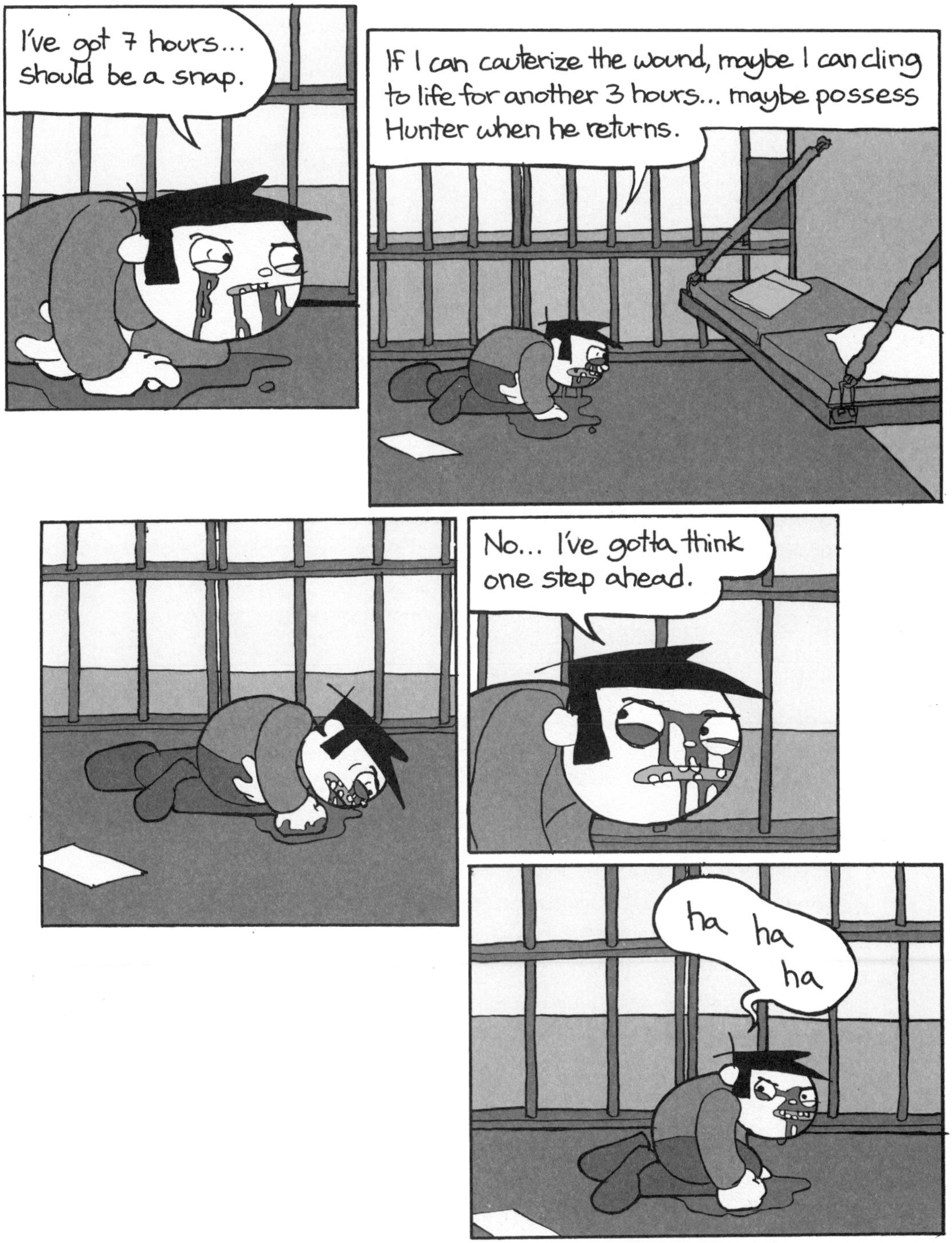
I've got 7 hours...
should be a snap.
If I can cauterize the wound, maybe I can cling to life for another 3 hours... maybe possess Hunter when he returns.
No... I've gotta think one step ahead.
ha ha ha

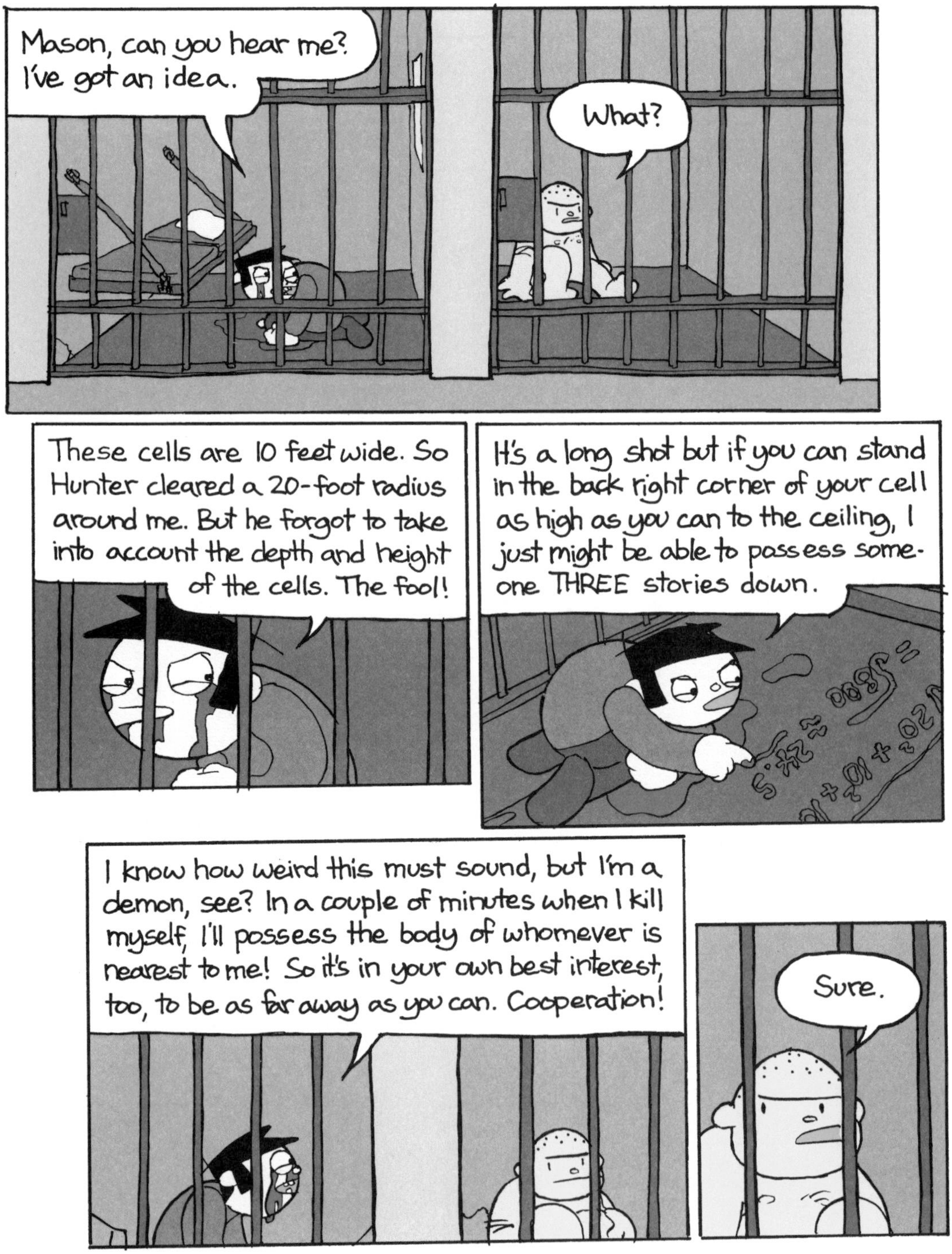
Mason, can you hear me? I've got an idea.
What?
These cells are 10 feet wide. So Hunter cleared a 20-foot radius around me. But he forgot to take into account the depth and height of the cells. The fool!
It's a long shot but if you can stand in the back right corner of your cell as high as you can to the ceiling, I just might be able to possess some-one THREE stories down.
I know how weird this must sound, but I'm a demon, see? In a couple of minutes when I kill myself, I'll possess the body of whomever is nearest to me! So it's in your own best interest, too, to be as far away as you can. Cooperation!
Sure.

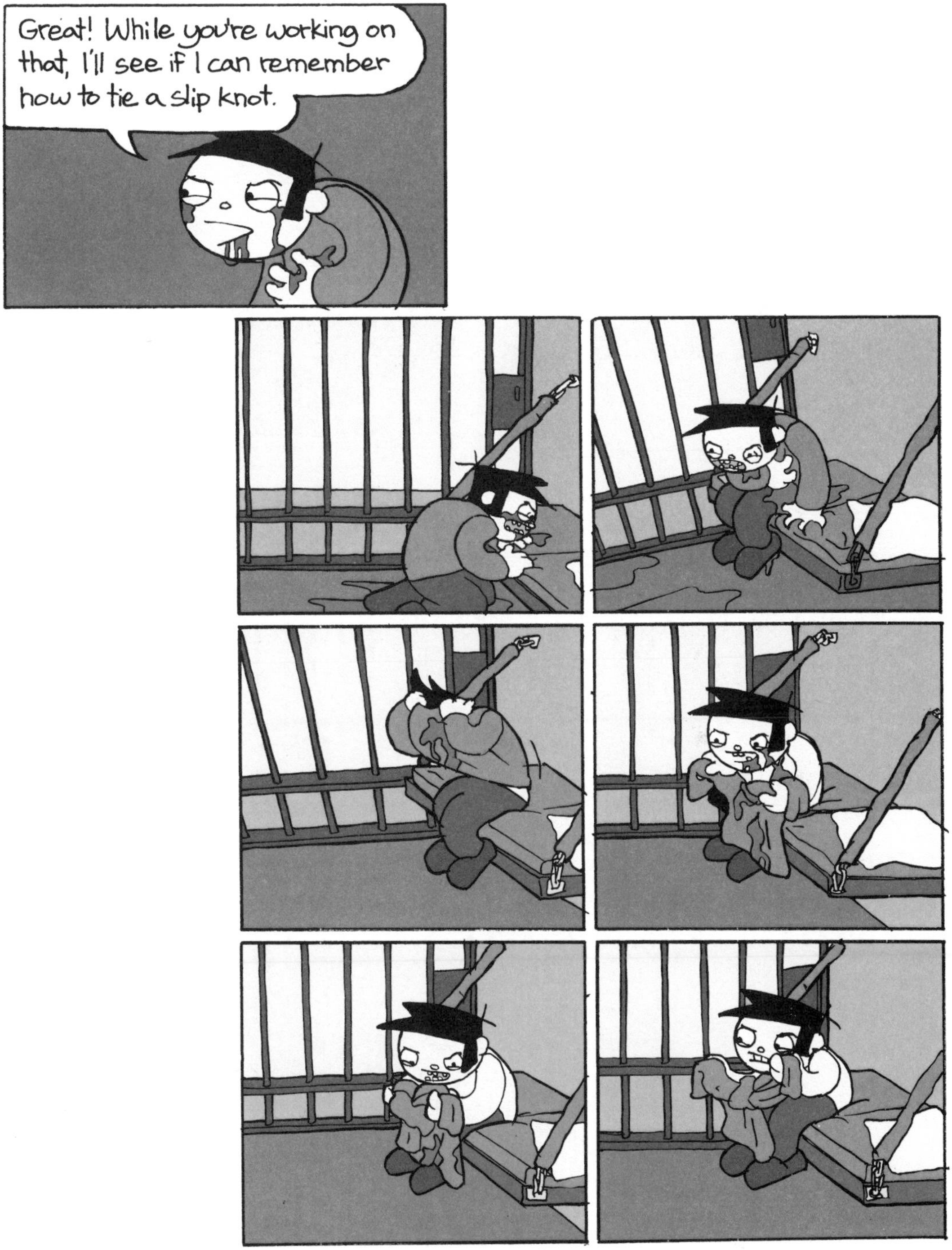
Great! While you're working on that, I'll see if I can remember how to tie a slip knot.

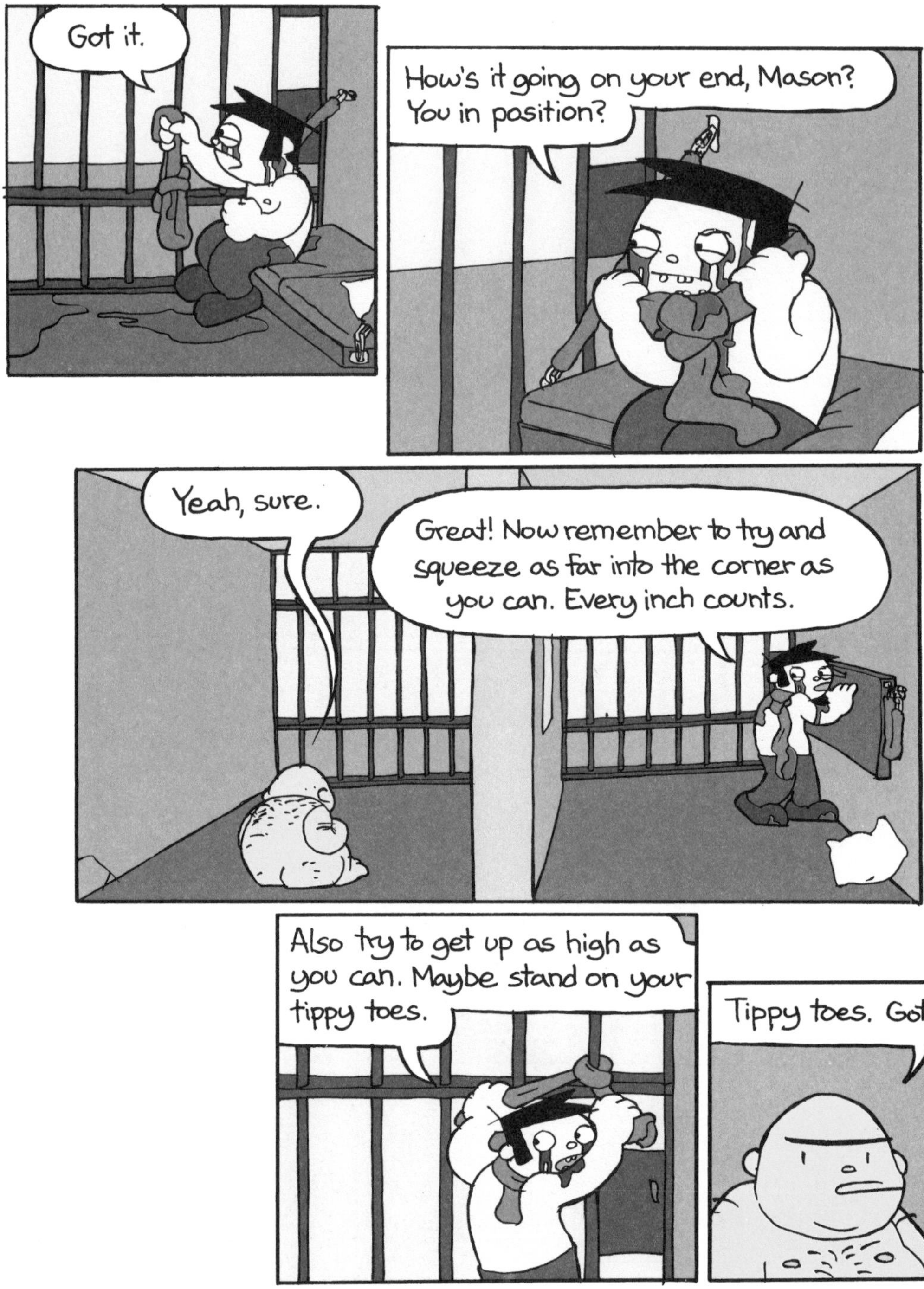
Got it.
How's it going on your end, Mason? You in position?
Yeah, sure.
Great! Now remember to try and squeeze as far into the corner as you can. Every inch counts.
Also try to get up as high as you can. Maybe stand on your tippy toes.
Tippy toes. Got it.

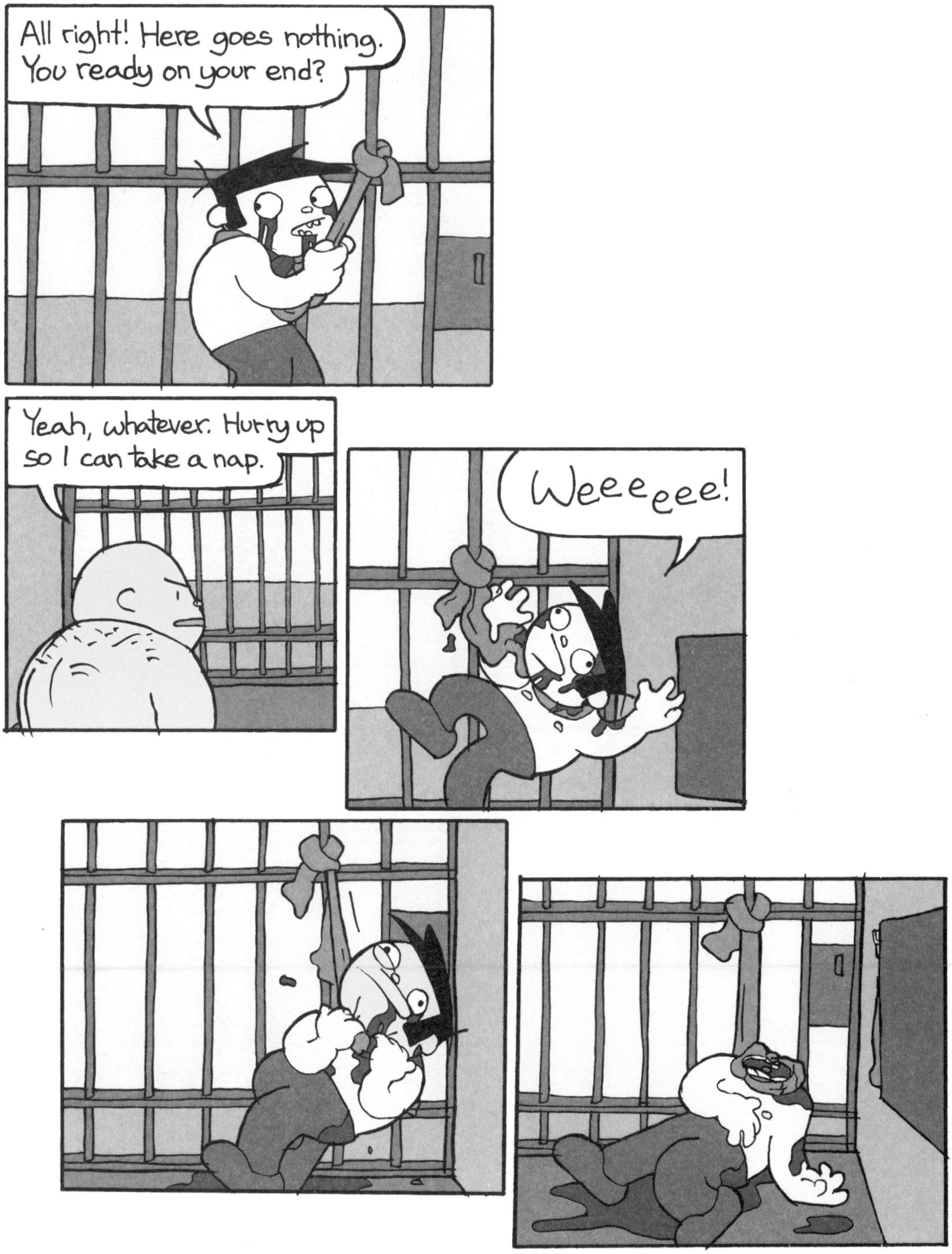
All right! Here goes nothing. You ready on your end?
Yeah, whatever. Hurry up so I can take a nap.
Weeeeee!

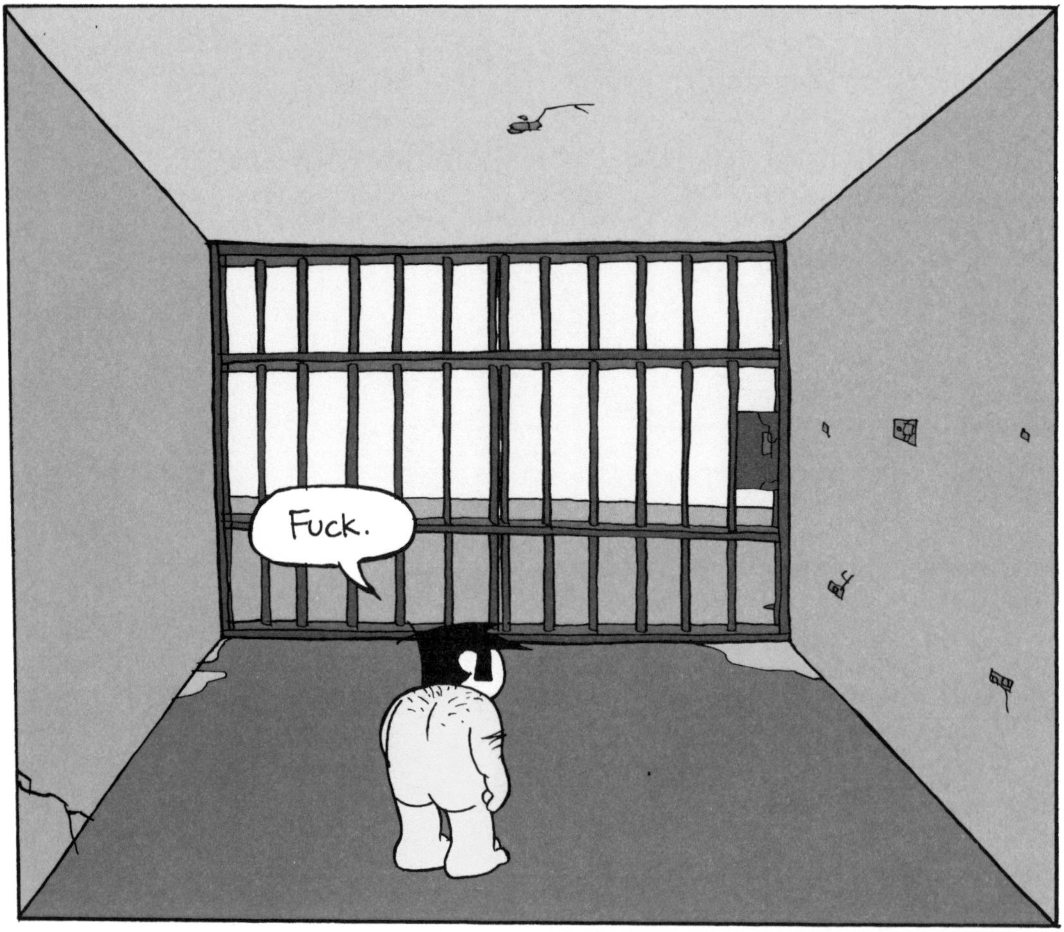
Fuck.

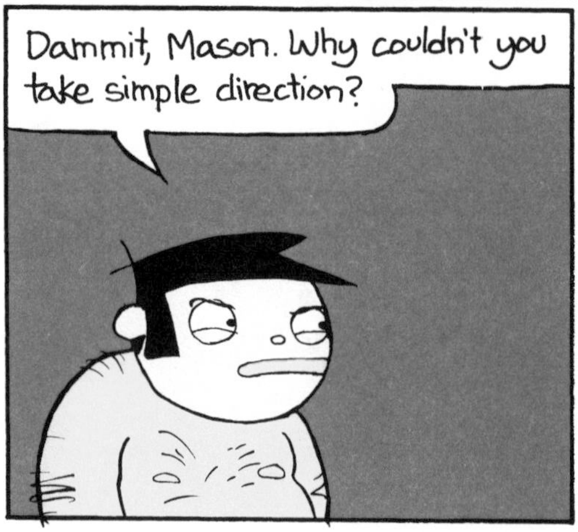
Dammit, Mason. Why couldn't you take simple direction?

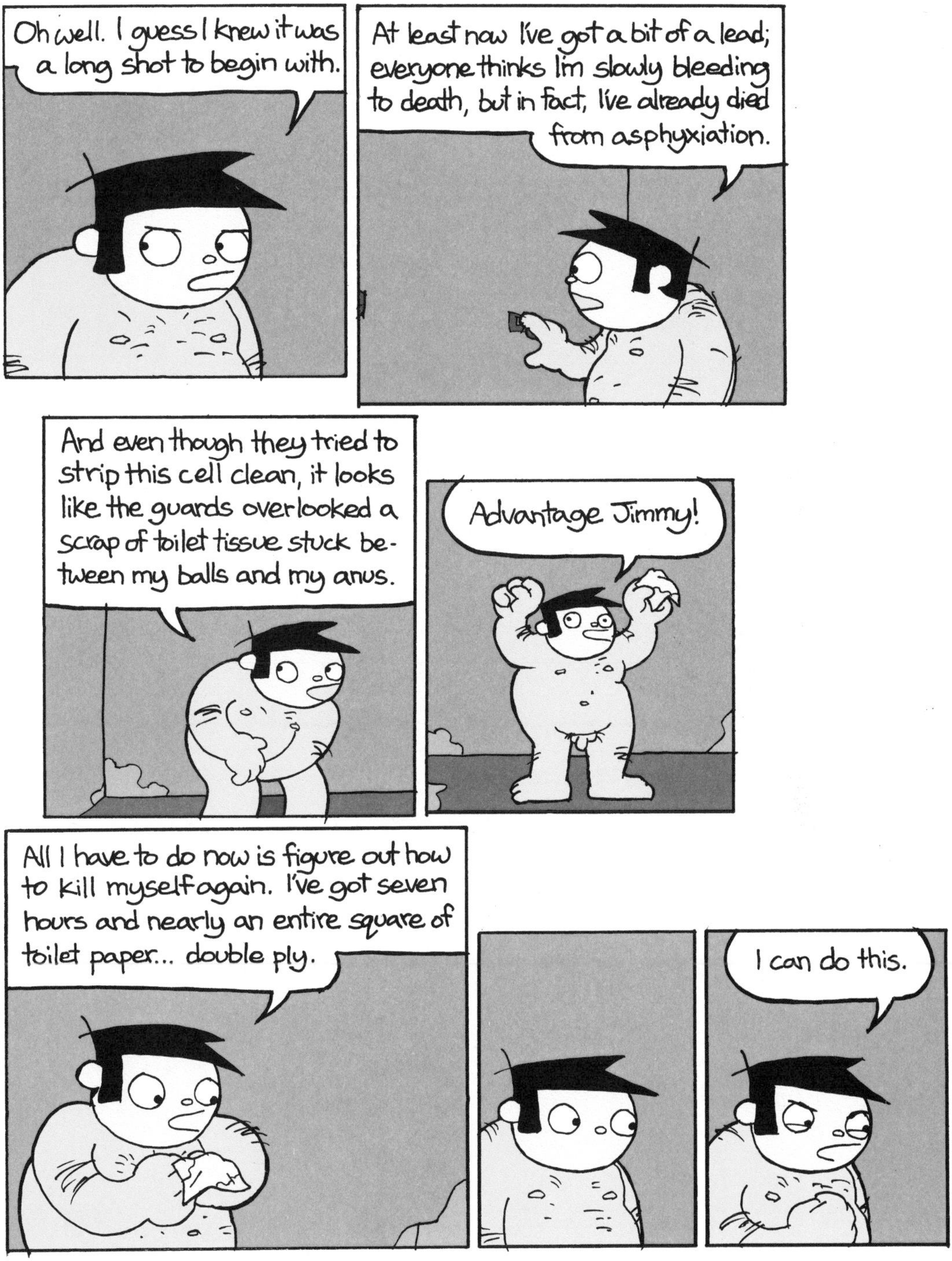
Oh well. I guess I knew it was a long shot to begin with.
At least now I've got a bit of a lead; everyone thinks I'm slowly bleeding to death, but in fact, I've already died from asphyxiation.
And even though they tried to strip this cell clean, it looks like the guards overlooked a scrap of toilet tissue stuck be-tween my balls and my anus.
Advantage Jimmy!
All I have to do now is figure out how to kill myself again. I've got seven hours and nearly an entire square of toilet paper... double ply.
I can do this.

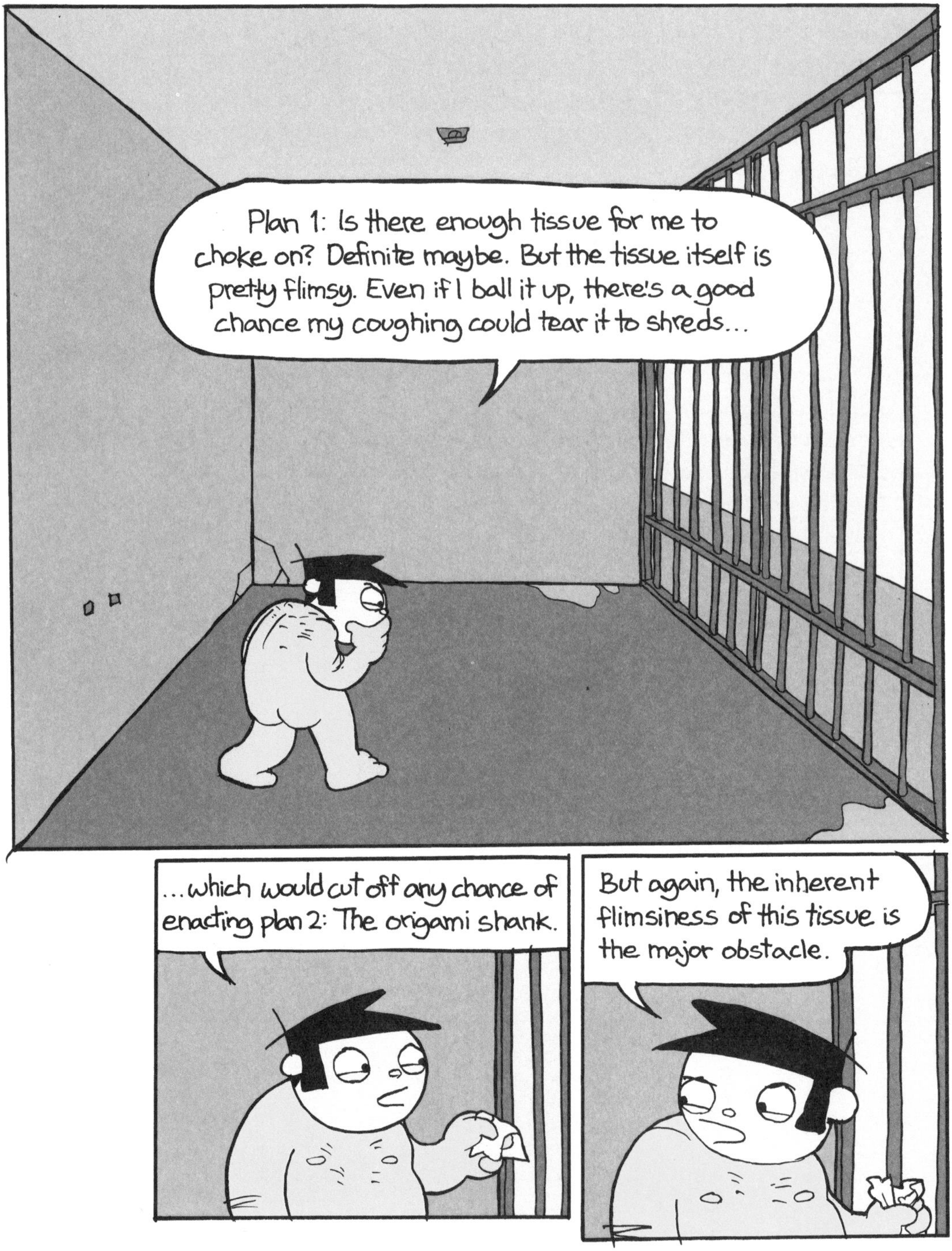
Plan 1: Is there enough tissue for me to choke on? Definite maybe. But the tissue itself is pretty flimsy. Even if I ball it up, there's a good chance my coughing could tear it to shreds...
...which would cut off any chance of enacting plan 2: The origami shank.
But again, the inherent flimsiness of this tissue is the major obstacle.

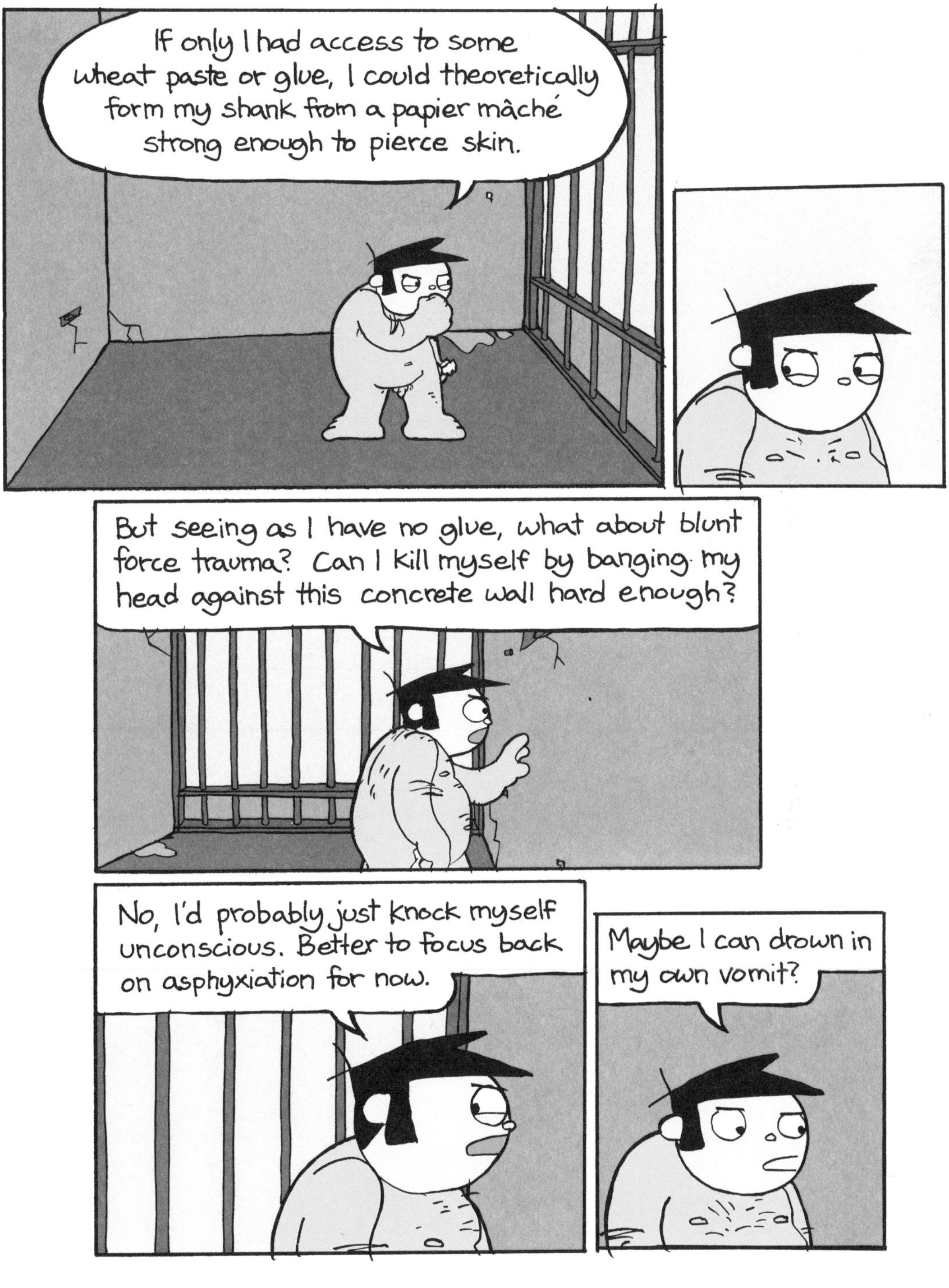
If only I had access to some wheat paste or glue, I could theoretically form my shank from a papier mâché strong enough to pierce skin.
But seeing as I have no glue, what about blunt force trauma? Can I kill myself by banging my head against this concrete wall hard enough?
No, I'd probably just knock myself unconscious. Better to focus back on asphyxiation for now.
Maybe I can drown in my own vomit?

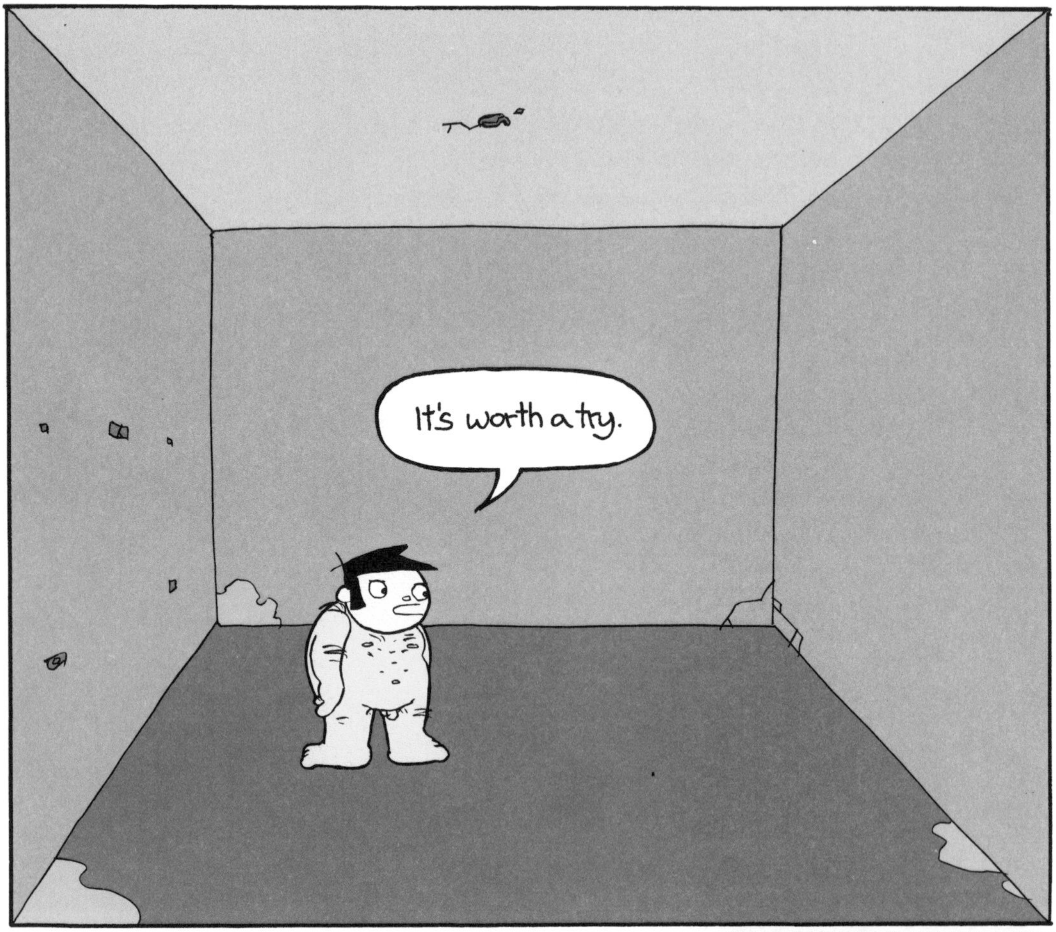
It's worth a try.

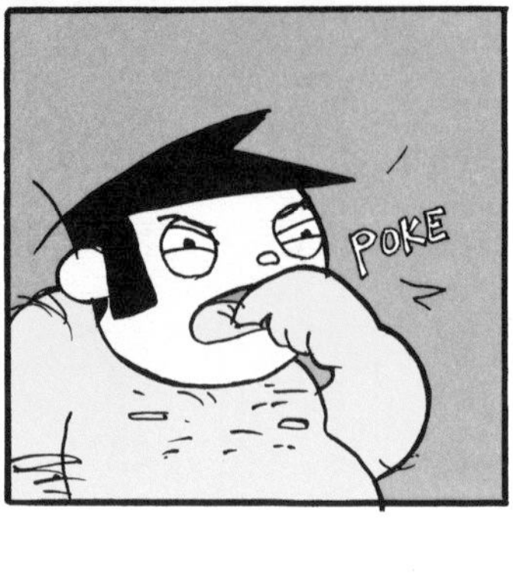
POKE

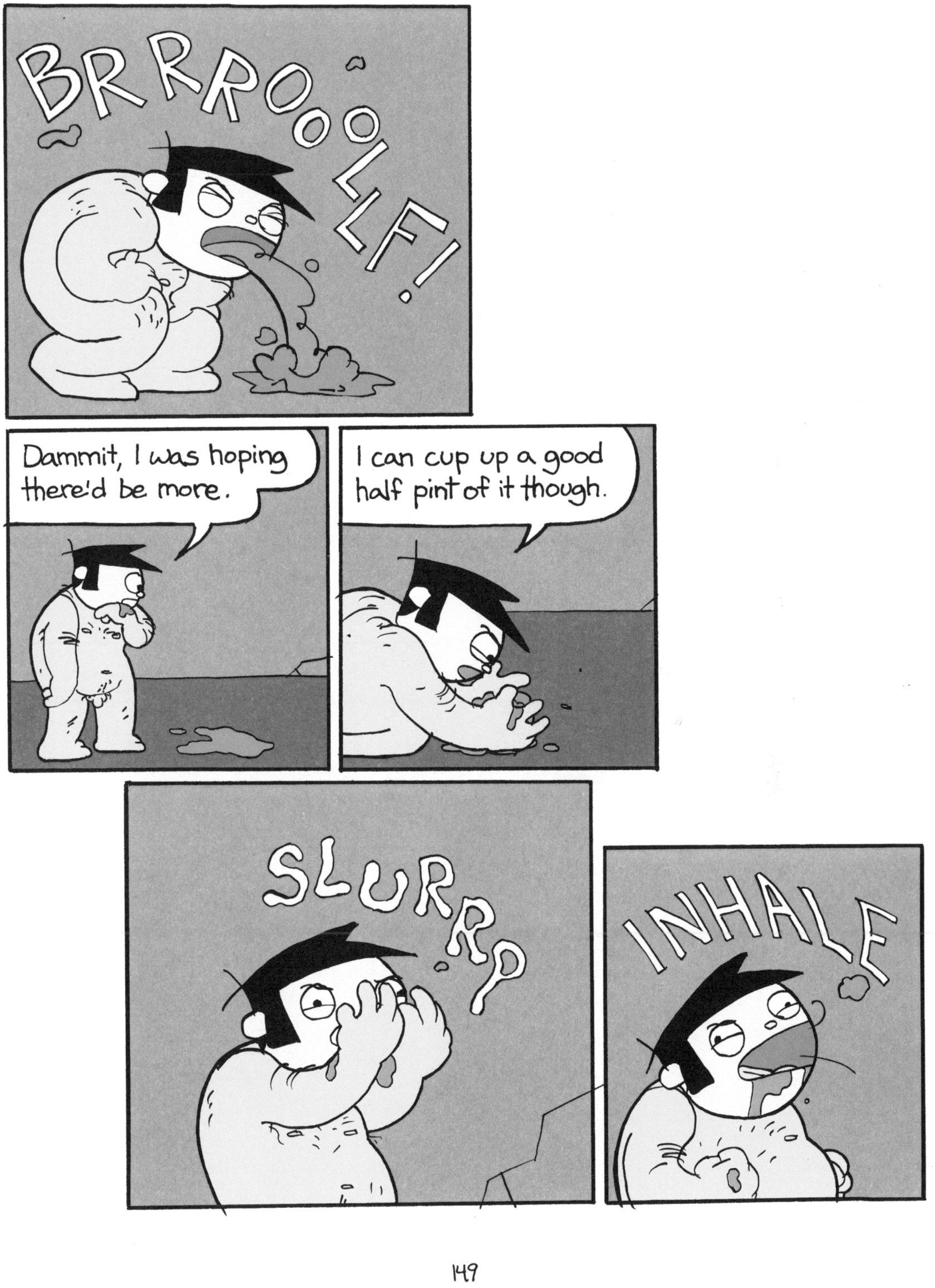
BRRROOOLLF!
Dammit, I was hoping there'd be more.
I can cup up a good half pint of it though.
SLURRP
INHALE

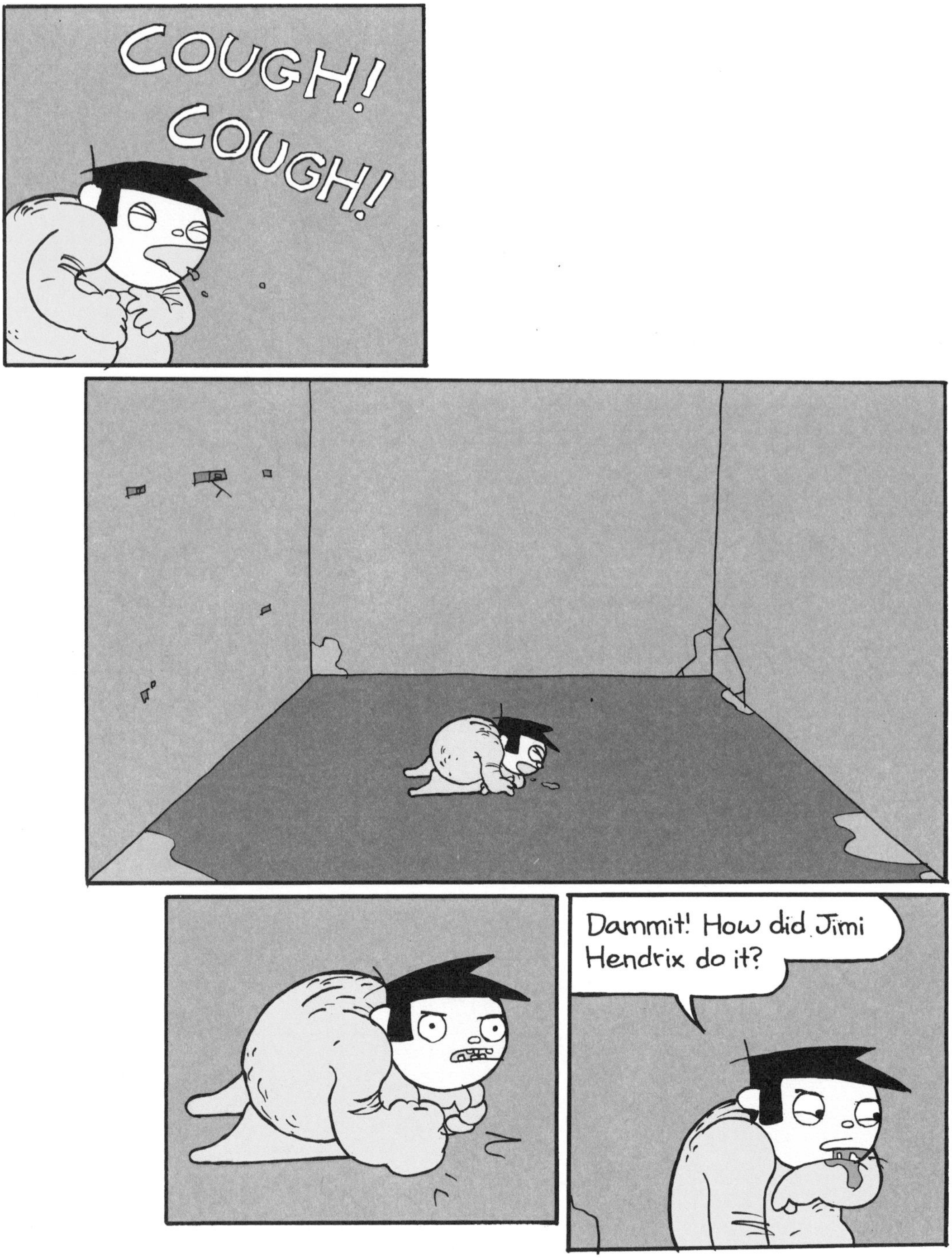
COUGH! COUGH!
Dammit! How did Jimi Hendrix do it?

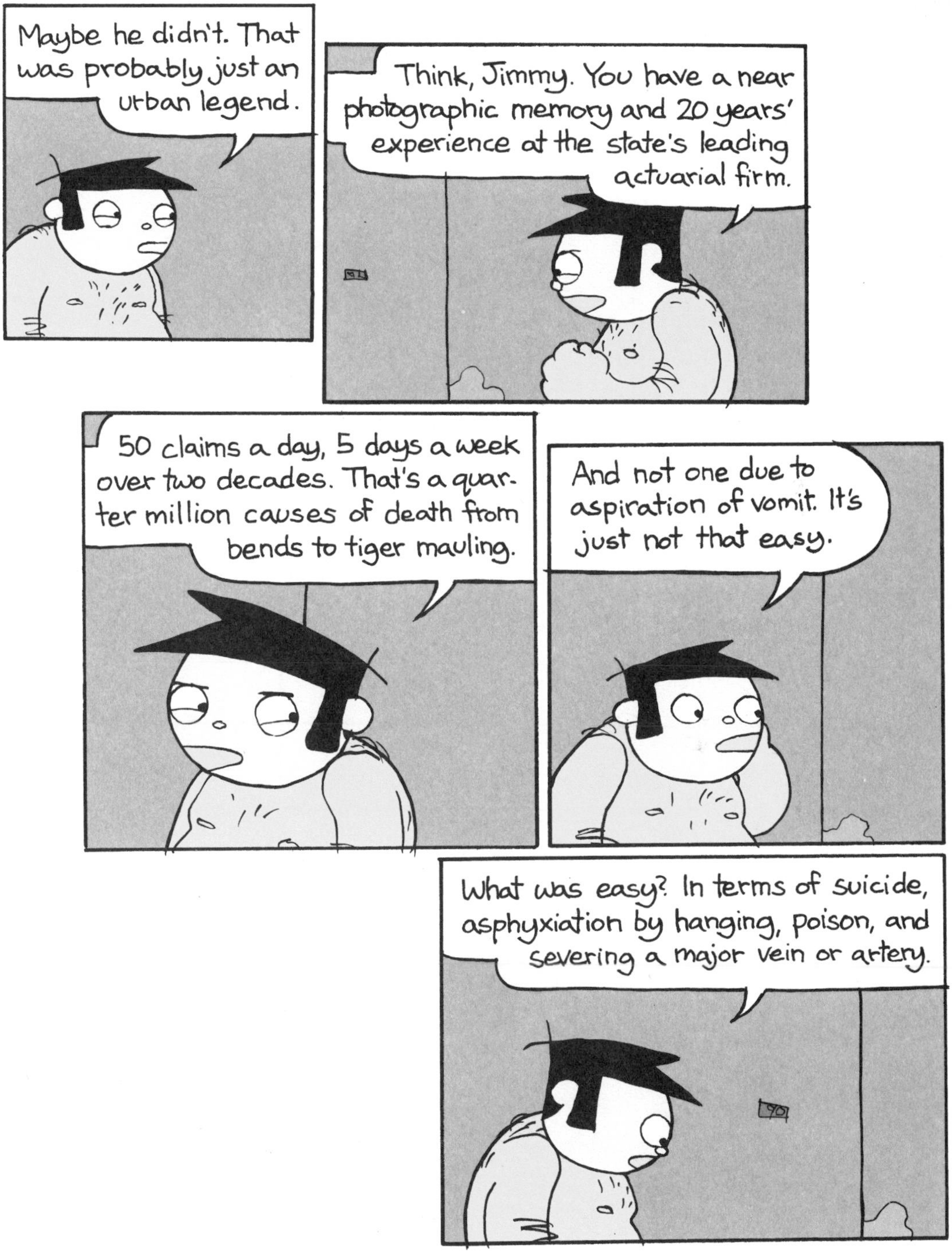
Maybe he didn't. That was probably just an urban legend.
Think, Jimmy. You have a near photographic memory and 20 years' experience at the state's leading actuarial firm.
50 claims a day, 5 days a week over two decades. That's a quarter million causes of death from bends to tiger mauling.
And not one due to aspiration of vomit. It's just not that easy.
What was easy? In terms of suicide, asphyxiation by hanging, poison, and severing a major vein or artery.

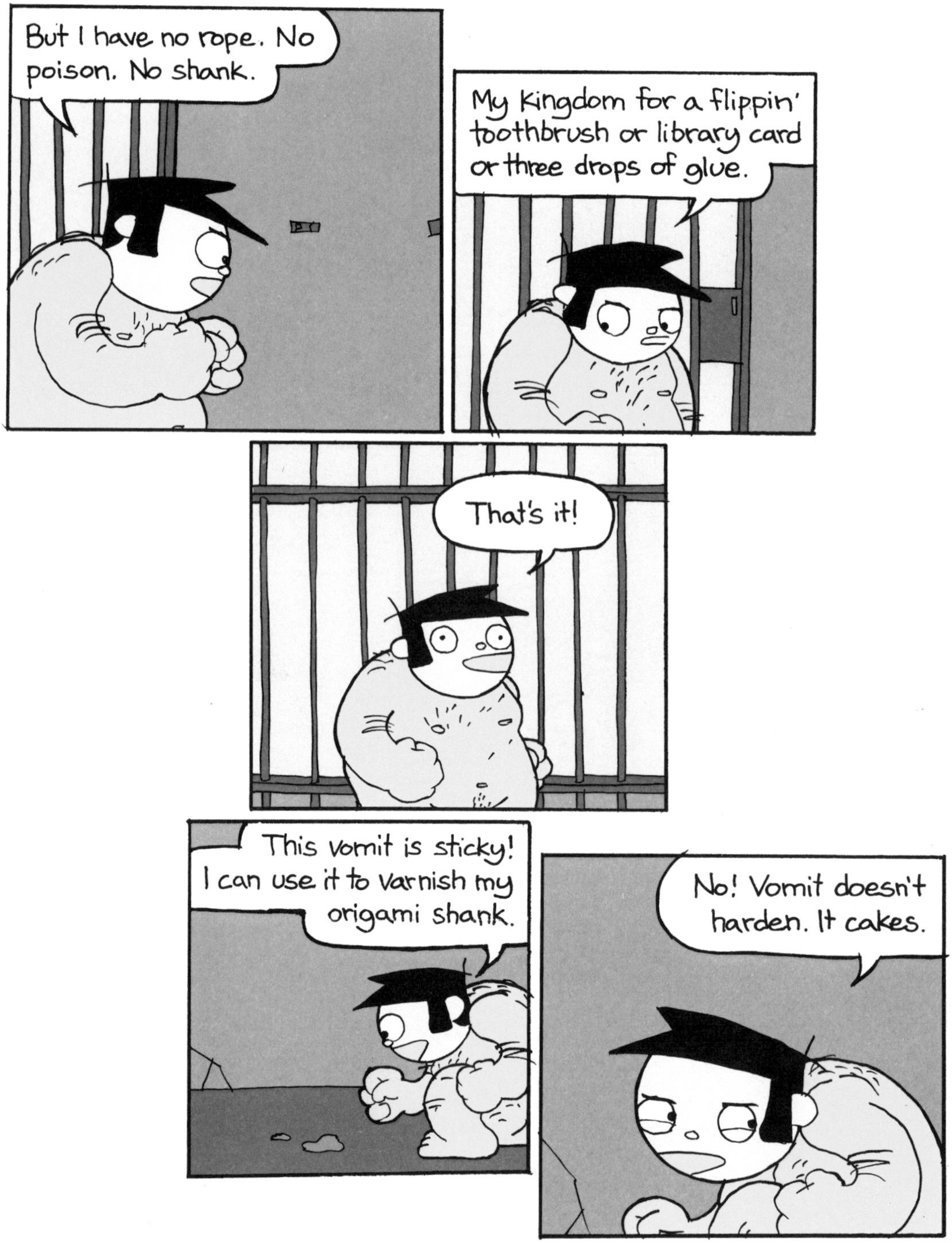
But I have no rope. No poison. No shank.
My Kingdom for a flippin' toothbrush or library card or three drops of glue.
That's it!
This vomit is sticky! I can use it to varnish my origami shank.
No! Vomit doesn't harden. It cakes.

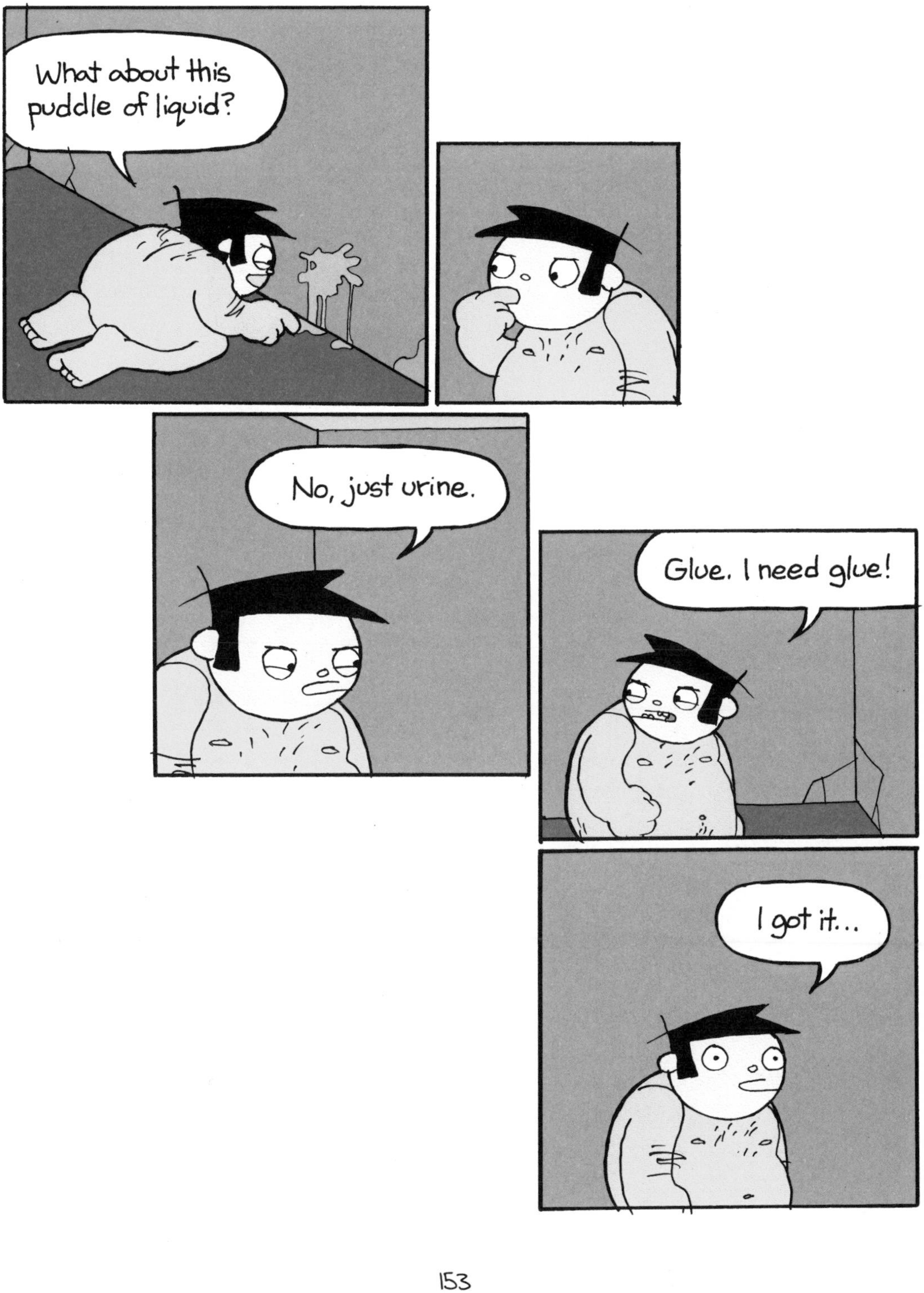
What about this puddle of liquid?
No, just urine.
Glue. I need glue!
I got it...

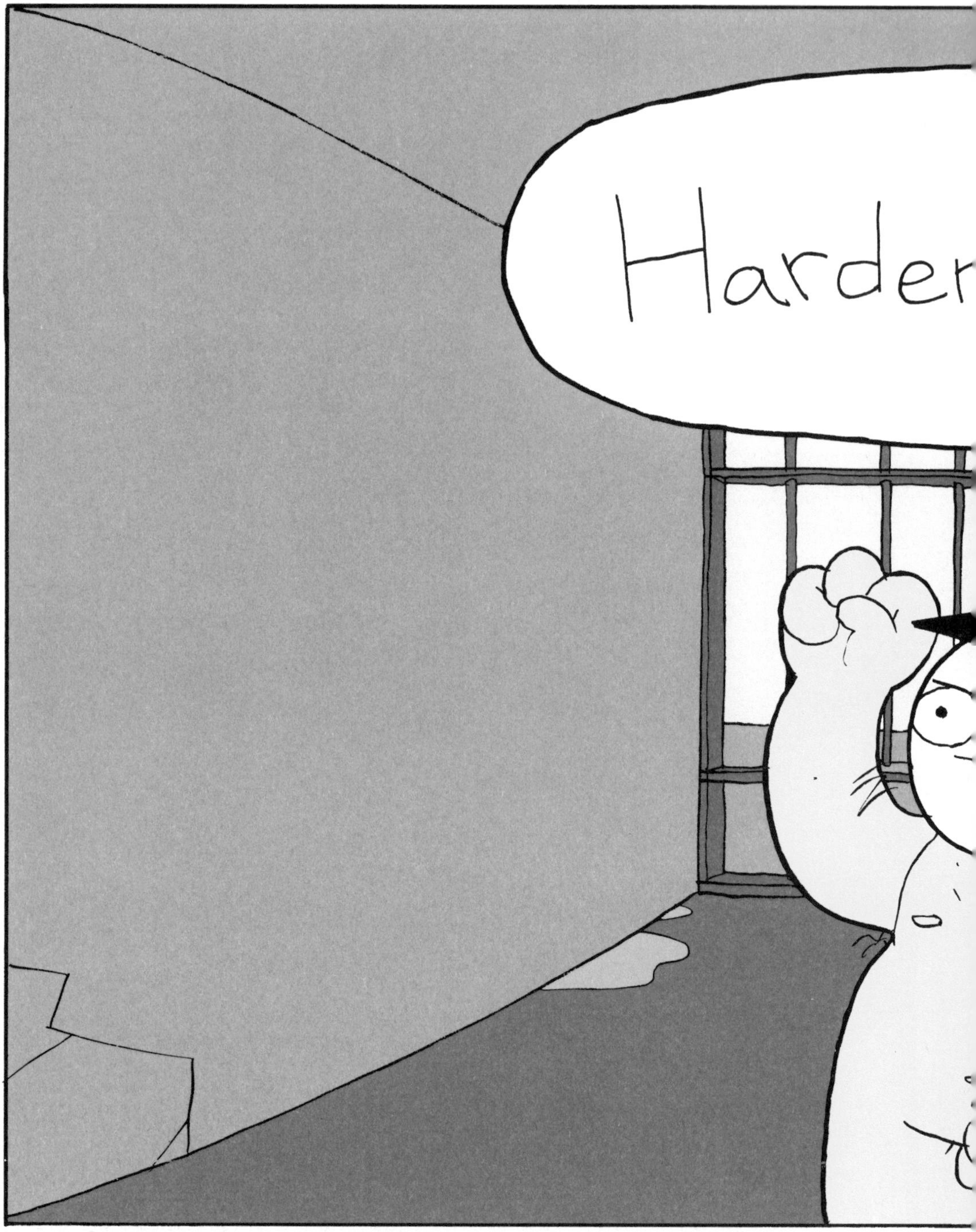
Harder

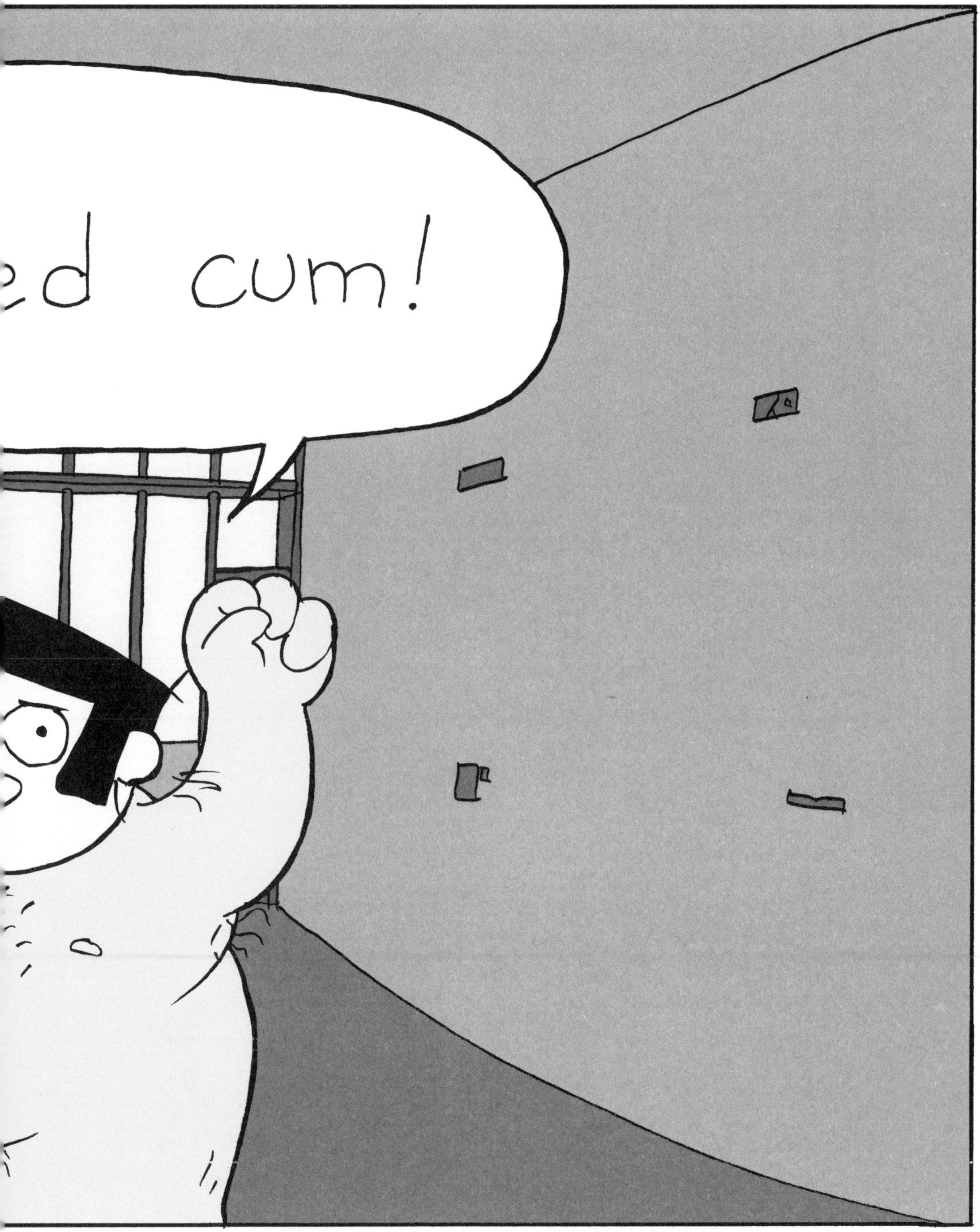
ed cum!

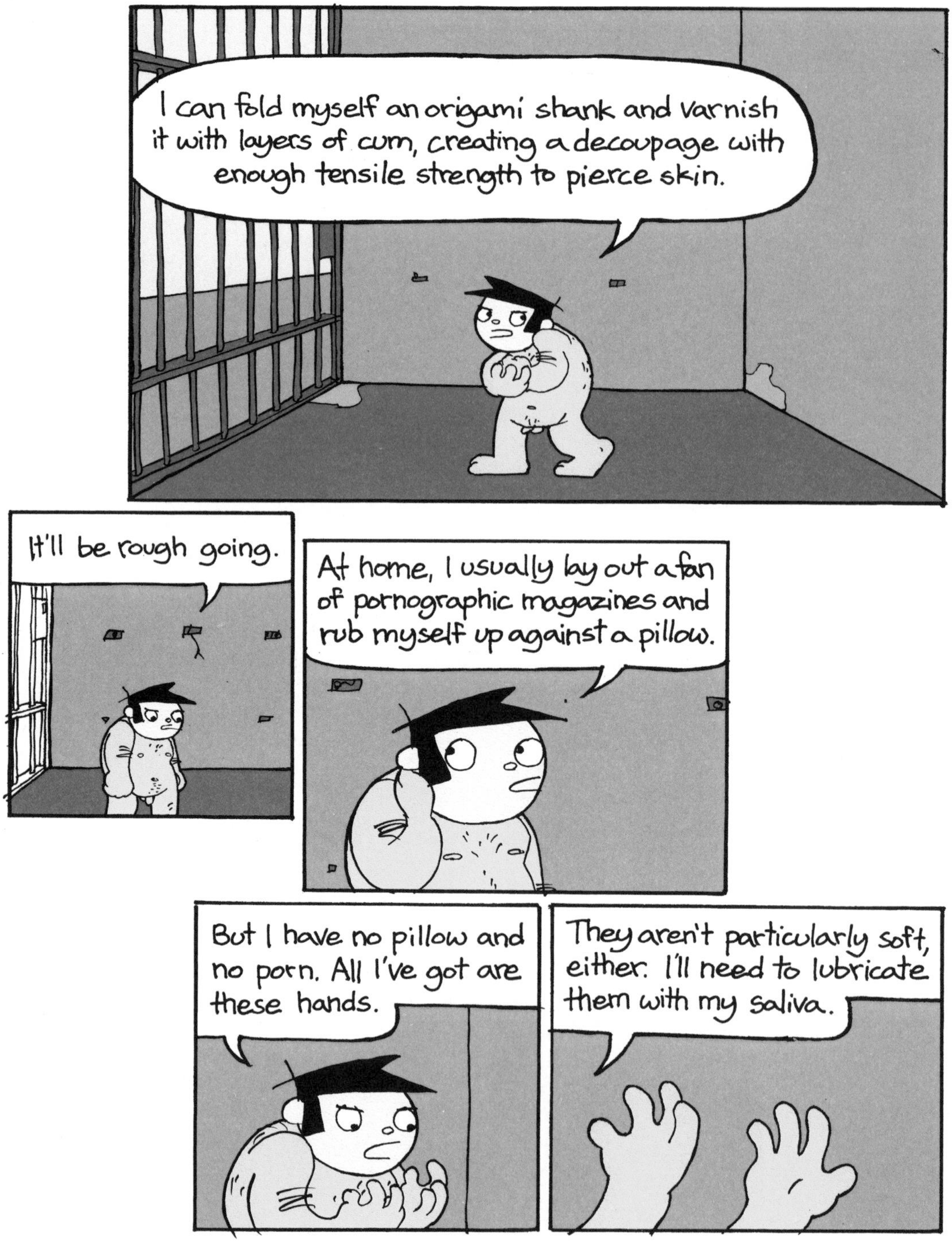
I can fold myself an origami shank and varnish it with layers of cum, creating a decoupage with enough tensile strength to pierce skin.
It'll be rough going.
At home, I usually lay out a fan of pornographic magazines and rub myself up against a pillow.
But I have no pillow and no porn. All I've got are these hands.
They aren't particularly soft, either. I'll need to lubricate them with my saliva.

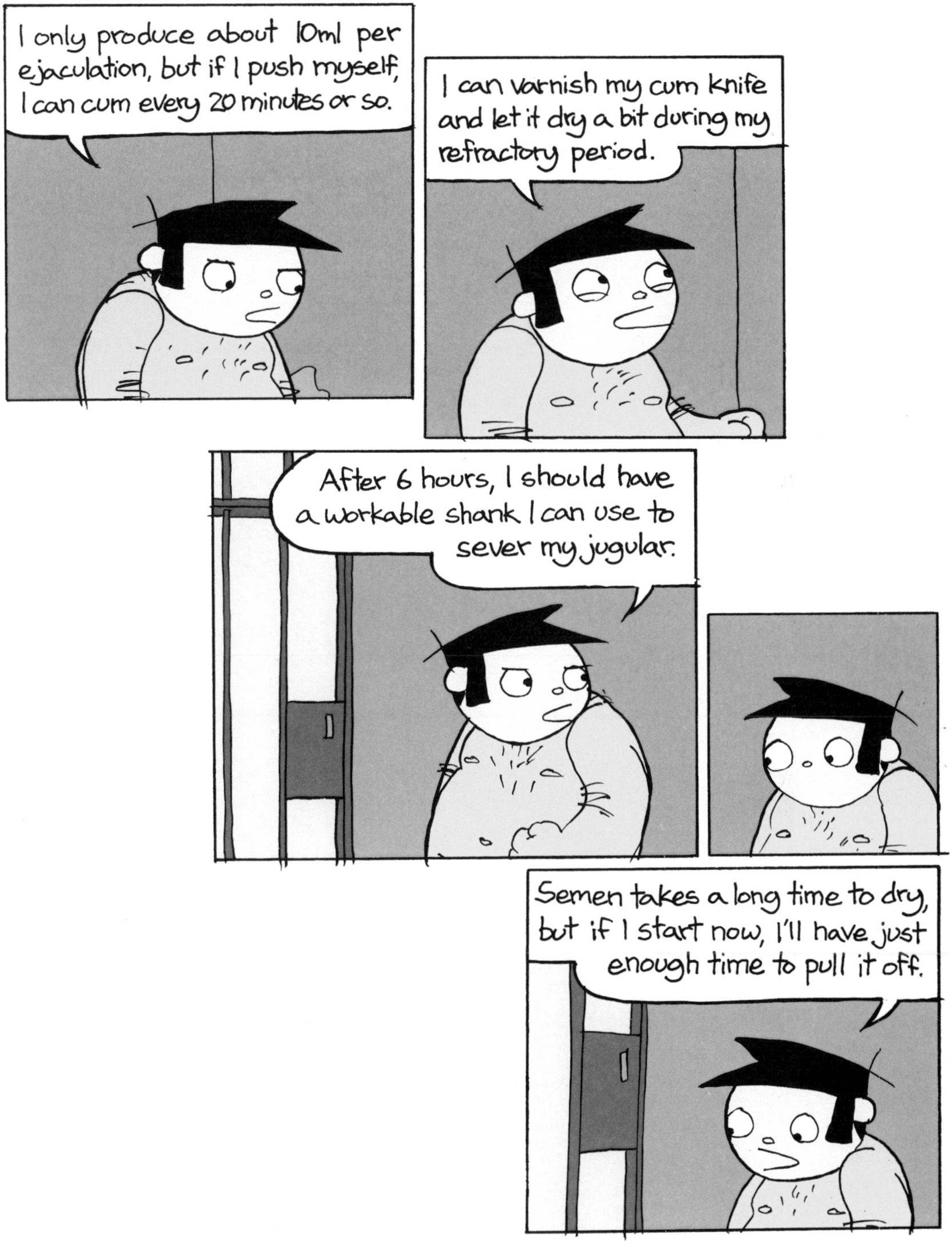
I only produce about 10ml per ejaculation, but if I push myself, I can cum every 20 minutes or so.
I can varnish my cum knife and let it dry a bit during my refractory period.
After 6 hours, I should have a workable shank I can use to sever my jugular.
Semen takes a long time to dry, but if I start now, I'll have just enough time to pull it off.

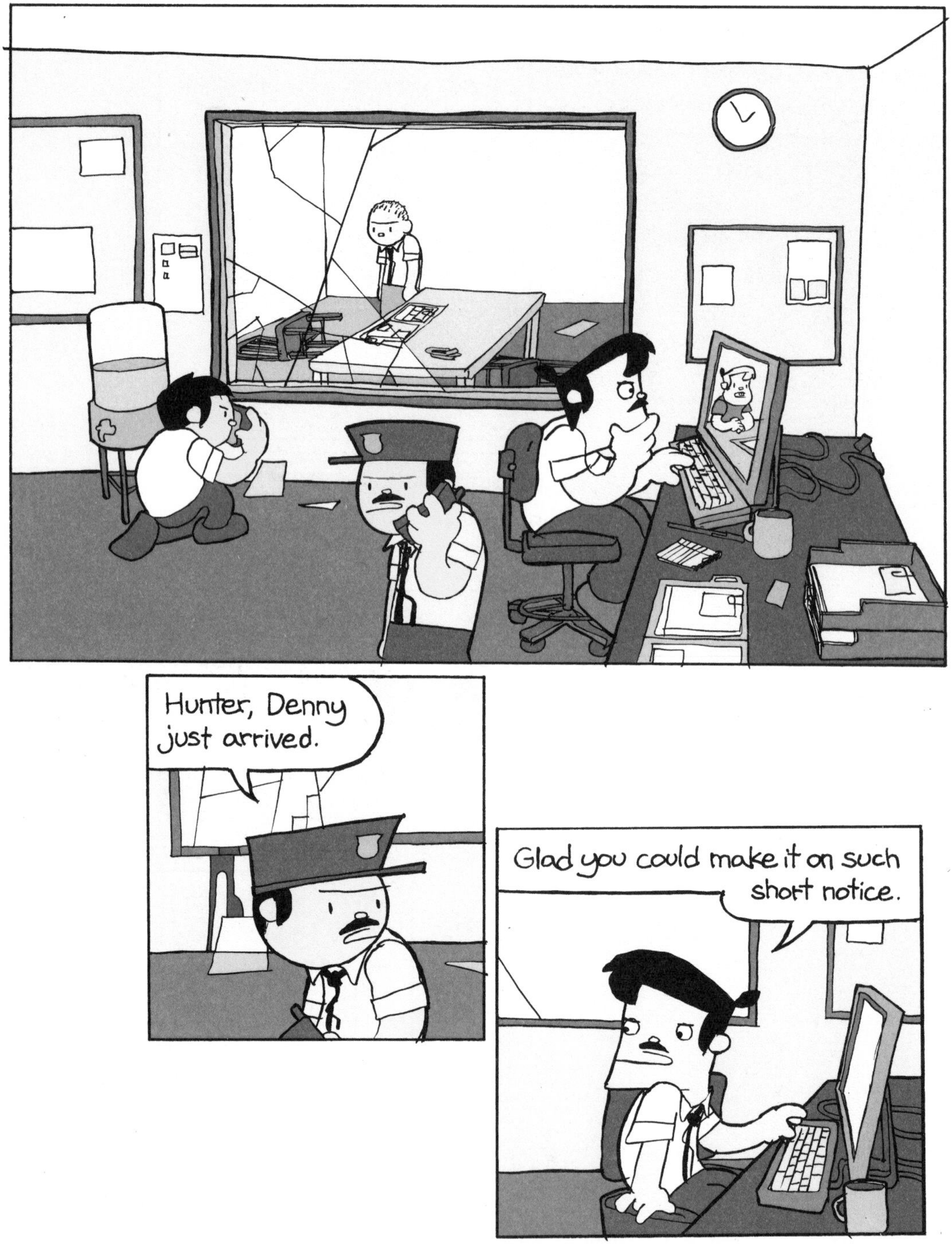
Hunter, Denny just arrived.
Glad you could make it on such short notice.

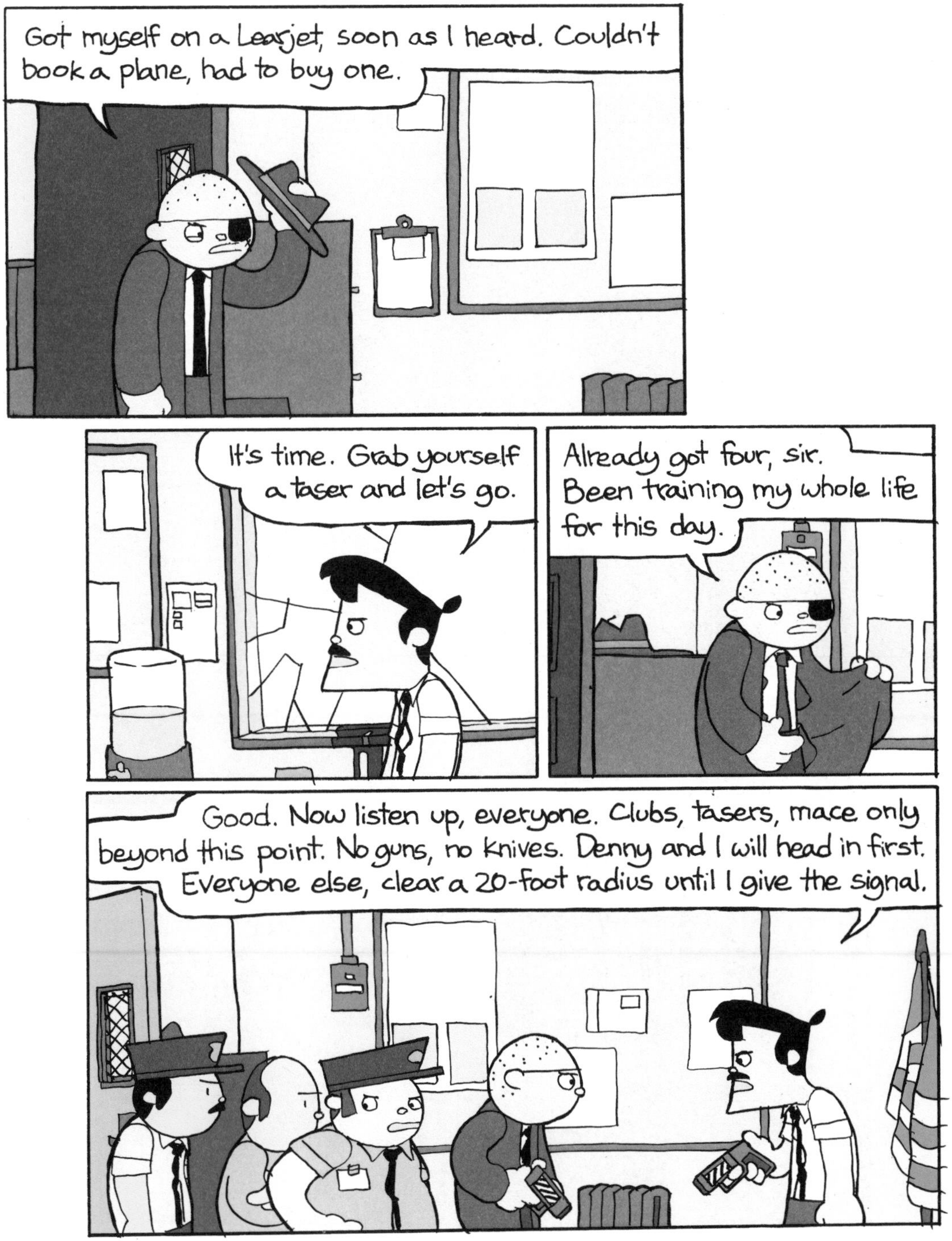
Got myself on a Learjet, soon as I heard. Couldn't book a plane, had to buy one.
It's time. Grab yourself a taser and let's go.
Already got four, sir. Been training my whole life for this day.
Good. Now listen up, everyone. Clubs, tasers, mace only beyond this point. No guns, no knives. Denny and I will head in first. Everyone else, clear a 20-foot radius until I give the signal.

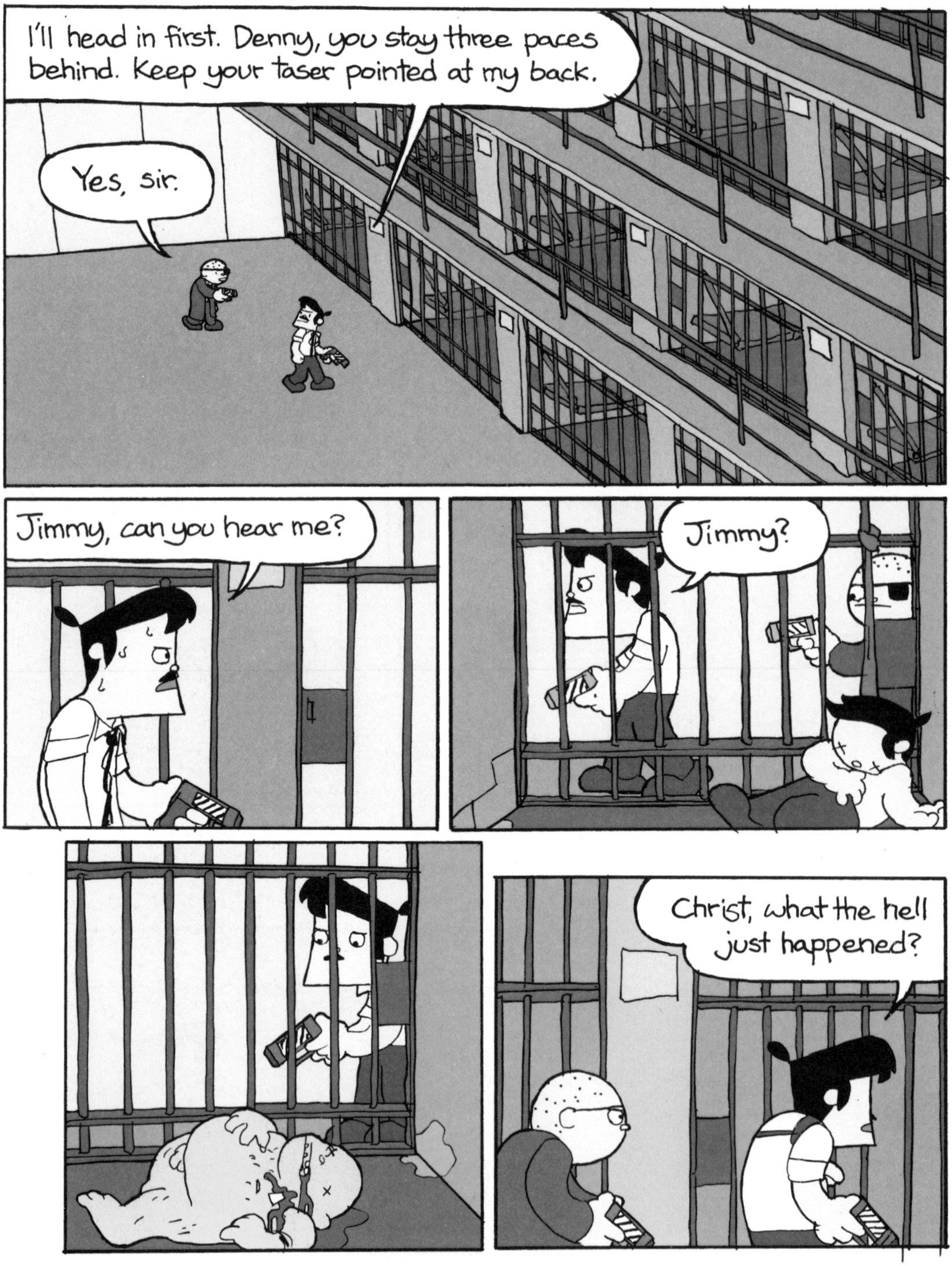
I'll head in first. Denny, you stay three paces behind. Keep your taser pointed at my back.
Yes, sir.
Jimmy, can you hear me?
Jimmy?
Christ, what the hell just happened?

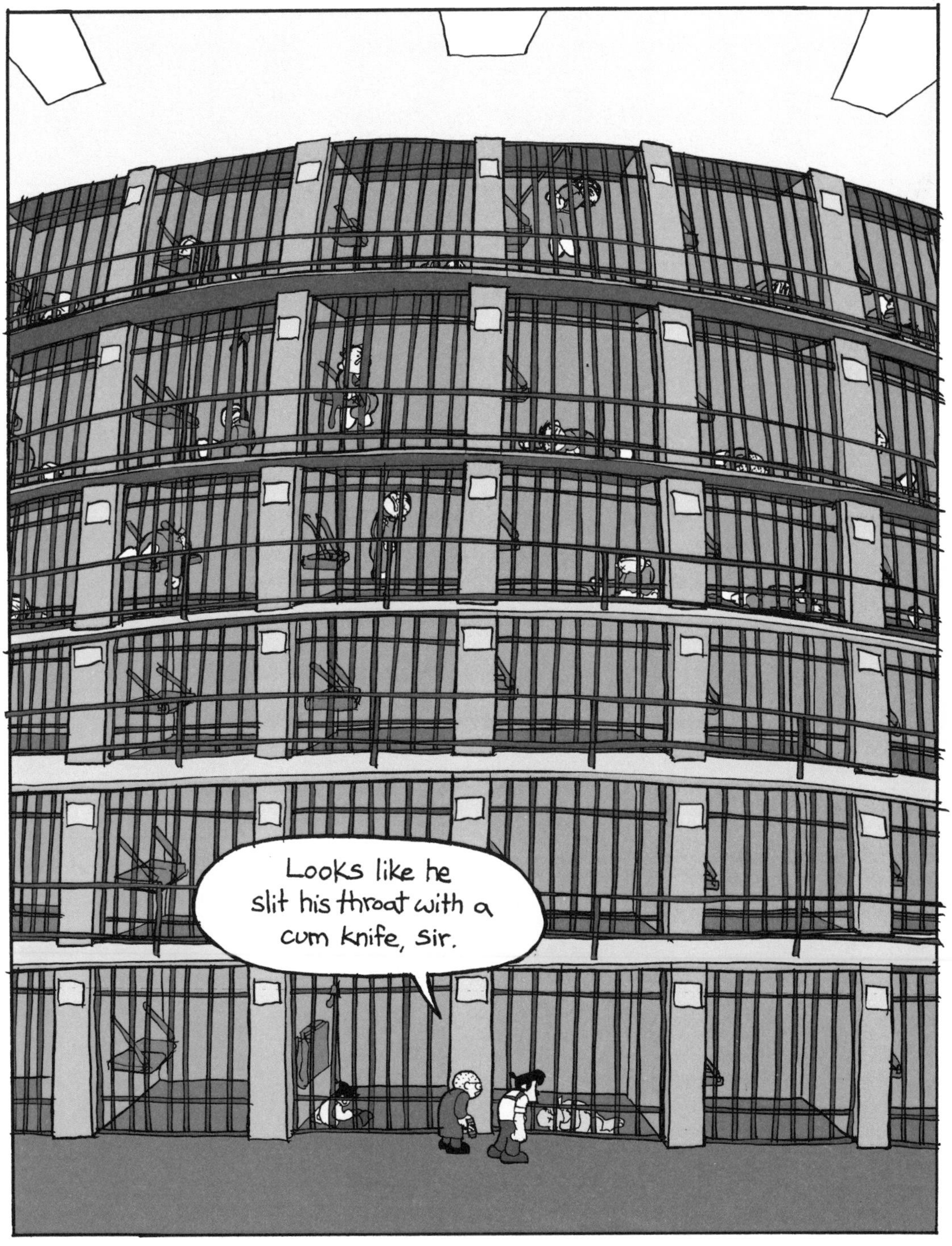
Looks like he slit his throat with a cum knife, sir.

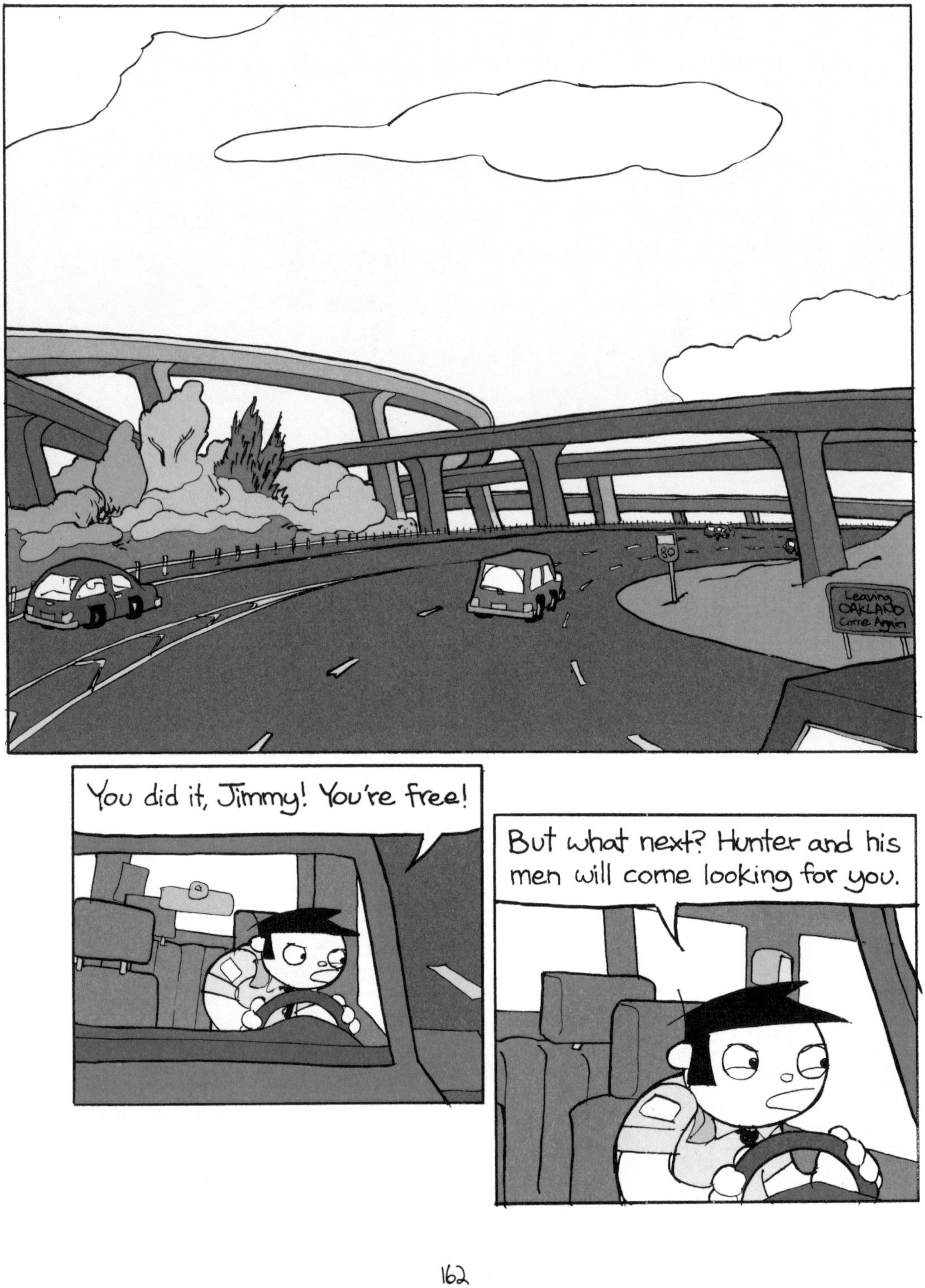
80
Leaving OAKLAND Come Again
You did it, Jimmy! You're free!
But what next? Hunter and his men will come looking for you.

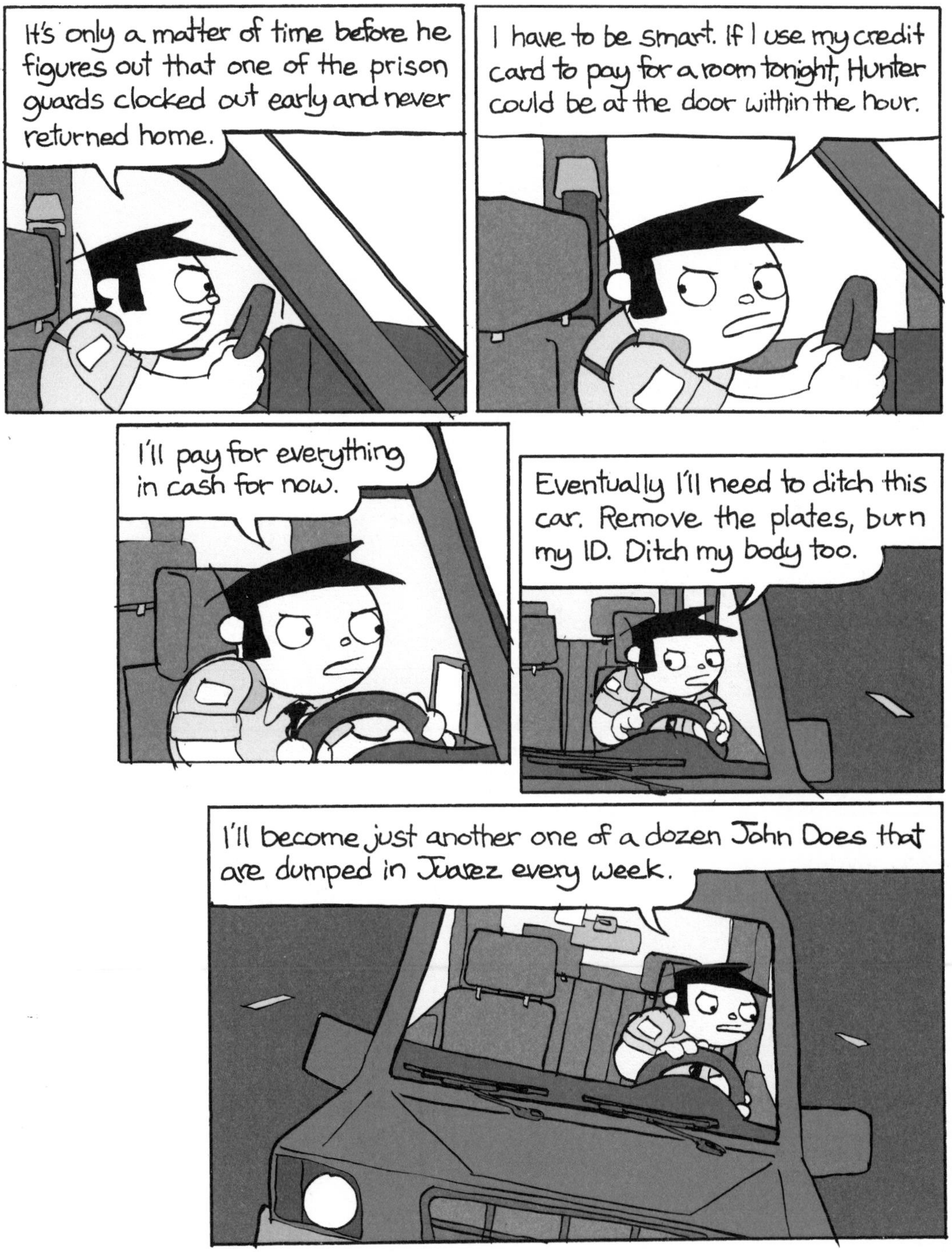

It's only a matter of time before he figures out that one of the prison guards clocked out early and never returned home.
I have to be smart. If I use my credit card to pay for a room tonight, Hunter could be at the door within the hour.
I'll pay for everything in cash for now.
Eventually I'll need to ditch this car. Remove the plates, burn my ID. Ditch my body too.
I'll become just another one of a dozen John Does that are dumped in Juarez every week.

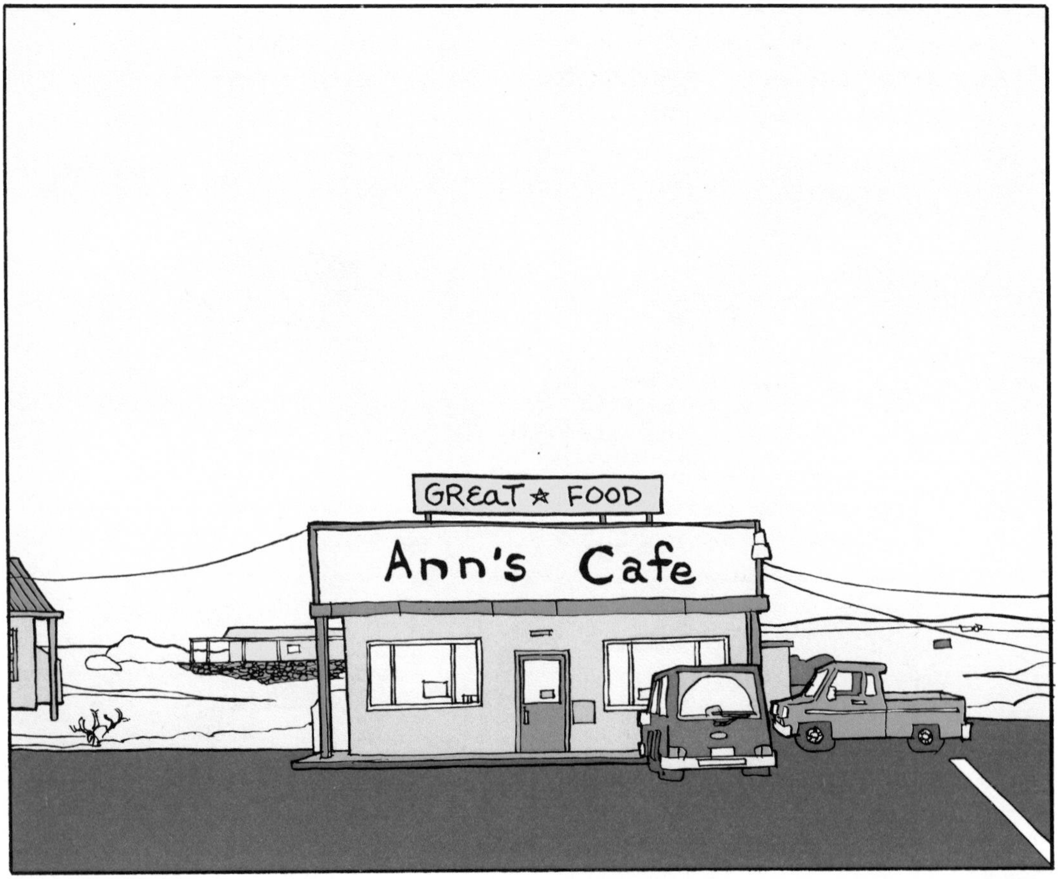
GREaT ★ FOOD
Ann's Cafe

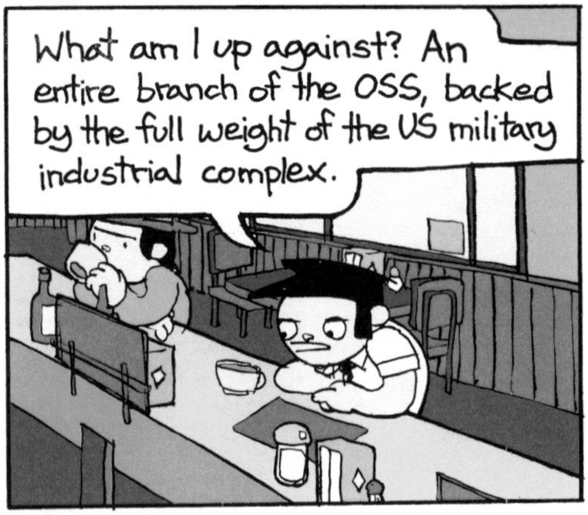
What am I up against? An entire branch of the OSS, backed by the full weight of the US military industrial complex.

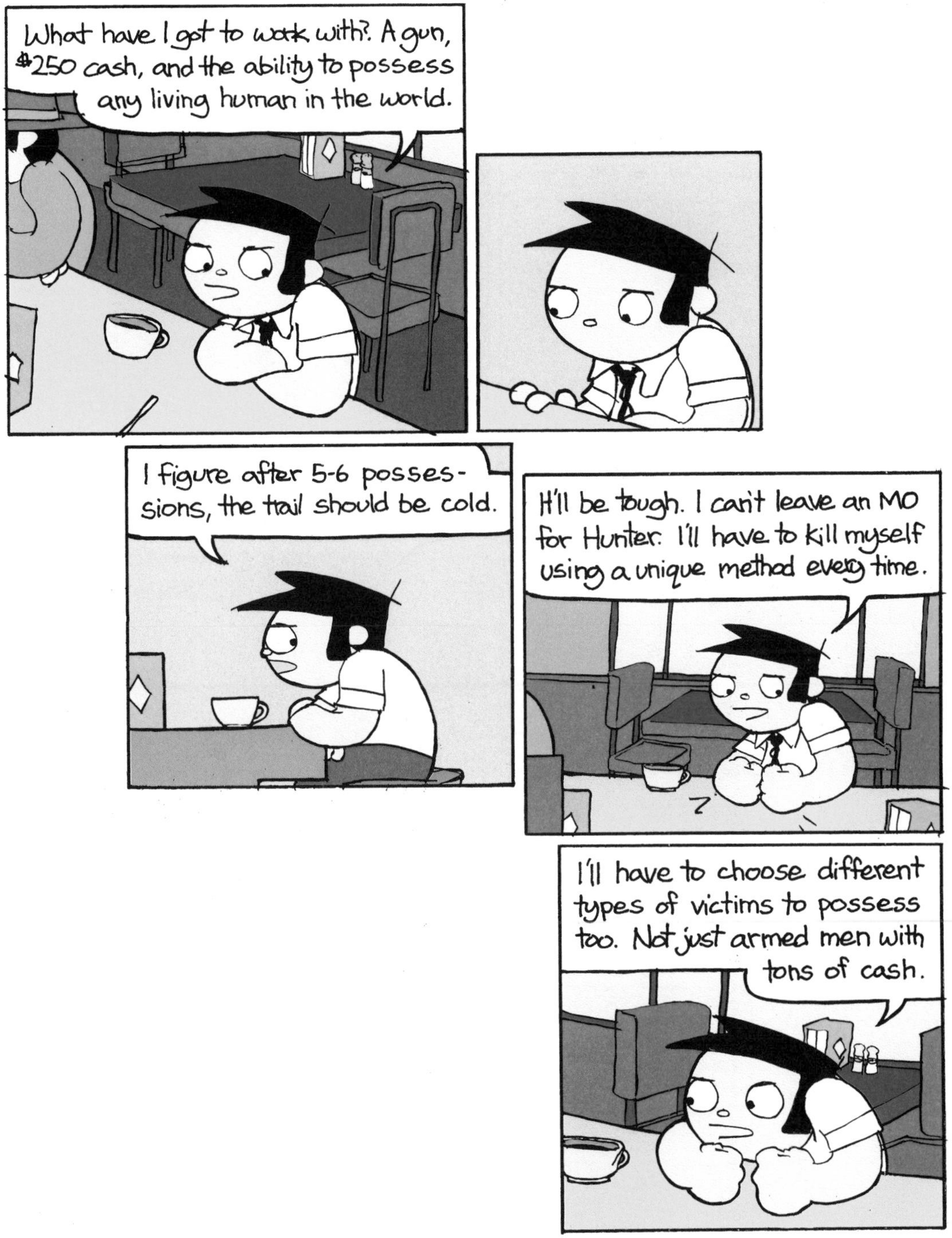
What have I got to work with? A gun, $250 cash, and the ability to possess any living human in the world.
I figure after 5-6 posses-sions, the trail should be cold.
It'll be tough. I can't leave an MO for Hunter. I'll have to kill myself using a unique method every time.
I'll have to choose different types of victims to possess too. Not just armed men with tons of cash.

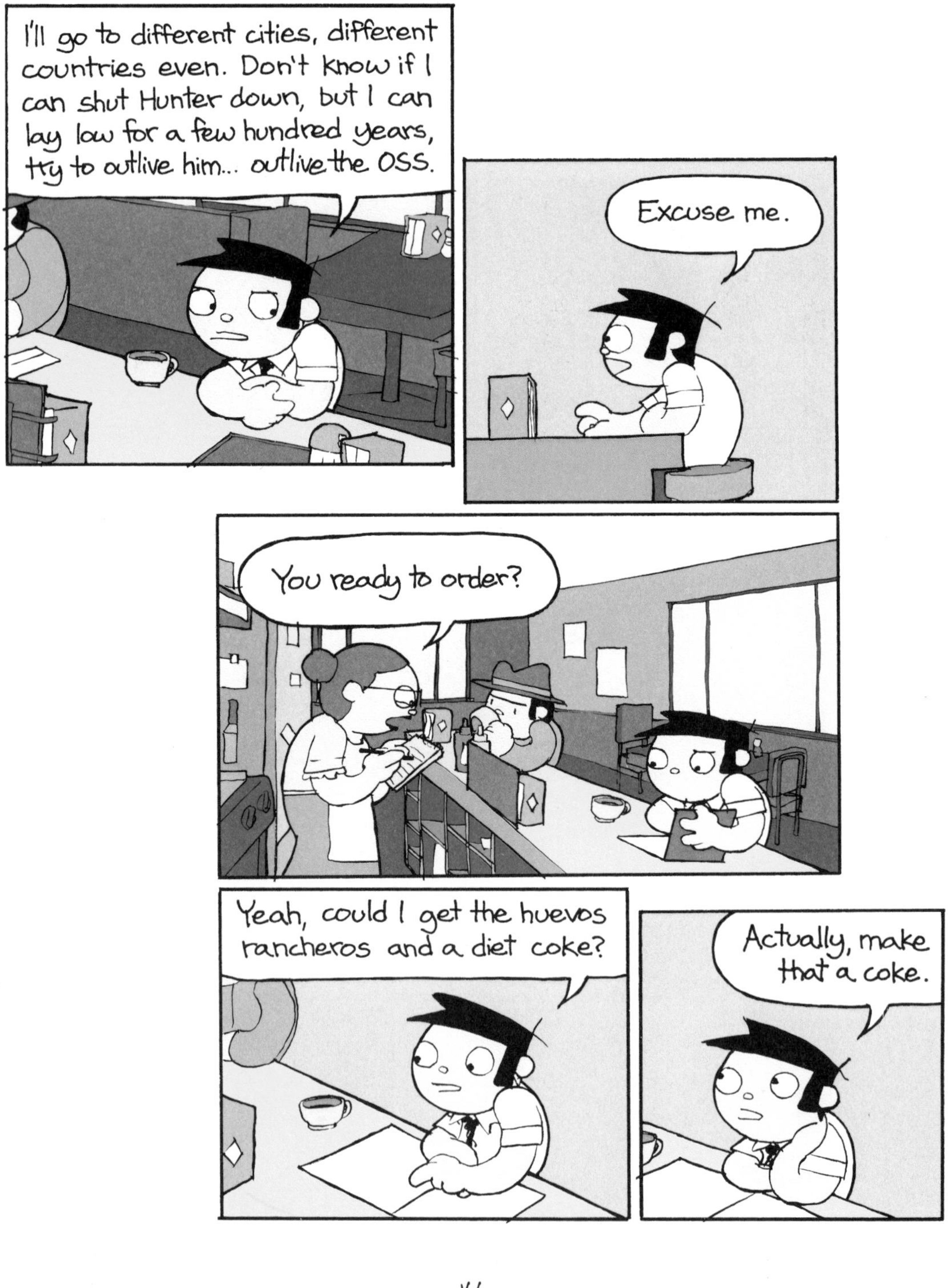
I'll go to different cities, different countries even. Don't know if I can shut Hunter down, but I can lay low for a few hundred years, try to outlive him... outlive the OSS.
Excuse me.
You ready to order?
Yeah, could I get the huevos rancheros and a diet coke?
Actually, make that a coke.